OKKO

THE CYCLE OF EARTH

ARCHAIA ENTERTAINMENT, LLC
WWW.ARCHAIA.COM

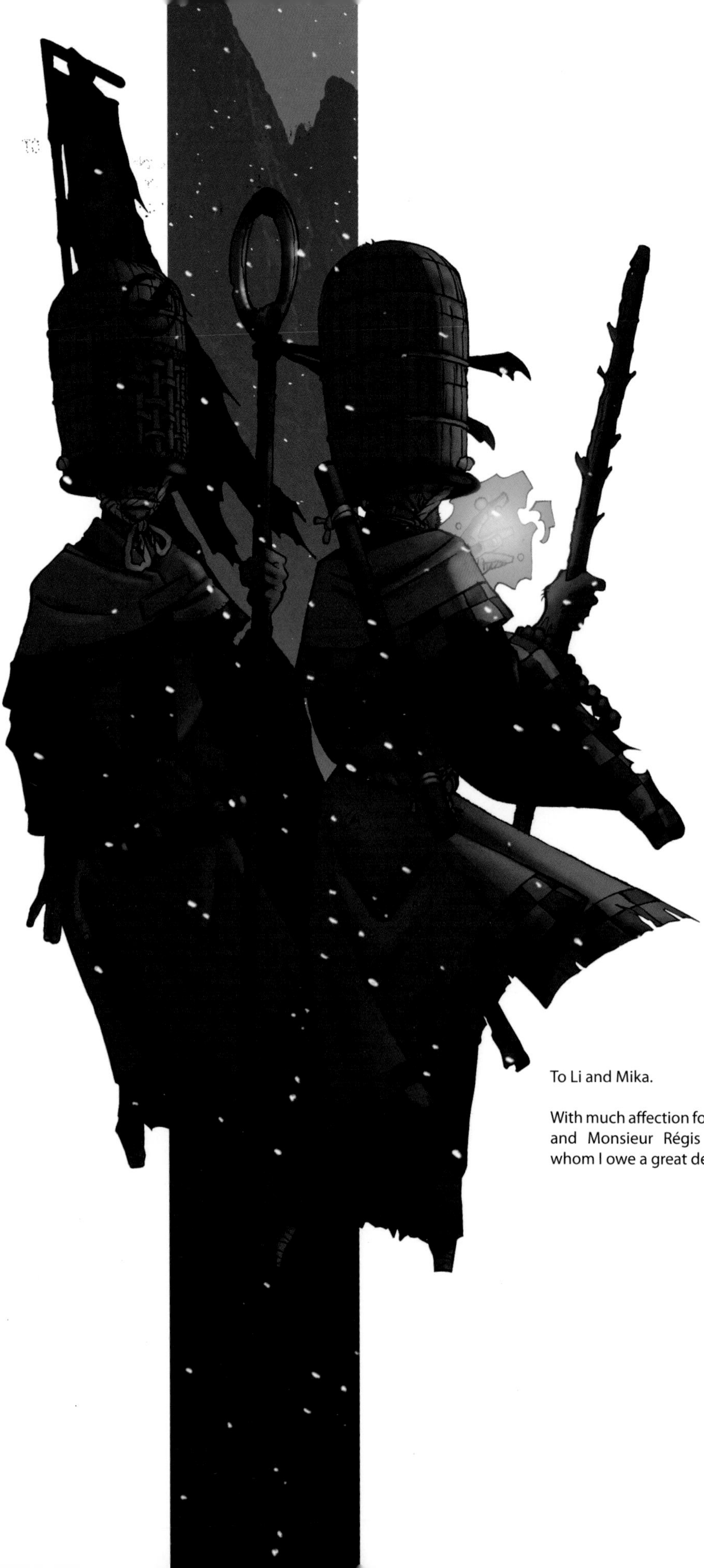

To Li and Mika.

With much affection for Jean Bouyer and Monsieur Régis Delolme, to whom I owe a great deal.

— Hub

OKKO

THE CYCLE OF EARTH

WRITTEN & ILLUSTRATED BY
HUB

STORYBOARDS BY
EMMANUEL MICHALAK & HUB

COLORS BY
HUB & STEPHAN PELAYO

For this edition book design and layout by
Scott Newman & Mark Smylie

Published by Archaia

PJ Bickett, President
Mark Smylie, Publisher
Stephen Christy III, Director of Development
Kraig Thompson, Director of Sales
Paul Morrissey, Editor
Mel Caylo, Marketing Manager
Scott Newman, Production Manager
Danielle Bonadona, Munika S. Lay, Loren Morgenstern
& Jeff Prezenkowski, Interns

Archaia Entertainment, LLC
1680 Vine Street, Suite 912
Los Angeles, California, 90028, USA
www.Archaia.com

OKKO: THE CYCLE OF EARTH

May 2010

FIRST PRINTING

10 9 8 7 6 5 4 3 2 1
ISBN 1-932386-55-6

ISBN-13 978-1-932386-55-4

ARCHAIA ™

the CYCLE OF EARth

Part One

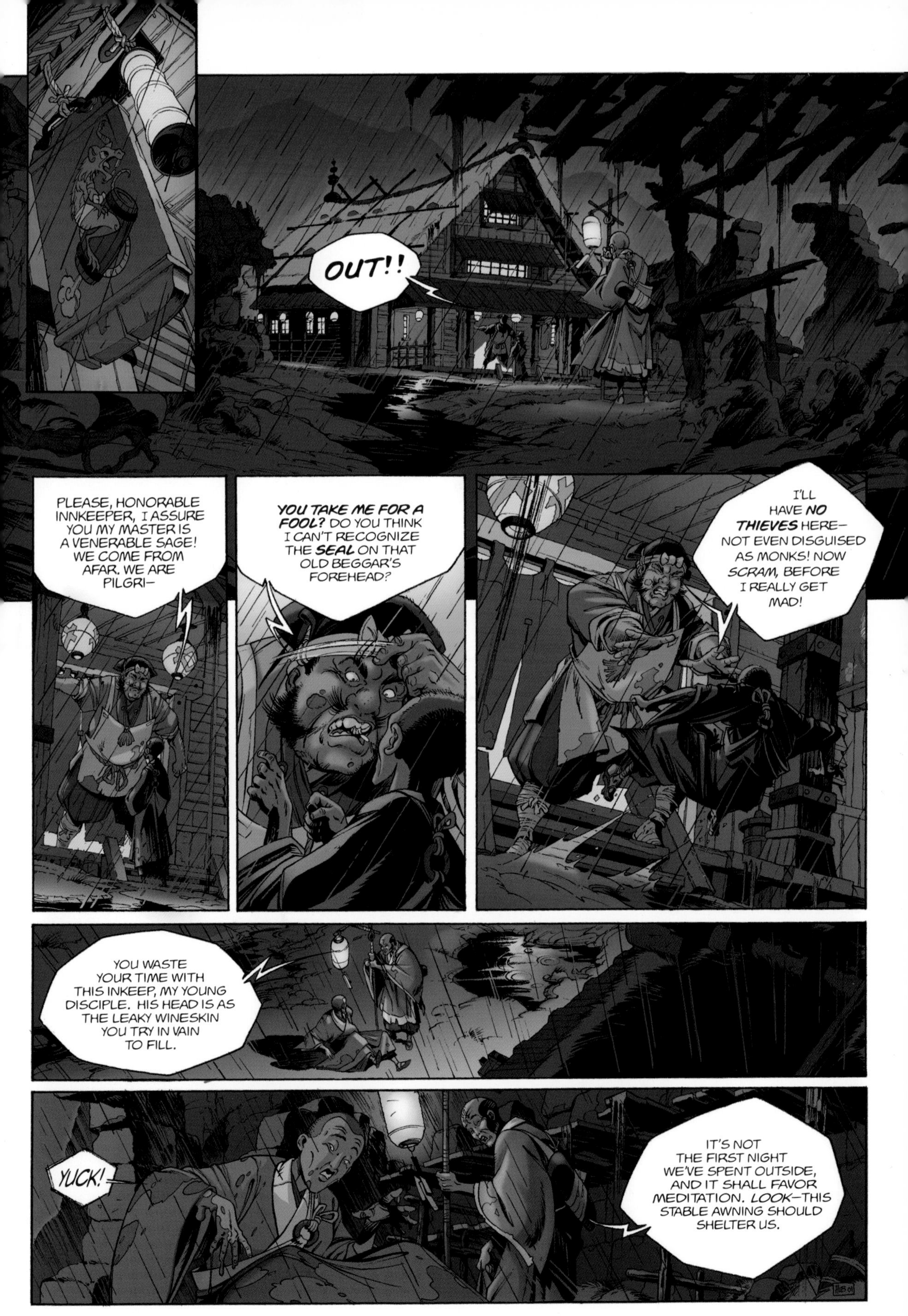
OUT!!
PLEASE, HONORABLE INNKEEPER, I ASSURE YOU MY MASTER IS A VENERABLE SAGE! WE COME FROM AFAR. WE ARE PILGRI–
YOU TAKE ME FOR A FOOL? DO YOU THINK I CAN'T RECOGNIZE THE SEAL ON THAT OLD BEGGAR'S FOREHEAD?
I'LL HAVE NO THIEVES HERE– NOT EVEN DISGUISED AS MONKS! NOW SCRAM, BEFORE I REALLY GET MAD!
YOU WASTE YOUR TIME WITH THIS INKEEP, MY YOUNG DISCIPLE. HIS HEAD IS AS THE LEAKY WINESKIN YOU TRY IN VAIN TO FILL.
YUCK!
IT'S NOT THE FIRST NIGHT WE'VE SPENT OUTSIDE, AND IT SHALL FAVOR MEDITATION. LOOK–THIS STABLE AWNING SHOULD SHELTER US.

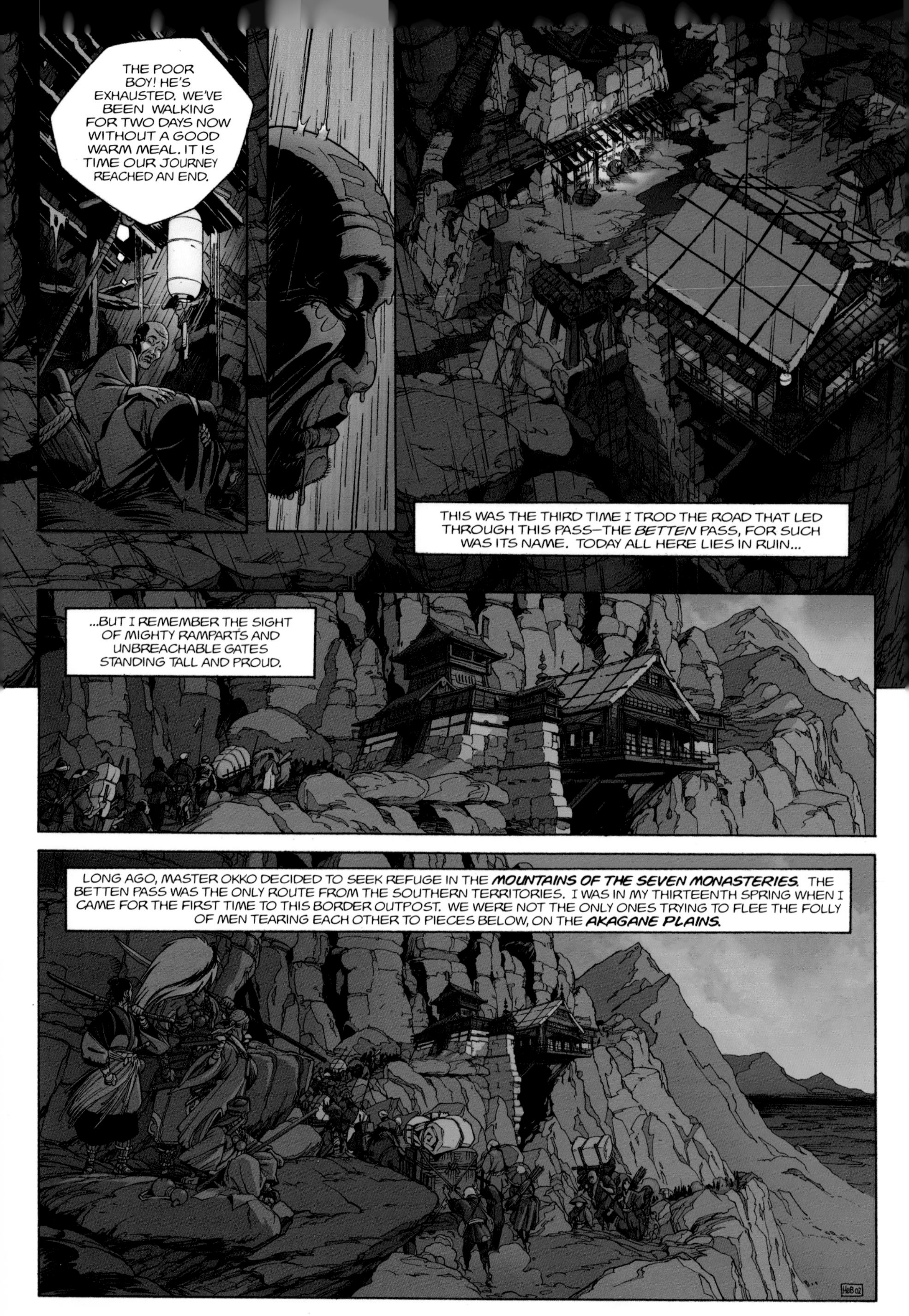
THE POOR BOY! HE'S EXHAUSTED. WE'VE BEEN WALKING FOR TWO DAYS NOW WITHOUT A GOOD WARM MEAL. IT IS TIME OUR JOURNEY REACHED AN END.
THIS WAS THE THIRD TIME I TROD THE ROAD THAT LED THROUGH THIS PASS—THE *BETTEN* PASS, FOR SUCH WAS ITS NAME. TODAY ALL HERE LIES IN RUIN...
...BUT I REMEMBER THE SIGHT OF MIGHTY RAMPARTS AND UNBREACHABLE GATES STANDING TALL AND PROUD.
LONG AGO, MASTER OKKO DECIDED TO SEEK REFUGE IN THE ***MOUNTAINS OF THE SEVEN MONASTERIES***. THE BETTEN PASS WAS THE ONLY ROUTE FROM THE SOUTHERN TERRITORIES. I WAS IN MY THIRTEENTH SPRING WHEN I CAME FOR THE FIRST TIME TO THIS BORDER OUTPOST. WE WERE NOT THE ONLY ONES TRYING TO FLEE THE FOLLY OF MEN TEARING EACH OTHER TO PIECES BELOW, ON THE ***AKAGANE PLAINS***.
HUB 02

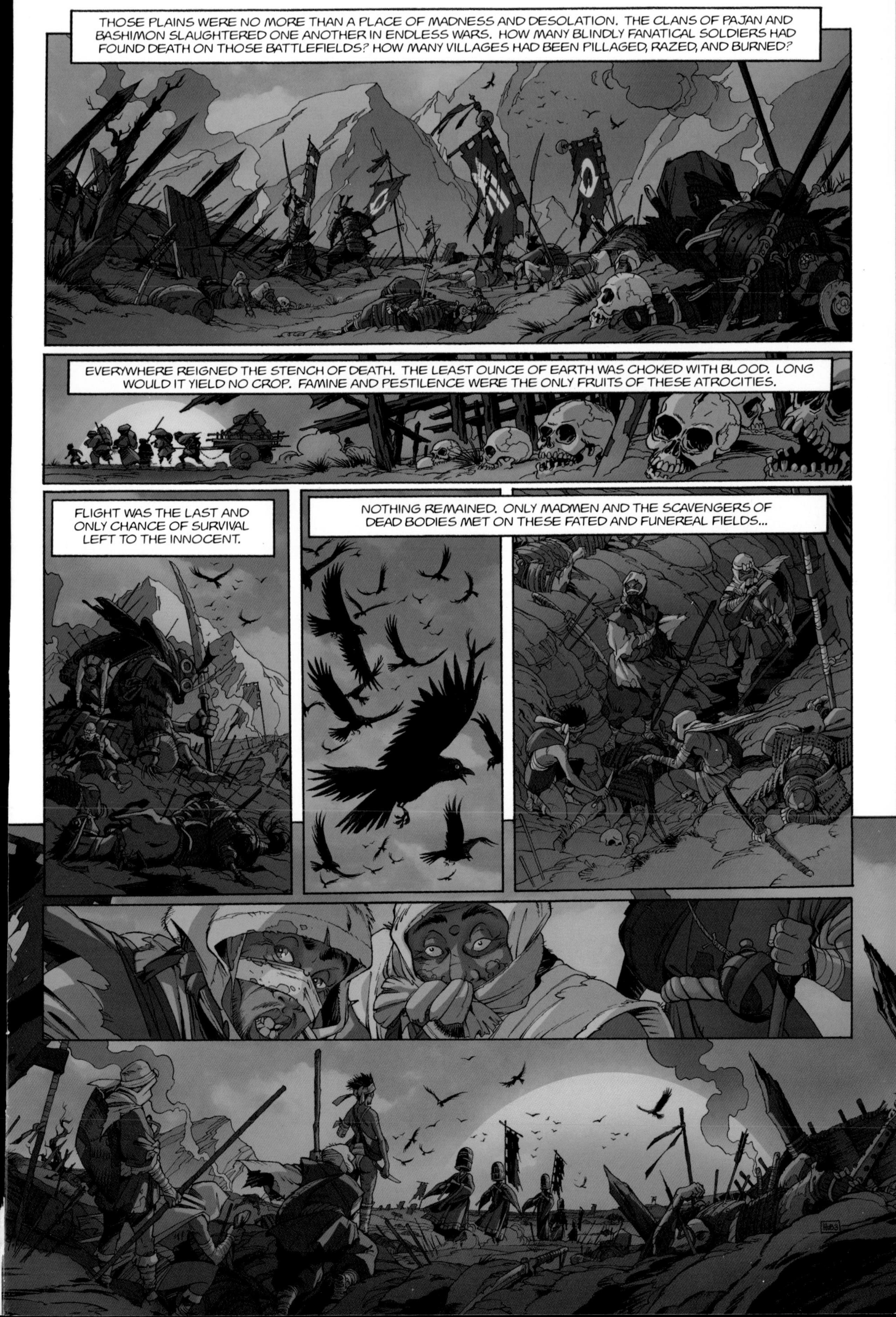
THOSE PLAINS WERE NO MORE THAN A PLACE OF MADNESS AND DESOLATION. THE CLANS OF PAJAN AND BASHIMON SLAUGHTERED ONE ANOTHER IN ENDLESS WARS. HOW MANY BLINDLY FANATICAL SOLDIERS HAD FOUND DEATH ON THOSE BATTLEFIELDS? HOW MANY VILLAGES HAD BEEN PILLAGED, RAZED, AND BURNED?
EVERYWHERE REIGNED THE STENCH OF DEATH. THE LEAST OUNCE OF EARTH WAS CHOKED WITH BLOOD. LONG WOULD IT YIELD NO CROP. FAMINE AND PESTILENCE WERE THE ONLY FRUITS OF THESE ATROCITIES.
FLIGHT WAS THE LAST AND ONLY CHANCE OF SURVIVAL LEFT TO THE INNOCENT.
NOTHING REMAINED. ONLY MADMEN AND THE SCAVENGERS OF DEAD BODIES MET ON THESE FATED AND FUNEREAL FIELDS...

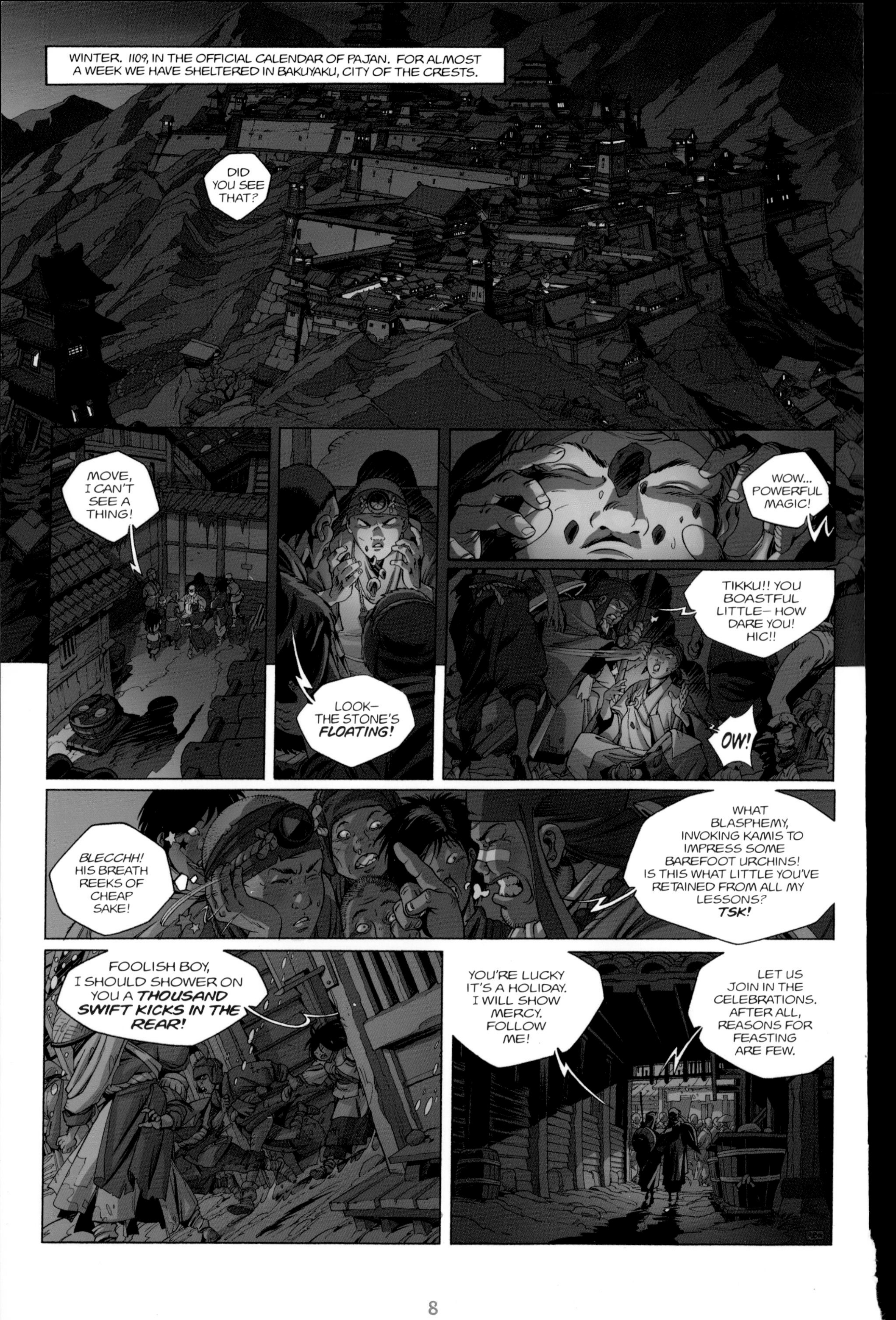
WINTER. 1109, IN THE OFFICIAL CALENDAR OF PAJAN. FOR ALMOST A WEEK WE HAVE SHELTERED IN BAKUYAKU, CITY OF THE CRESTS.
DID YOU SEE THAT?
MOVE, I CAN'T SEE A THING!
LOOK— THE STONE'S *FLOATING!*
WOW... POWERFUL MAGIC!
TIKKU!! YOU BOASTFUL LITTLE— HOW DARE YOU! HIC!!
OW!
BLECCHH! HIS BREATH REEKS OF CHEAP SAKE!
WHAT BLASPHEMY, INVOKING KAMIS TO IMPRESS SOME BAREFOOT URCHINS! IS THIS WHAT LITTLE YOU'VE RETAINED FROM ALL MY LESSONS? *TSK!*
FOOLISH BOY, I SHOULD SHOWER ON YOU A *THOUSAND SWIFT KICKS IN THE REAR!*
YOU'RE LUCKY IT'S A HOLIDAY. I WILL SHOW MERCY. FOLLOW ME!
LET US JOIN IN THE CELEBRATIONS. AFTER ALL, REASONS FOR FEASTING ARE FEW.

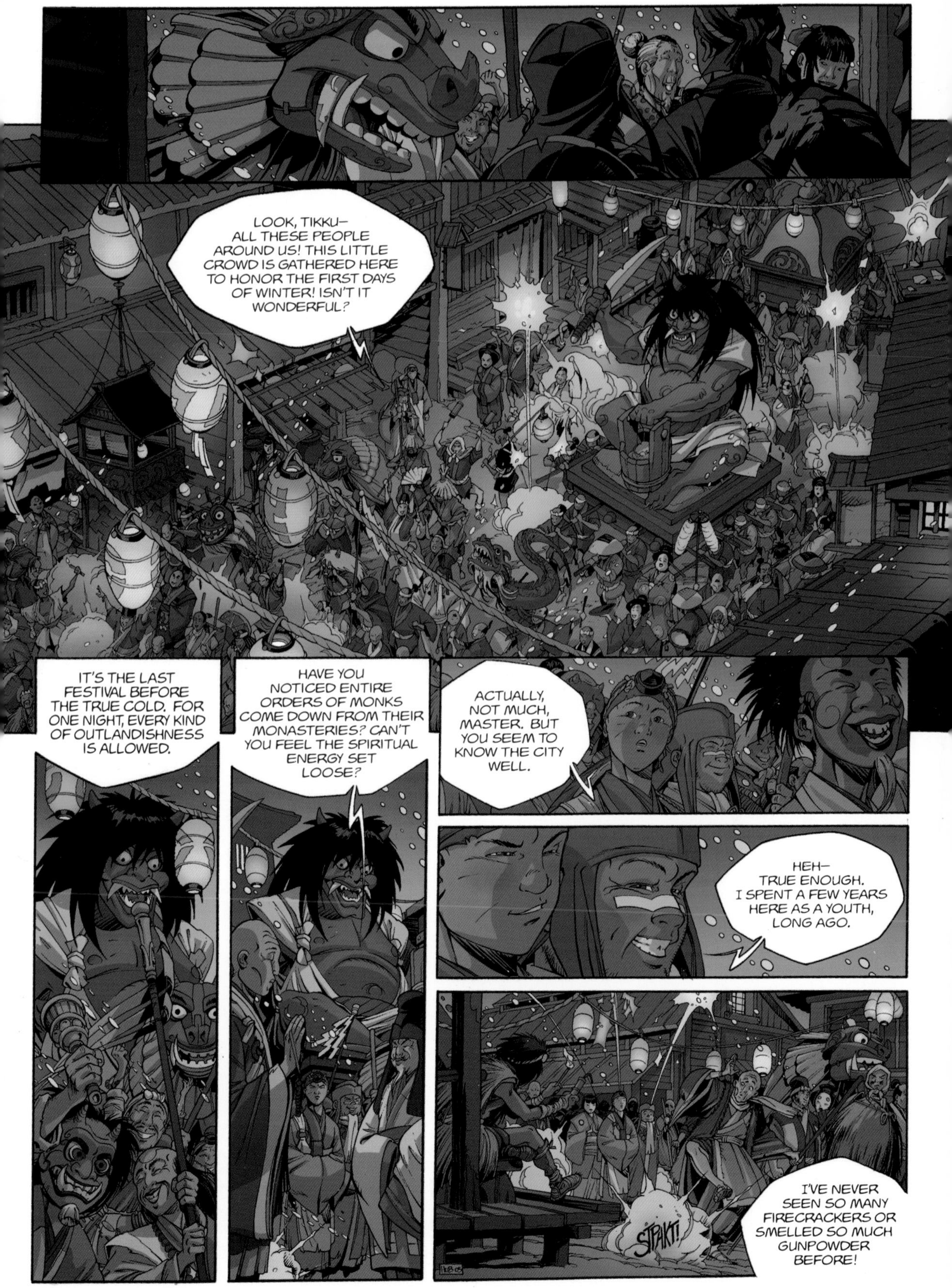
LOOK, TIKKU— ALL THESE PEOPLE AROUND US! THIS LITTLE CROWD IS GATHERED HERE TO HONOR THE FIRST DAYS OF WINTER! ISN'T IT WONDERFUL?
IT'S THE LAST FESTIVAL BEFORE THE TRUE COLD. FOR ONE NIGHT, EVERY KIND OF OUTLANDISHNESS IS ALLOWED.
HAVE YOU NOTICED ENTIRE ORDERS OF MONKS COME DOWN FROM THEIR MONASTERIES? CAN'T YOU FEEL THE SPIRITUAL ENERGY SET LOOSE?
ACTUALLY, NOT MUCH, MASTER. BUT YOU SEEM TO KNOW THE CITY WELL.
HEH— TRUE ENOUGH. I SPENT A FEW YEARS HERE AS A YOUTH, LONG AGO.
STRAK!
I'VE NEVER SEEN SO MANY FIRECRACKERS OR SMELLED SO MUCH GUNPOWDER BEFORE!

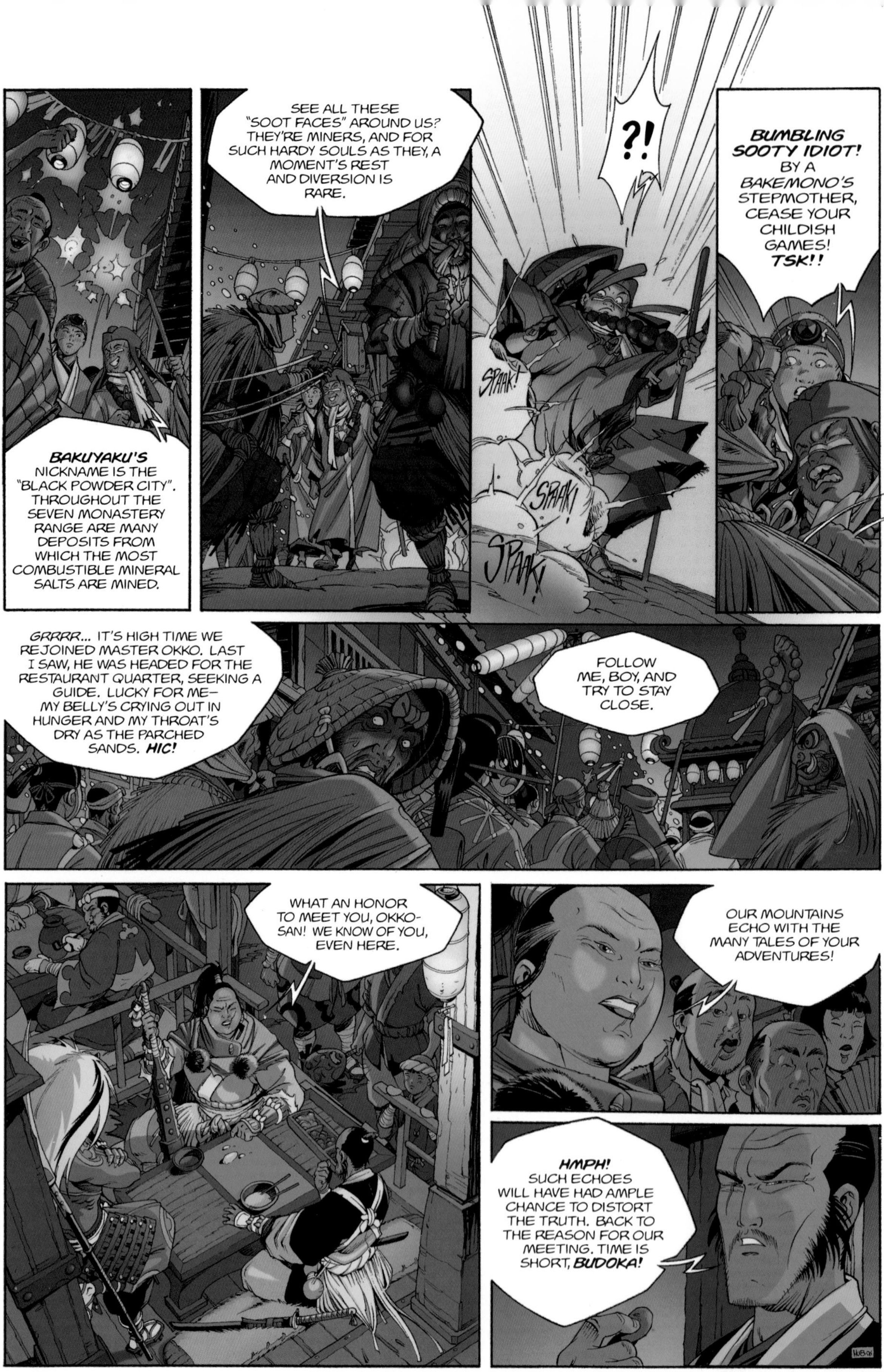
BAKUYAKU'S NICKNAME IS THE "BLACK POWDER CITY". THROUGHOUT THE SEVEN MONASTERY RANGE ARE MANY DEPOSITS FROM WHICH THE MOST COMBUSTIBLE MINERAL SALTS ARE MINED.
SEE ALL THESE "SOOT FACES" AROUND US? THEY'RE MINERS, AND FOR SUCH HARDY SOULS AS THEY, A MOMENT'S REST AND DIVERSION IS RARE.
?!
SPAAK!
SPAAK!
SPAAK!
BUMBLING SOOTY IDIOT! BY A BAKEMONO'S STEPMOTHER, CEASE YOUR CHILDISH GAMES! TSK!!
GRRRR... IT'S HIGH TIME WE REJOINED MASTER OKKO. LAST I SAW, HE WAS HEADED FOR THE RESTAURANT QUARTER, SEEKING A GUIDE. LUCKY FOR ME– MY BELLY'S CRYING OUT IN HUNGER AND MY THROAT'S DRY AS THE PARCHED SANDS. HIC!
FOLLOW ME, BOY, AND TRY TO STAY CLOSE.
WHAT AN HONOR TO MEET YOU, OKKO-SAN! WE KNOW OF YOU, EVEN HERE.
OUR MOUNTAINS ECHO WITH THE MANY TALES OF YOUR ADVENTURES!
HMPH! SUCH ECHOES WILL HAVE HAD AMPLE CHANCE TO DISTORT THE TRUTH. BACK TO THE REASON FOR OUR MEETING. TIME IS SHORT, BUDOKA!

*BUDOKA: PEASANT WARRIOR

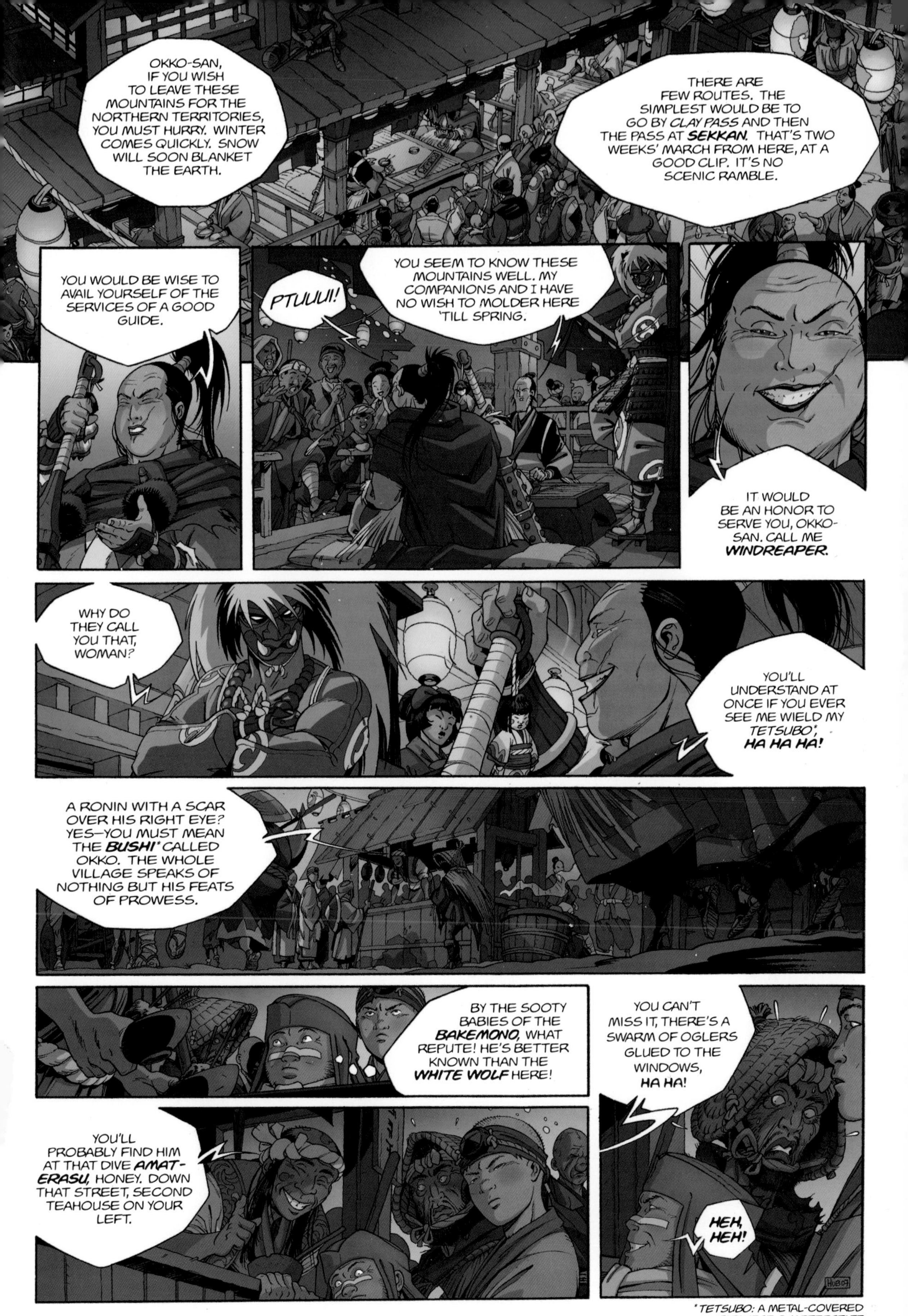
OKKO-SAN, IF YOU WISH TO LEAVE THESE MOUNTAINS FOR THE NORTHERN TERRITORIES, YOU MUST HURRY. WINTER COMES QUICKLY. SNOW WILL SOON BLANKET THE EARTH.
THERE ARE FEW ROUTES. THE SIMPLEST WOULD BE TO GO BY *CLAY PASS* AND THEN THE PASS AT **SEKKAN**. THAT'S TWO WEEKS' MARCH FROM HERE, AT A GOOD CLIP. IT'S NO SCENIC RAMBLE.
YOU WOULD BE WISE TO AVAIL YOURSELF OF THE SERVICES OF A GOOD GUIDE.
PTUUUI!
YOU SEEM TO KNOW THESE MOUNTAINS WELL. MY COMPANIONS AND I HAVE NO WISH TO MOLDER HERE 'TILL SPRING.
IT WOULD BE AN HONOR TO SERVE YOU, OKKO-SAN. CALL ME **WINDREAPER**.
WHY DO THEY CALL YOU THAT, WOMAN?
YOU'LL UNDERSTAND AT ONCE IF YOU EVER SEE ME WIELD MY *TETSUBO**, **HA HA HA!**
A RONIN WITH A SCAR OVER HIS RIGHT EYE? YES—YOU MUST MEAN THE **BUSHI*** CALLED OKKO. THE WHOLE VILLAGE SPEAKS OF NOTHING BUT HIS FEATS OF PROWESS.
BY THE SOOTY BABIES OF THE **BAKEMONO**, WHAT REPUTE! HE'S BETTER KNOWN THAN THE **WHITE WOLF** HERE!
YOU CAN'T MISS IT, THERE'S A SWARM OF OGLERS GLUED TO THE WINDOWS, **HA HA!**
YOU'LL PROBABLY FIND HIM AT THAT DIVE **AMATERASU**, HONEY. DOWN THAT STREET, SECOND TEAHOUSE ON YOUR LEFT.
HEH, HEH!
HUB07

*TETSUBO: A METAL-COVERED JAPANESE QUARTERSTAFF
*BUSHI: WARRIOR

THANK YOU, MY GOOD—

HEY, WHAT—?!

EVER HEAR OF "EXCUSE ME"? TSK!!

STUPID—??

THREE *KOKUS*', YOU SAY? HMM...

DEAL, OKKO-SAN! I SHALL BE DEEPLY HONORED TO GUIDE YOU AND YOUR FRIENDS TO THE PASS AT SEKKAN.

OKKO-SAN! I MUST SPEAK WITH YOU!

?

THEY'RE HERE, I CAN FEEL IT! THEIR MADNESS IS *BLACK AS THE DARKEST RAVEN'S WING!*

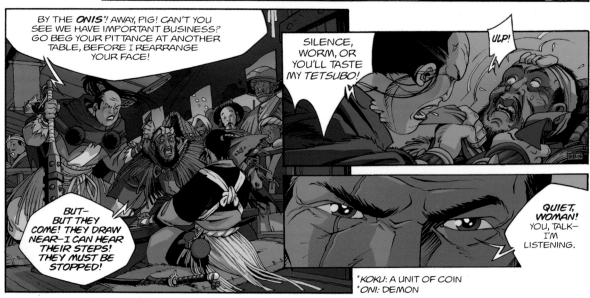

BY THE *ONIS*'! AWAY, PIG! CAN'T YOU SEE WE HAVE IMPORTANT BUSINESS? GO BEG YOUR PITTANCE AT ANOTHER TABLE, BEFORE I REARRANGE YOUR FACE!

SILENCE, WORM, OR YOU'LL TASTE MY *TETSUBO!*

ULP!

BUT— BUT THEY COME! THEY DRAW NEAR—I CAN HEAR THEIR STEPS! THEY MUST BE STOPPED!

QUIET, WOMAN! YOU, TALK— I'M LISTENING.

*KOKU: A UNIT OF COIN
*ONI: DEMON

12

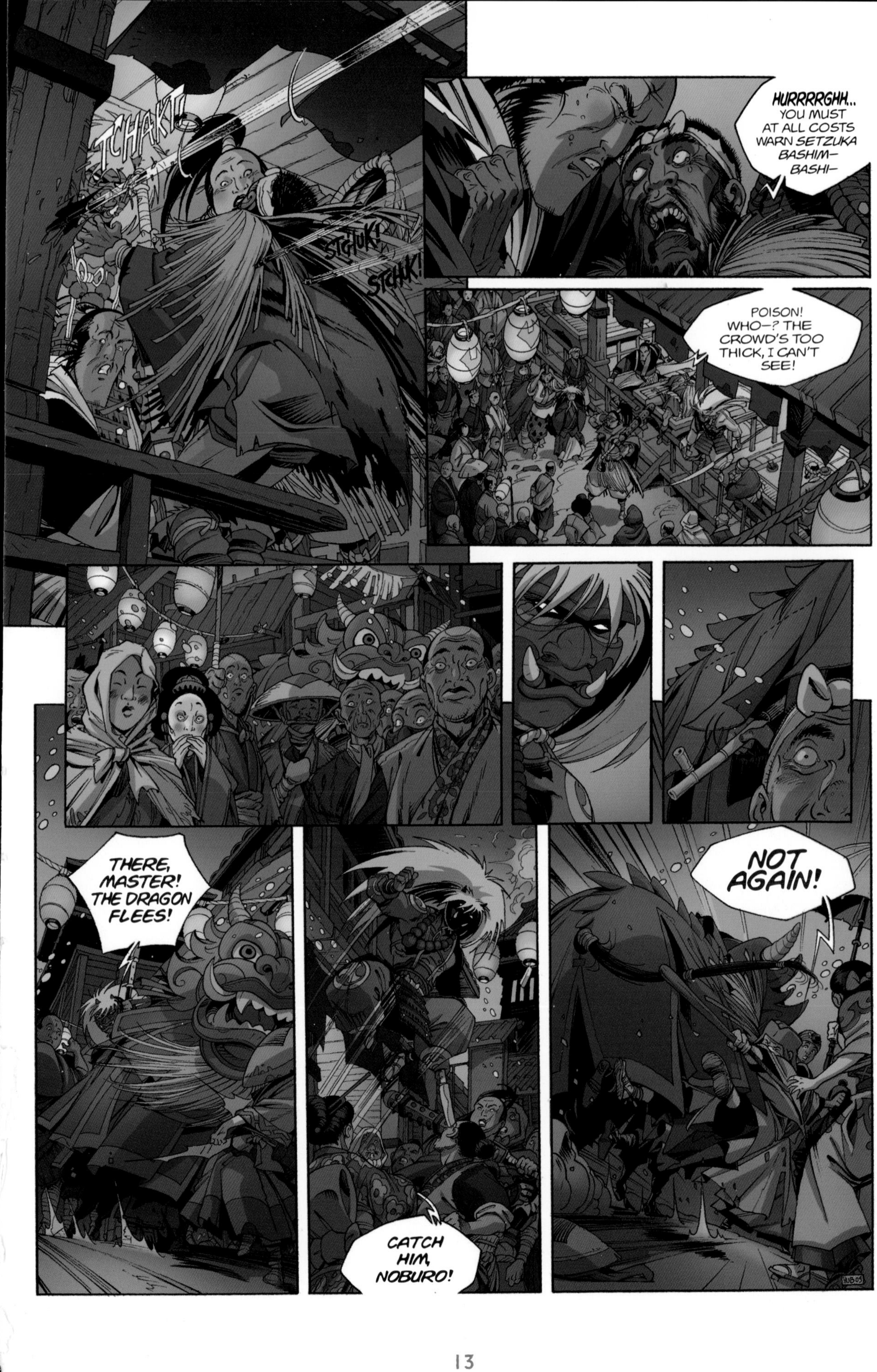
TCHAK!
STCHUK!
STCHK!
HURRRRGHH... YOU MUST AT ALL COSTS WARN SETZUKA BASHIM-BASHI–
POISON! WHO–? THE CROWD'S TOO THICK, I CAN'T SEE!
THERE, MASTER! THE DRAGON FLEES!
CATCH HIM, NOBURO!
NOT AGAIN!

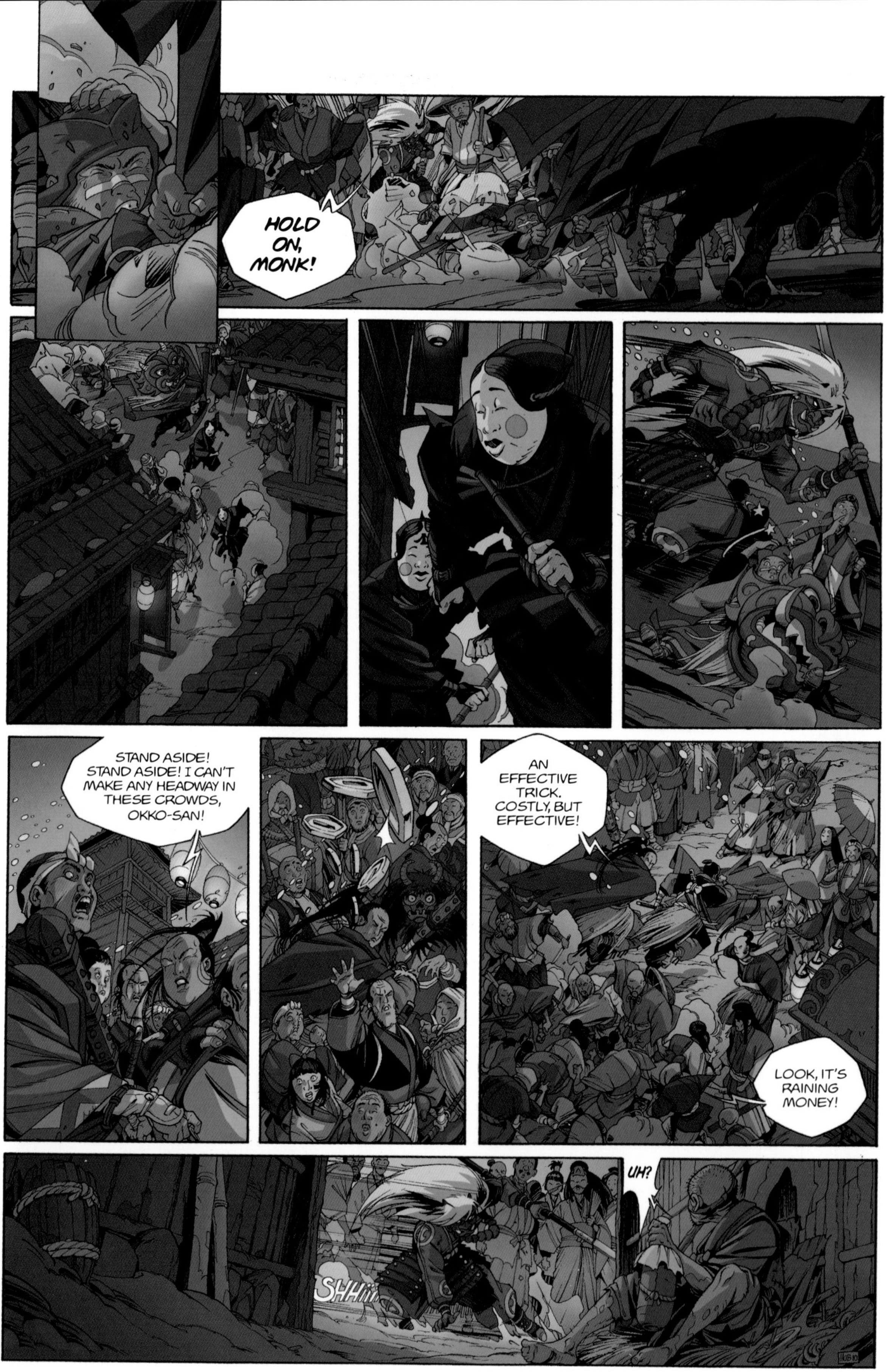
HOLD ON, MONK!
STAND ASIDE! STAND ASIDE! I CAN'T MAKE ANY HEADWAY IN THESE CROWDS, OKKO-SAN!
AN EFFECTIVE TRICK. COSTLY, BUT EFFECTIVE!
LOOK, IT'S RAINING MONEY!
UH?
SHHiii

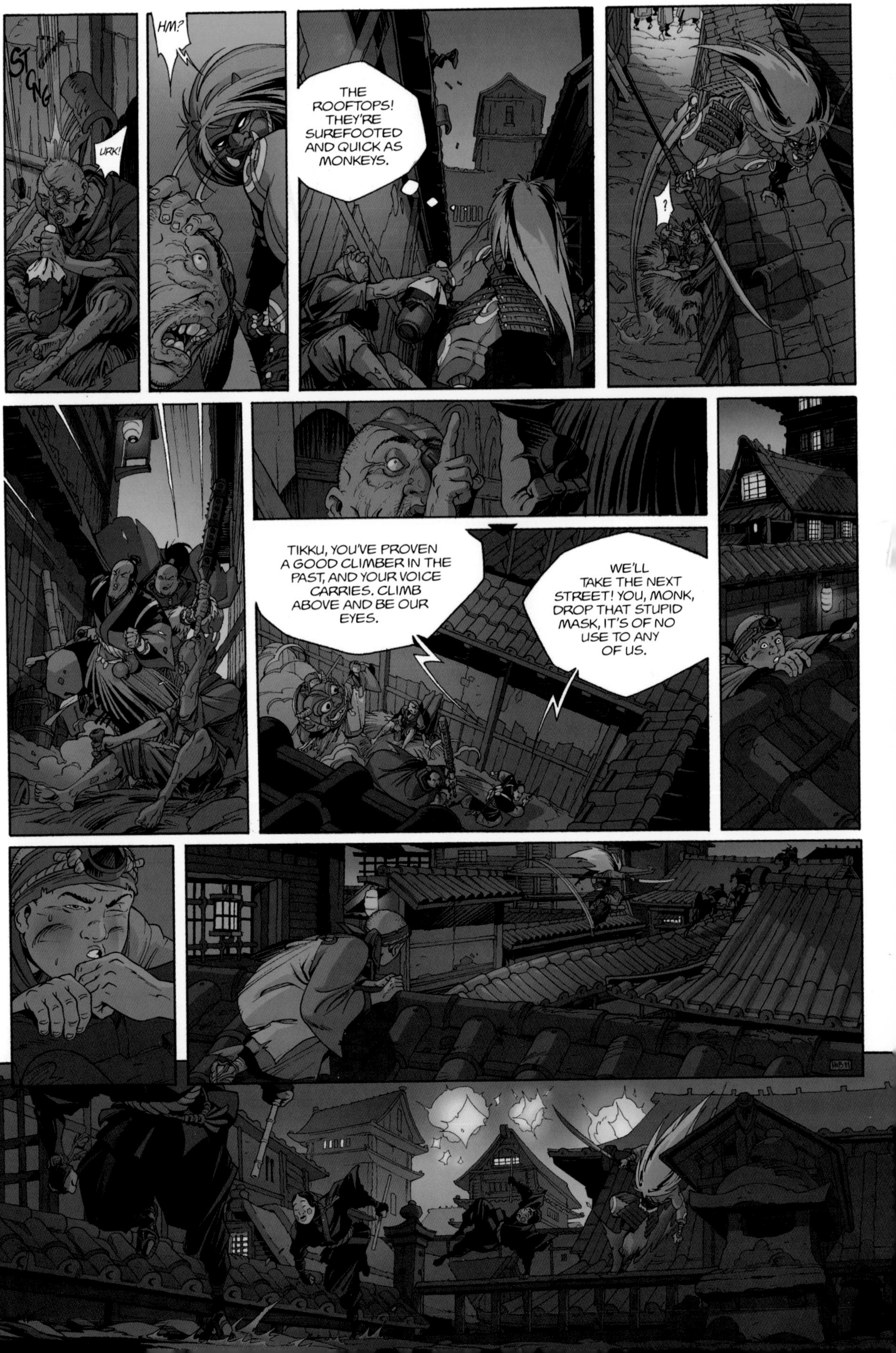
STCNG
URK!
HM?
THE ROOFTOPS! THEY'RE SUREFOOTED AND QUICK AS MONKEYS.
?
TIKKU, YOU'VE PROVEN A GOOD CLIMBER IN THE PAST, AND YOUR VOICE CARRIES. CLIMB ABOVE AND BE OUR EYES.
WE'LL TAKE THE NEXT STREET! YOU, MONK, DROP THAT STUPID MASK, IT'S OF NO USE TO ANY OF US.

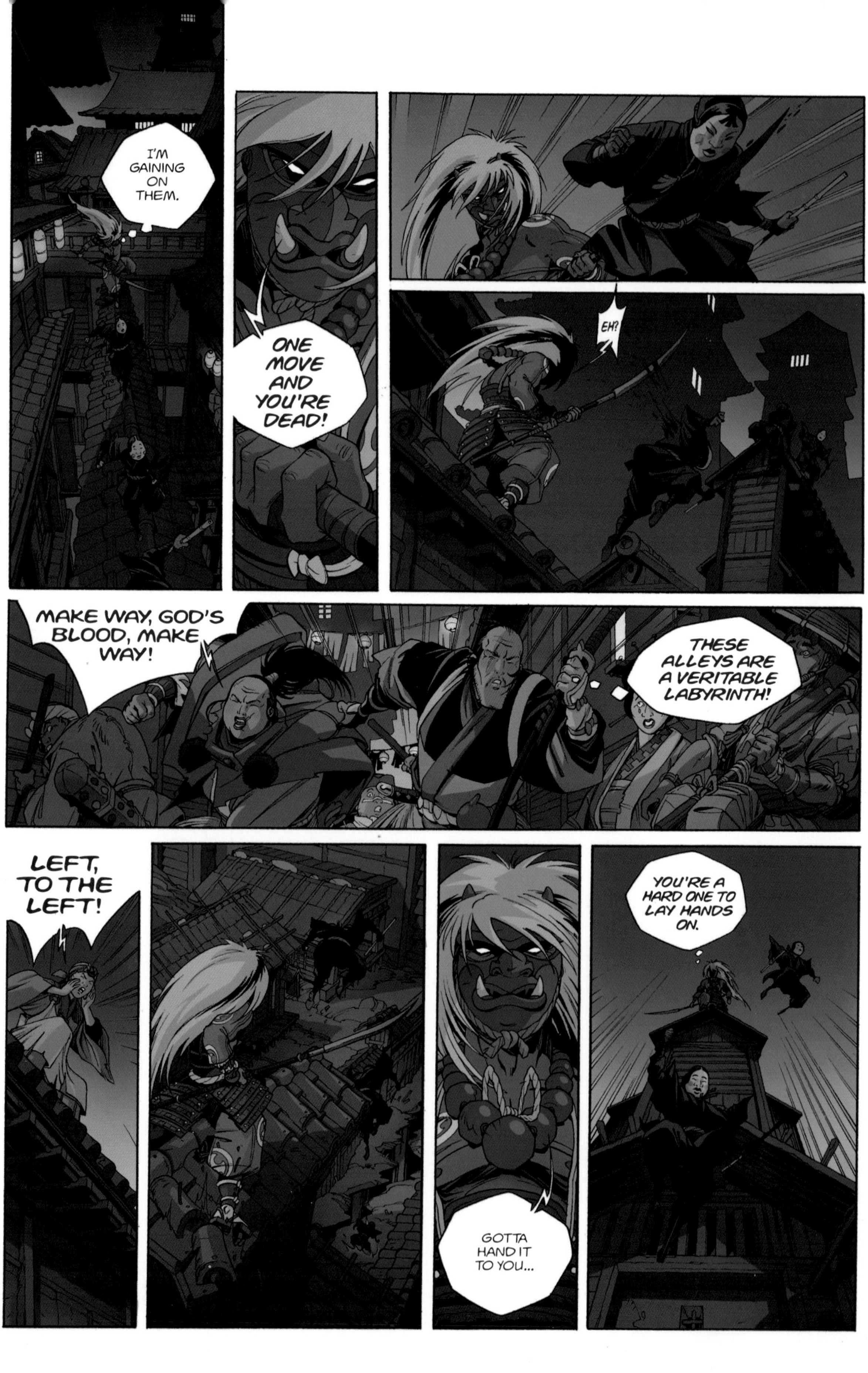
I'M GAINING ON THEM.
ONE MOVE AND YOU'RE DEAD!
EH?
MAKE WAY, GOD'S BLOOD, MAKE WAY!
THESE ALLEYS ARE A VERITABLE LABYRINTH!
LEFT, TO THE LEFT!
GOTTA HAND IT TO YOU...
YOU'RE A HARD ONE TO LAY HANDS ON.

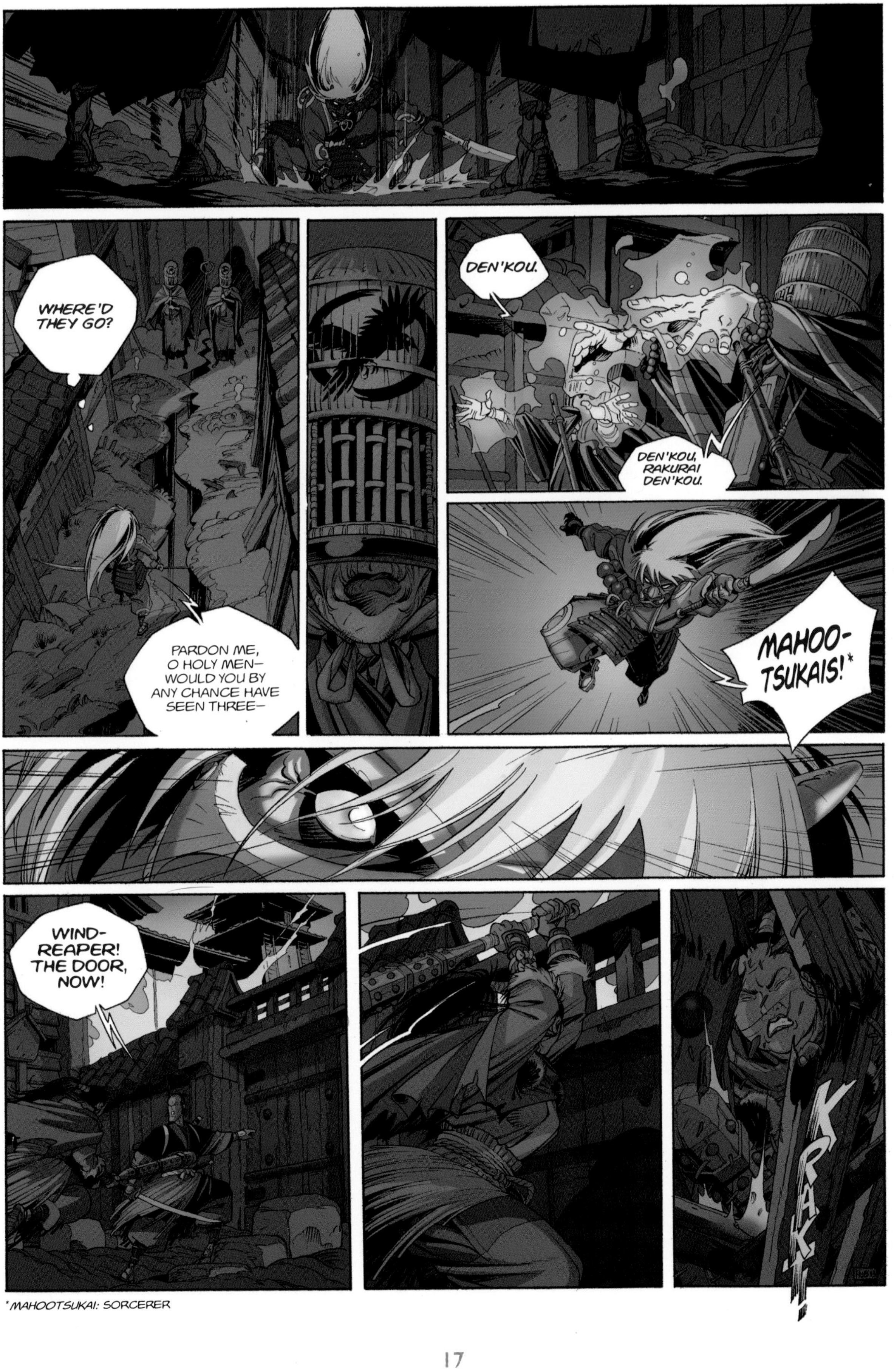
WHERE'D THEY GO?
PARDON ME, O HOLY MEN— WOULD YOU BY ANY CHANCE HAVE SEEN THREE—
DEN'KOU.
DEN'KOU, RAKURAI DEN'KOU.
MAHOO-TSUKAIS!*
WIND-REAPER! THE DOOR, NOW!
KRAKT!

*MAHOOTSUKAI: SORCERER

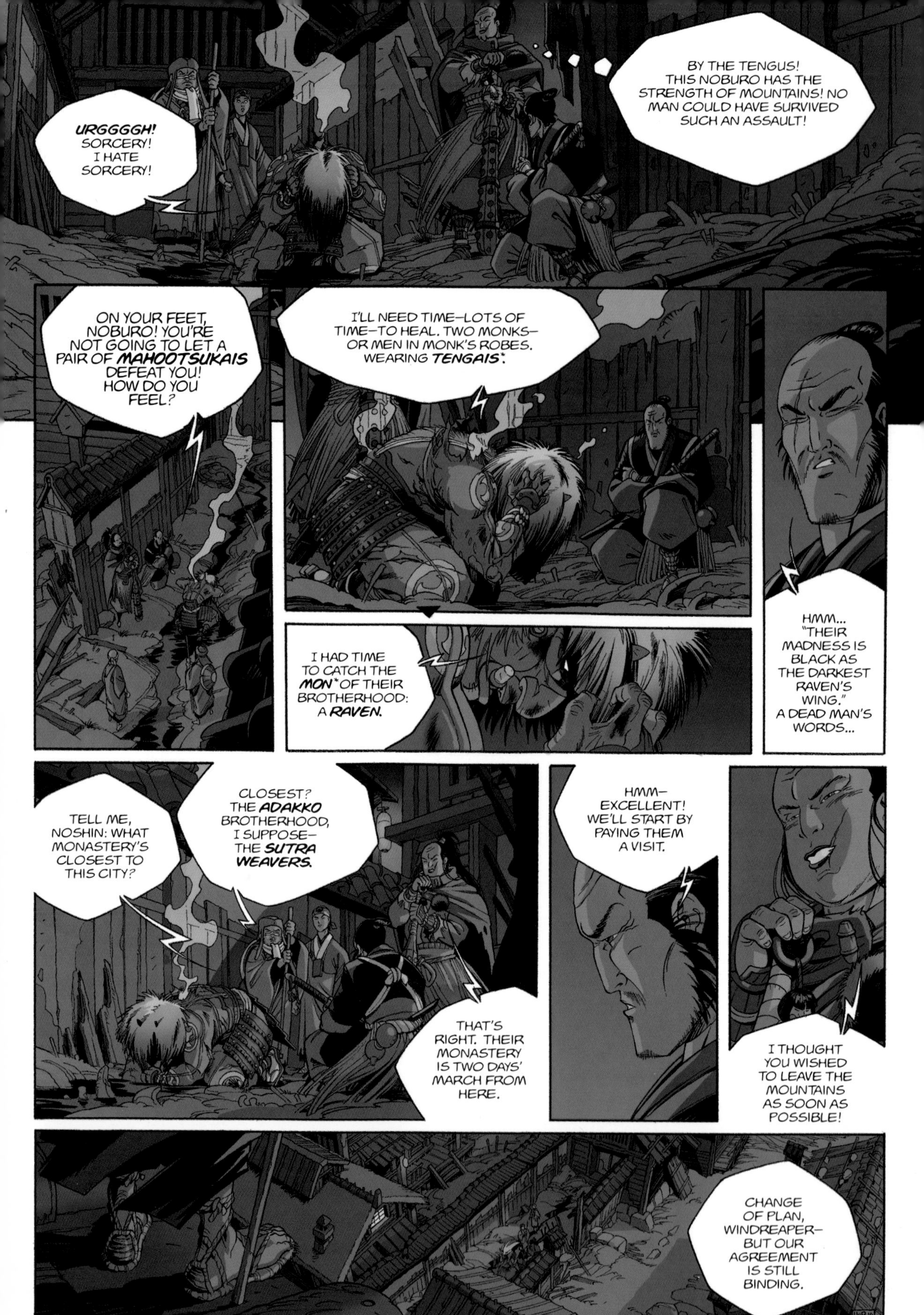
URGGGGH! SORCERY! I HATE SORCERY!
BY THE TENGUS! THIS NOBURO HAS THE STRENGTH OF MOUNTAINS! NO MAN COULD HAVE SURVIVED SUCH AN ASSAULT!
ON YOUR FEET, NOBURO! YOU'RE NOT GOING TO LET A PAIR OF MAHOOTSUKAIS DEFEAT YOU! HOW DO YOU FEEL?
I'LL NEED TIME—LOTS OF TIME—TO HEAL. TWO MONKS—OR MEN IN MONK'S ROBES. WEARING TENGAIS*.
I HAD TIME TO CATCH THE MON* OF THEIR BROTHERHOOD: A RAVEN.
HMM... "THEIR MADNESS IS BLACK AS THE DARKEST RAVEN'S WING." A DEAD MAN'S WORDS...
TELL ME, NOSHIN: WHAT MONASTERY'S CLOSEST TO THIS CITY?
CLOSEST? THE ADAKKO BROTHERHOOD, I SUPPOSE—THE SUTRA WEAVERS.
THAT'S RIGHT. THEIR MONASTERY IS TWO DAYS' MARCH FROM HERE.
HMM—EXCELLENT! WE'LL START BY PAYING THEM A VISIT.
I THOUGHT YOU WISHED TO LEAVE THE MOUNTAINS AS SOON AS POSSIBLE!
CHANGE OF PLAN, WINDREAPER—BUT OUR AGREEMENT IS STILL BINDING.
HUB 14

*MON: HERALDIC EMBLEM
*TENGAI: A BASKETLIKE WICKER HAT WORN OVER THE HEAD

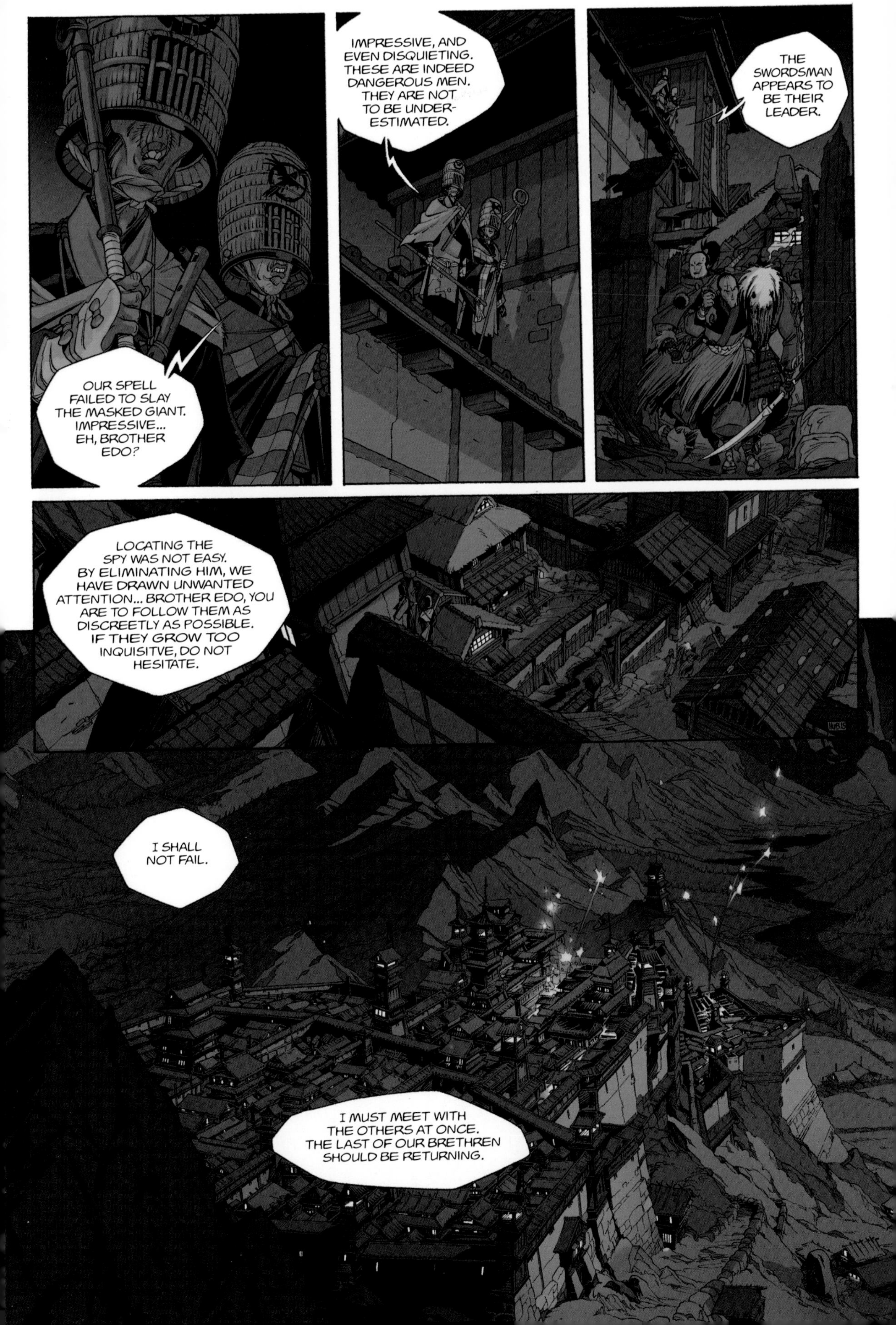
OUR SPELL FAILED TO SLAY THE MASKED GIANT. IMPRESSIVE... EH, BROTHER EDO?
IMPRESSIVE, AND EVEN DISQUIETING. THESE ARE INDEED DANGEROUS MEN. THEY ARE NOT TO BE UNDER-ESTIMATED.
THE SWORDSMAN APPEARS TO BE THEIR LEADER.
LOCATING THE SPY WAS NOT EASY. BY ELIMINATING HIM, WE HAVE DRAWN UNWANTED ATTENTION... BROTHER EDO, YOU ARE TO FOLLOW THEM AS DISCREETLY AS POSSIBLE. IF THEY GROW TOO INQUISITVE, DO NOT HESITATE.
I SHALL NOT FAIL.
I MUST MEET WITH THE OTHERS AT ONCE. THE LAST OF OUR BRETHREN SHOULD BE RETURNING.

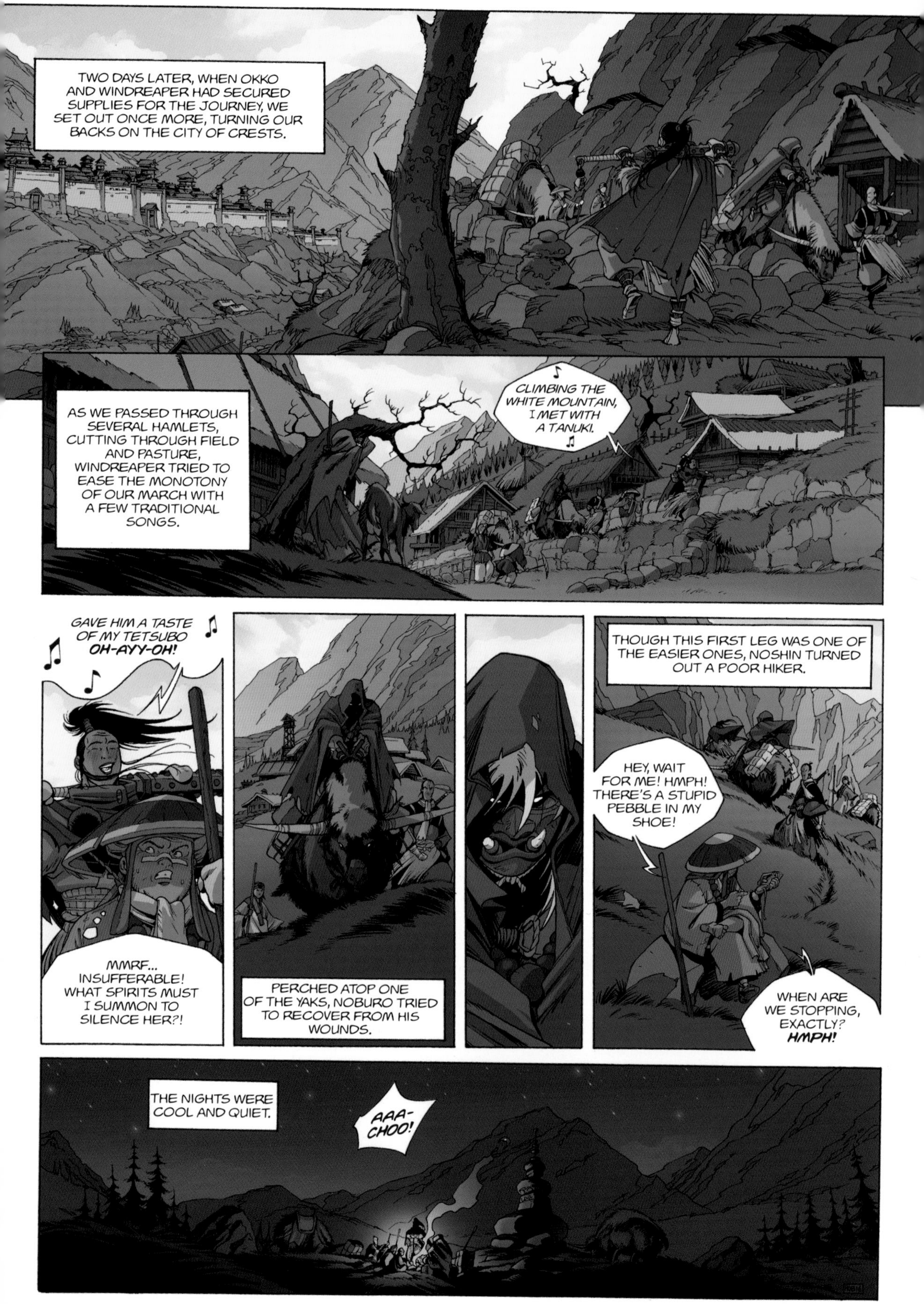
TWO DAYS LATER, WHEN OKKO AND WINDREAPER HAD SECURED SUPPLIES FOR THE JOURNEY, WE SET OUT ONCE MORE, TURNING OUR BACKS ON THE CITY OF CRESTS.
AS WE PASSED THROUGH SEVERAL HAMLETS, CUTTING THROUGH FIELD AND PASTURE, WINDREAPER TRIED TO EASE THE MONOTONY OF OUR MARCH WITH A FEW TRADITIONAL SONGS.
♪ CLIMBING THE WHITE MOUNTAIN, I MET WITH A TANUKI. ♫
GAVE HIM A TASTE OF MY TETSUBO **OH-AYY-OH!**
MMRF... INSUFFERABLE! WHAT SPIRITS MUST I SUMMON TO SILENCE HER?!
PERCHED ATOP ONE OF THE YAKS, NOBURO TRIED TO RECOVER FROM HIS WOUNDS.
THOUGH THIS FIRST LEG WAS ONE OF THE EASIER ONES, NOSHIN TURNED OUT A POOR HIKER.
HEY, WAIT FOR ME! HMPH! THERE'S A STUPID PEBBLE IN MY SHOE!
WHEN ARE WE STOPPING, EXACTLY? **HMPH!**
THE NIGHTS WERE COOL AND QUIET.
AAA-CHOO!

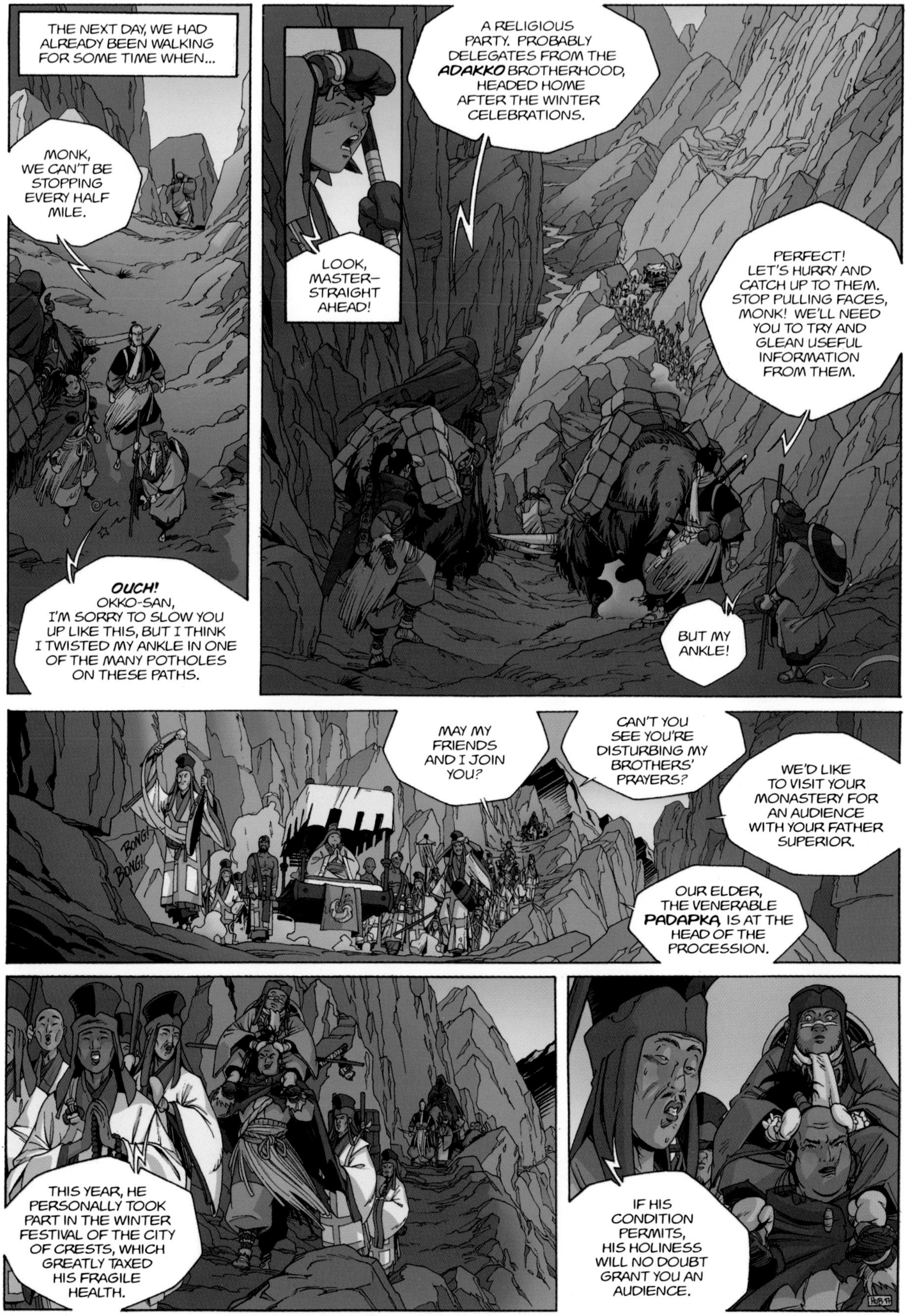
THE NEXT DAY, WE HAD ALREADY BEEN WALKING FOR SOME TIME WHEN...
MONK, WE CAN'T BE STOPPING EVERY HALF MILE.
OUCH! OKKO-SAN, I'M SORRY TO SLOW YOU UP LIKE THIS, BUT I THINK I TWISTED MY ANKLE IN ONE OF THE MANY POTHOLES ON THESE PATHS.
A RELIGIOUS PARTY. PROBABLY DELEGATES FROM THE ADAKKO BROTHERHOOD, HEADED HOME AFTER THE WINTER CELEBRATIONS.
LOOK, MASTER— STRAIGHT AHEAD!
PERFECT! LET'S HURRY AND CATCH UP TO THEM. STOP PULLING FACES, MONK! WE'LL NEED YOU TO TRY AND GLEAN USEFUL INFORMATION FROM THEM.
BUT MY ANKLE!
BONG! BONG!
MAY MY FRIENDS AND I JOIN YOU?
CAN'T YOU SEE YOU'RE DISTURBING MY BROTHERS' PRAYERS?
WE'D LIKE TO VISIT YOUR MONASTERY FOR AN AUDIENCE WITH YOUR FATHER SUPERIOR.
OUR ELDER, THE VENERABLE PADAPKA, IS AT THE HEAD OF THE PROCESSION.
THIS YEAR, HE PERSONALLY TOOK PART IN THE WINTER FESTIVAL OF THE CITY OF CRESTS, WHICH GREATLY TAXED HIS FRAGILE HEALTH.
IF HIS CONDITION PERMITS, HIS HOLINESS WILL NO DOUBT GRANT YOU AN AUDIENCE.

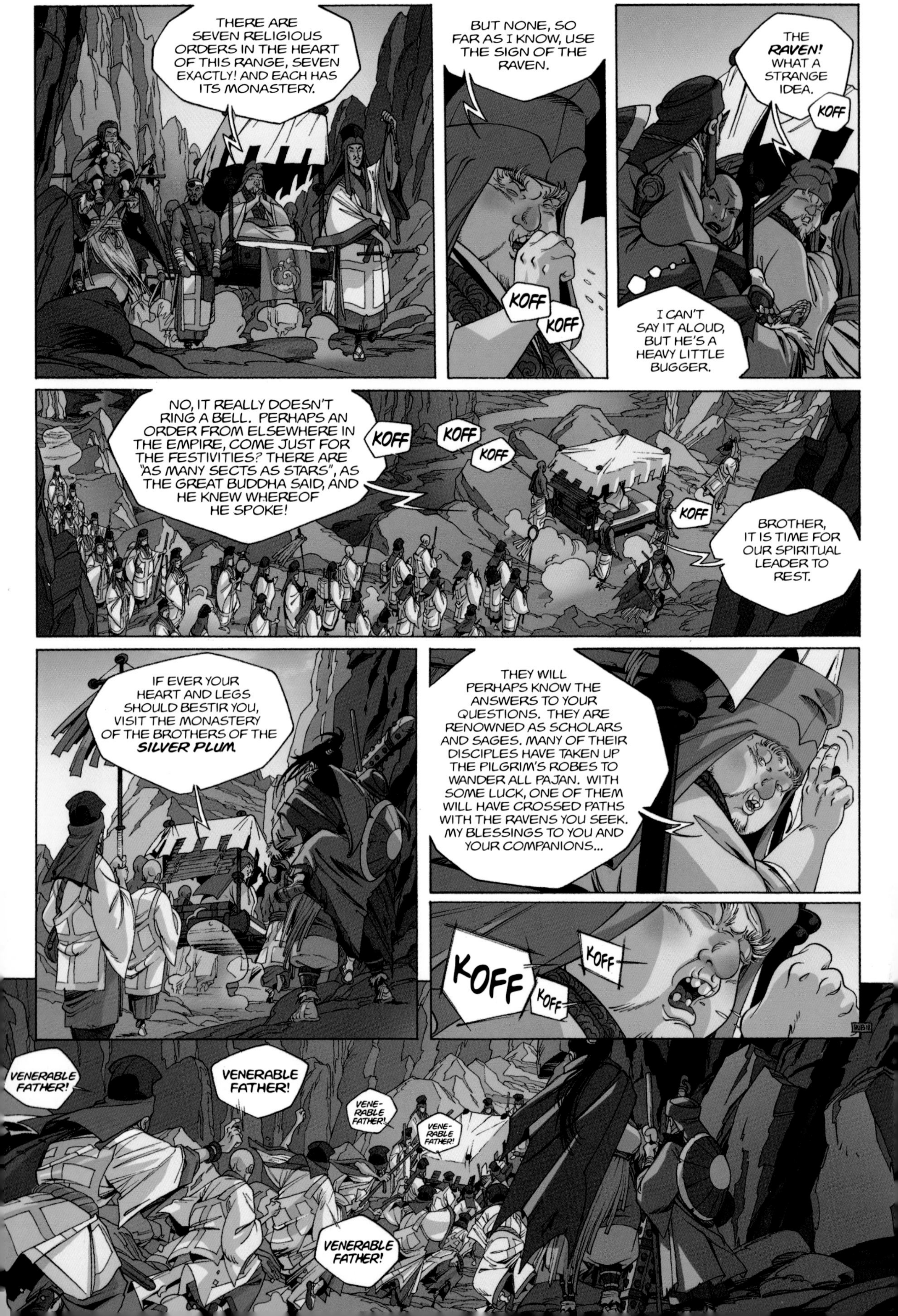
THERE ARE SEVEN RELIGIOUS ORDERS IN THE HEART OF THIS RANGE, SEVEN EXACTLY! AND EACH HAS ITS MONASTERY.
BUT NONE, SO FAR AS I KNOW, USE THE SIGN OF THE RAVEN.
KOFF
KOFF
THE RAVEN! WHAT A STRANGE IDEA.
KOFF
I CAN'T SAY IT ALOUD, BUT HE'S A HEAVY LITTLE BUGGER.
NO, IT REALLY DOESN'T RING A BELL. PERHAPS AN ORDER FROM ELSEWHERE IN THE EMPIRE, COME JUST FOR THE FESTIVITIES? THERE ARE "AS MANY SECTS AS STARS", AS THE GREAT BUDDHA SAID, AND HE KNEW WHEREOF HE SPOKE!
KOFF
KOFF
KOFF
KOFF
BROTHER, IT IS TIME FOR OUR SPIRITUAL LEADER TO REST.
IF EVER YOUR HEART AND LEGS SHOULD BESTIR YOU, VISIT THE MONASTERY OF THE BROTHERS OF THE SILVER PLUM.
THEY WILL PERHAPS KNOW THE ANSWERS TO YOUR QUESTIONS. THEY ARE RENOWNED AS SCHOLARS AND SAGES. MANY OF THEIR DISCIPLES HAVE TAKEN UP THE PILGRIM'S ROBES TO WANDER ALL PAJAN. WITH SOME LUCK, ONE OF THEM WILL HAVE CROSSED PATHS WITH THE RAVENS YOU SEEK. MY BLESSINGS TO YOU AND YOUR COMPANIONS...
KOFF
KOFF
KOFF
VENERABLE FATHER!
VENERABLE FATHER!
VENE-RABLE FATHER!
VENE-RABLE FATHER!
VENERABLE FATHER!

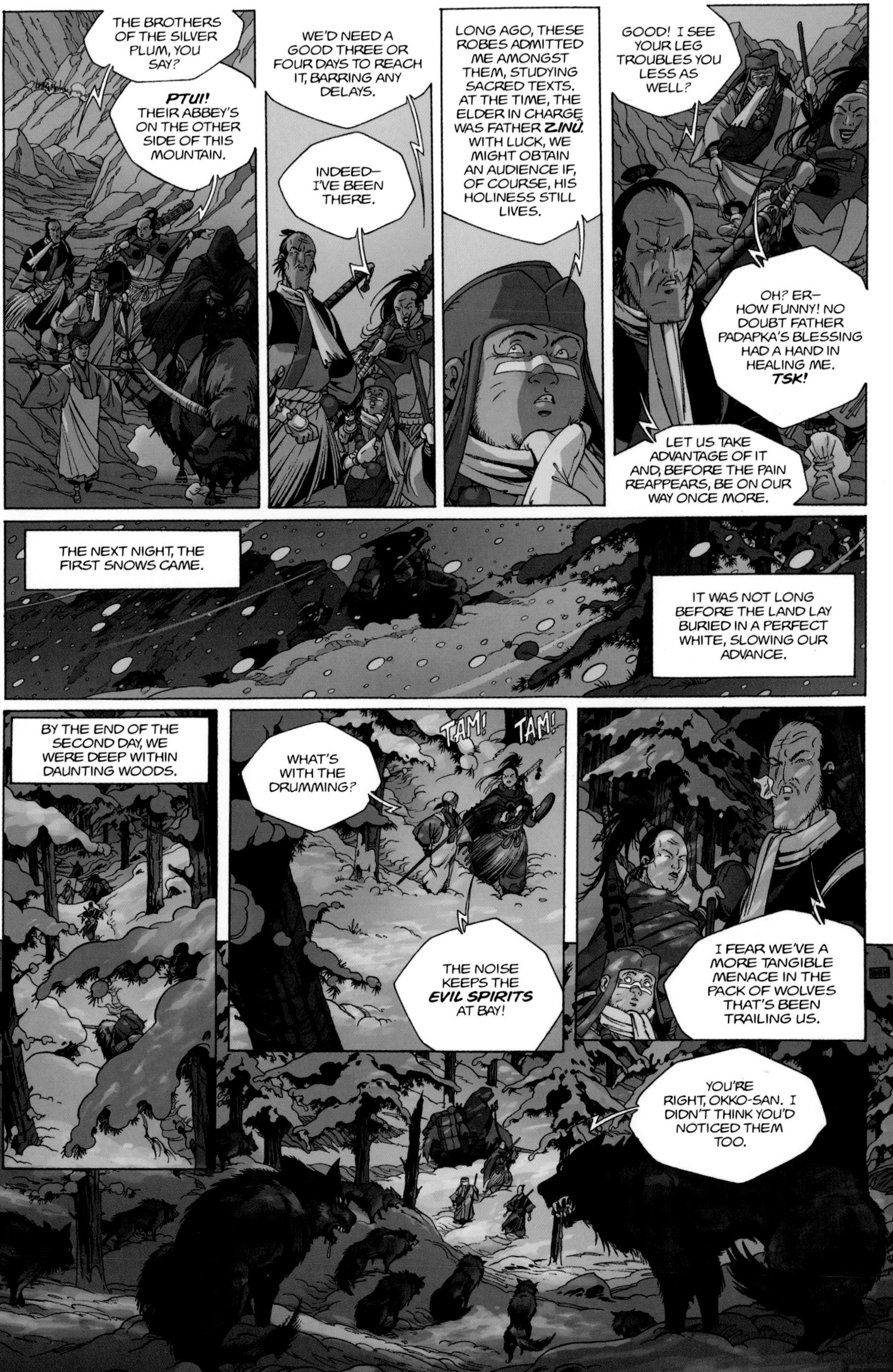

THE BROTHERS OF THE SILVER PLUM, YOU SAY?
PTUI! THEIR ABBEY'S ON THE OTHER SIDE OF THIS MOUNTAIN.
WE'D NEED A GOOD THREE OR FOUR DAYS TO REACH IT, BARRING ANY DELAYS.
INDEED— I'VE BEEN THERE.
LONG AGO, THESE ROBES ADMITTED ME AMONGST THEM, STUDYING SACRED TEXTS. AT THE TIME, THE ELDER IN CHARGE WAS FATHER ZINÛ. WITH LUCK, WE MIGHT OBTAIN AN AUDIENCE IF, OF COURSE, HIS HOLINESS STILL LIVES.
GOOD! I SEE YOUR LEG TROUBLES YOU LESS AS WELL?
OH? ER— HOW FUNNY! NO DOUBT FATHER PADAPKA'S BLESSING HAD A HAND IN HEALING ME. TSK!
LET US TAKE ADVANTAGE OF IT AND, BEFORE THE PAIN REAPPEARS, BE ON OUR WAY ONCE MORE.
THE NEXT NIGHT, THE FIRST SNOWS CAME.
IT WAS NOT LONG BEFORE THE LAND LAY BURIED IN A PERFECT WHITE, SLOWING OUR ADVANCE.
BY THE END OF THE SECOND DAY, WE WERE DEEP WITHIN DAUNTING WOODS.
TAM! TAM!
WHAT'S WITH THE DRUMMING?
THE NOISE KEEPS THE EVIL SPIRITS AT BAY!
I FEAR WE'VE A MORE TANGIBLE MENACE IN THE PACK OF WOLVES THAT'S BEEN TRAILING US.
YOU'RE RIGHT, OKKO-SAN. I DIDN'T THINK YOU'D NOTICED THEM TOO.

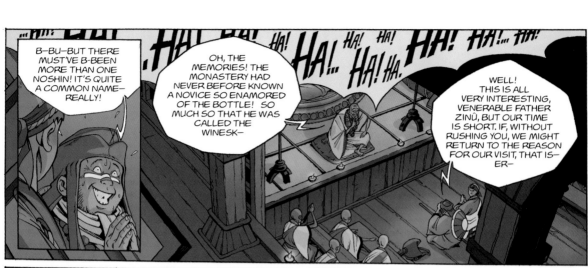

B—BU—BUT THERE MUST'VE B-BEEN MORE THAN ONE NOSHIN! IT'S QUITE A COMMON NAME—REALLY!

OH, THE MEMORIES! THE MONASTERY HAD NEVER BEFORE KNOWN A NOVICE SO ENAMORED OF THE BOTTLE! SO MUCH SO THAT HE WAS CALLED THE WINESK—

HA! HA! HA! HA! HA! HA! HA! HA!.. HA!

WELL! THIS IS ALL VERY INTERESTING, VENERABLE FATHER ZINÙ, BUT OUR TIME IS SHORT. IF, WITHOUT RUSHING YOU, WE MIGHT RETURN TO THE REASON FOR OUR VISIT, THAT IS—ER—

THE REASON? WHAT REASON? HEH HEH!

THE RAVEN—

OF COURSE, THE RAVENS! WHAT WAS I THINKING! A FASCINATING CREATURE, THE RAVEN.

BUT I KNOW NOT A SINGLE EMBLEM OR ARMS EVEN RESEMBLING OUR FEATHERED FRIEND!

CRANES AND NIGHTINGALES APLENTY, BUT NO RAVENS.

AND YOU, MY BROTHERS AND DISCIPLES? IN ALL YOUR MANY JOURNEYS, HAVE YOU EVER SEEN A SEAL OR COAT-OF-ARMS RESEMBLING SUCH AN ANIMAL?

NO.

NO.

NO.

NO.

NO.

NO.

NO.

NO.

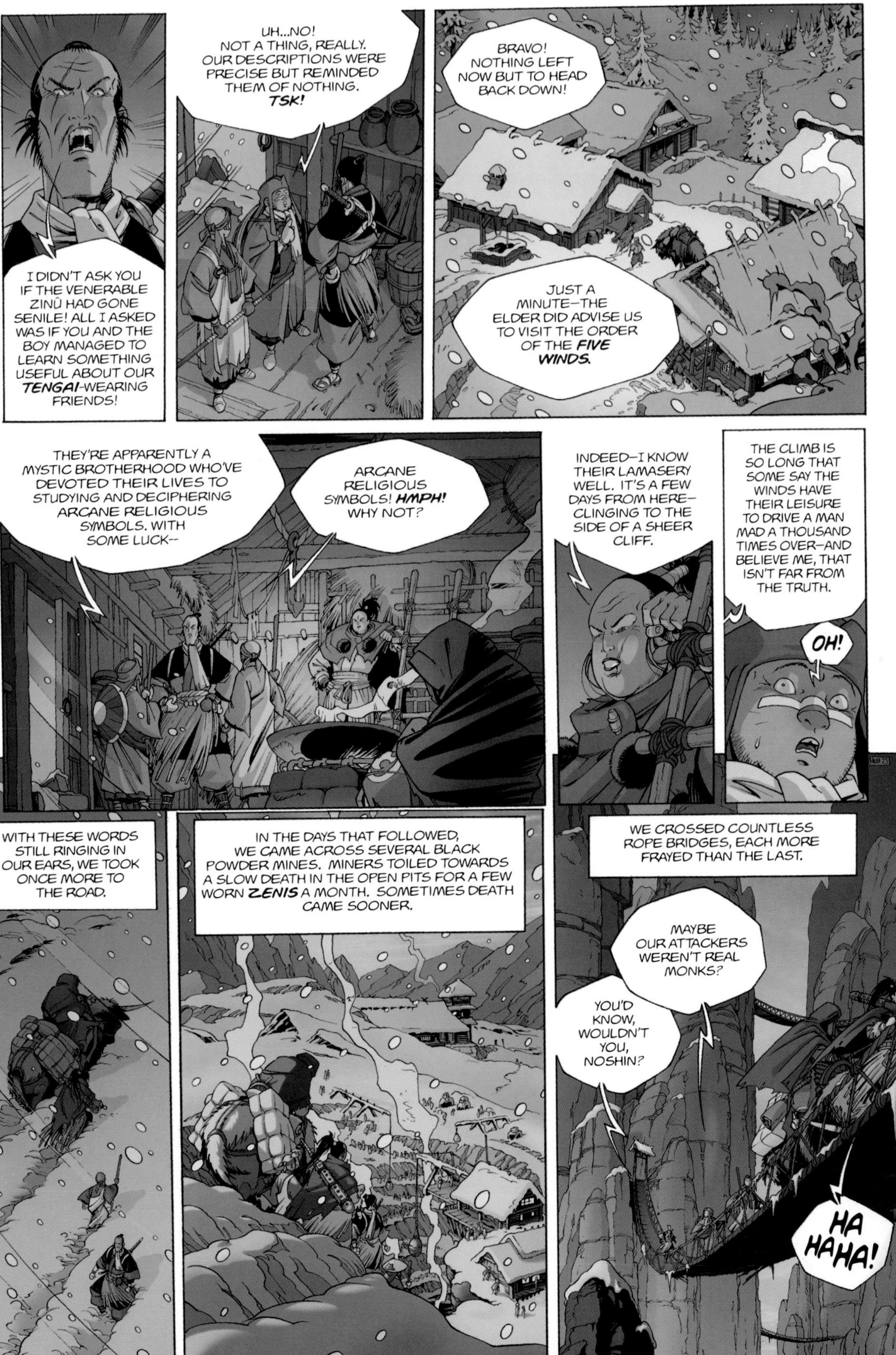
UH...NO! NOT A THING, REALLY. OUR DESCRIPTIONS WERE PRECISE BUT REMINDED THEM OF NOTHING. TSK!
I DIDN'T ASK YOU IF THE VENERABLE ZINÛ HAD GONE SENILE! ALL I ASKED WAS IF YOU AND THE BOY MANAGED TO LEARN SOMETHING USEFUL ABOUT OUR TENGAI-WEARING FRIENDS!
BRAVO! NOTHING LEFT NOW BUT TO HEAD BACK DOWN!
JUST A MINUTE—THE ELDER DID ADVISE US TO VISIT THE ORDER OF THE FIVE WINDS.
THEY'RE APPARENTLY A MYSTIC BROTHERHOOD WHO'VE DEVOTED THEIR LIVES TO STUDYING AND DECIPHERING ARCANE RELIGIOUS SYMBOLS. WITH SOME LUCK--
ARCANE RELIGIOUS SYMBOLS! HMPH! WHY NOT?
INDEED—I KNOW THEIR LAMASERY WELL. IT'S A FEW DAYS FROM HERE—CLINGING TO THE SIDE OF A SHEER CLIFF.
THE CLIMB IS SO LONG THAT SOME SAY THE WINDS HAVE THEIR LEISURE TO DRIVE A MAN MAD A THOUSAND TIMES OVER—AND BELIEVE ME, THAT ISN'T FAR FROM THE TRUTH.
OH!
WITH THESE WORDS STILL RINGING IN OUR EARS, WE TOOK ONCE MORE TO THE ROAD.
IN THE DAYS THAT FOLLOWED, WE CAME ACROSS SEVERAL BLACK POWDER MINES. MINERS TOILED TOWARDS A SLOW DEATH IN THE OPEN PITS FOR A FEW WORN ZENIS A MONTH. SOMETIMES DEATH CAME SOONER.
WE CROSSED COUNTLESS ROPE BRIDGES, EACH MORE FRAYED THAN THE LAST.
MAYBE OUR ATTACKERS WEREN'T REAL MONKS?
YOU'D KNOW, WOULDN'T YOU, NOSHIN?
HA HAHA!

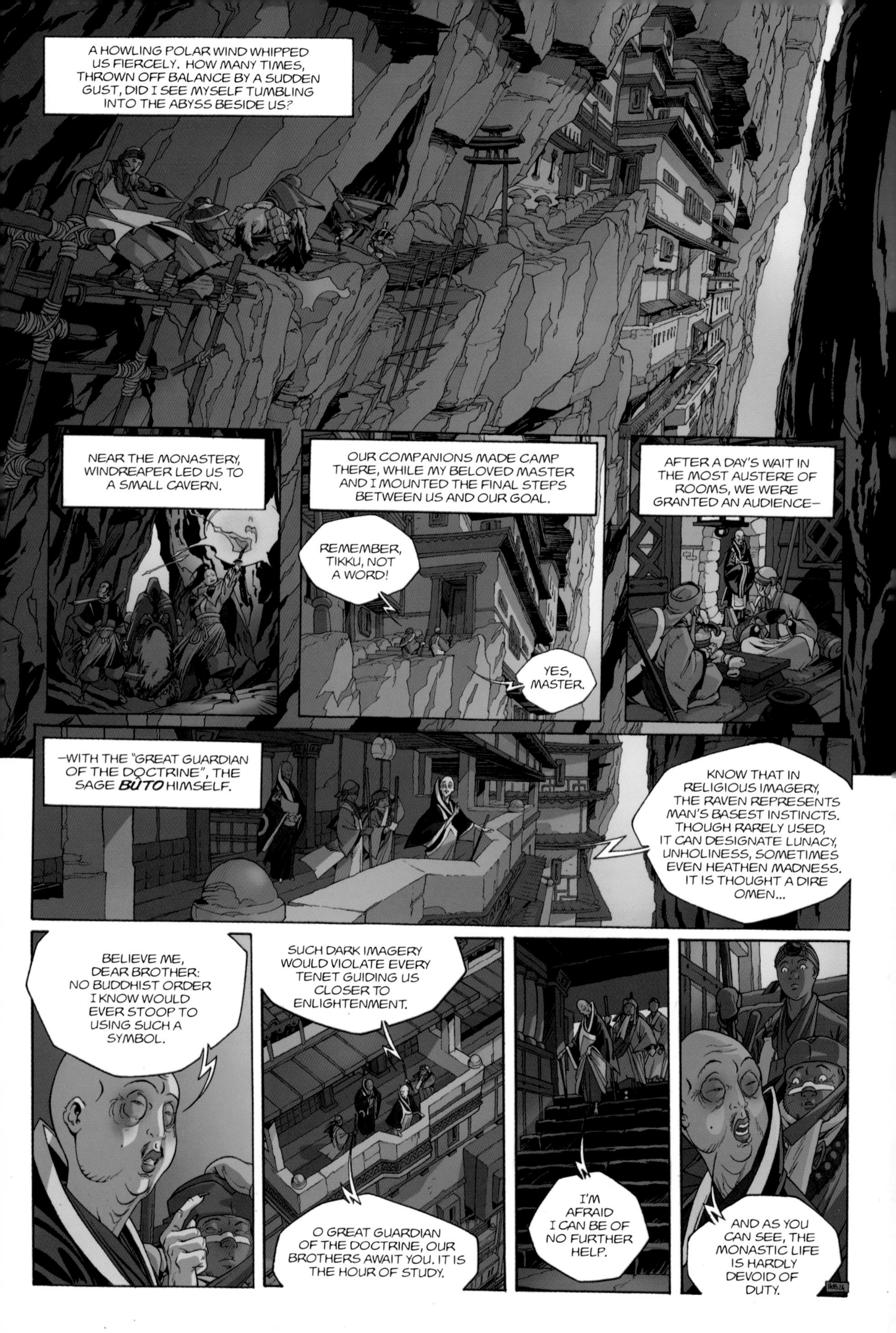
A HOWLING POLAR WIND WHIPPED US FIERCELY. HOW MANY TIMES, THROWN OFF BALANCE BY A SUDDEN GUST, DID I SEE MYSELF TUMBLING INTO THE ABYSS BESIDE US?
NEAR THE MONASTERY, WINDREAPER LED US TO A SMALL CAVERN.
OUR COMPANIONS MADE CAMP THERE, WHILE MY BELOVED MASTER AND I MOUNTED THE FINAL STEPS BETWEEN US AND OUR GOAL.
REMEMBER, TIKKU, NOT A WORD!
YES, MASTER.
AFTER A DAY'S WAIT IN THE MOST AUSTERE OF ROOMS, WE WERE GRANTED AN AUDIENCE—
—WITH THE "GREAT GUARDIAN OF THE DOCTRINE", THE SAGE **BÛTO** HIMSELF.
KNOW THAT IN RELIGIOUS IMAGERY, THE RAVEN REPRESENTS MAN'S BASEST INSTINCTS. THOUGH RARELY USED, IT CAN DESIGNATE LUNACY, UNHOLINESS, SOMETIMES EVEN HEATHEN MADNESS. IT IS THOUGHT A DIRE OMEN...
BELIEVE ME, DEAR BROTHER: NO BUDDHIST ORDER I KNOW WOULD EVER STOOP TO USING SUCH A SYMBOL.
SUCH DARK IMAGERY WOULD VIOLATE EVERY TENET GUIDING US CLOSER TO ENLIGHTENMENT.
O GREAT GUARDIAN OF THE DOCTRINE, OUR BROTHERS AWAIT YOU. IT IS THE HOUR OF STUDY.
I'M AFRAID I CAN BE OF NO FURTHER HELP.
AND AS YOU CAN SEE, THE MONASTIC LIFE IS HARDLY DEVOID OF DUTY.

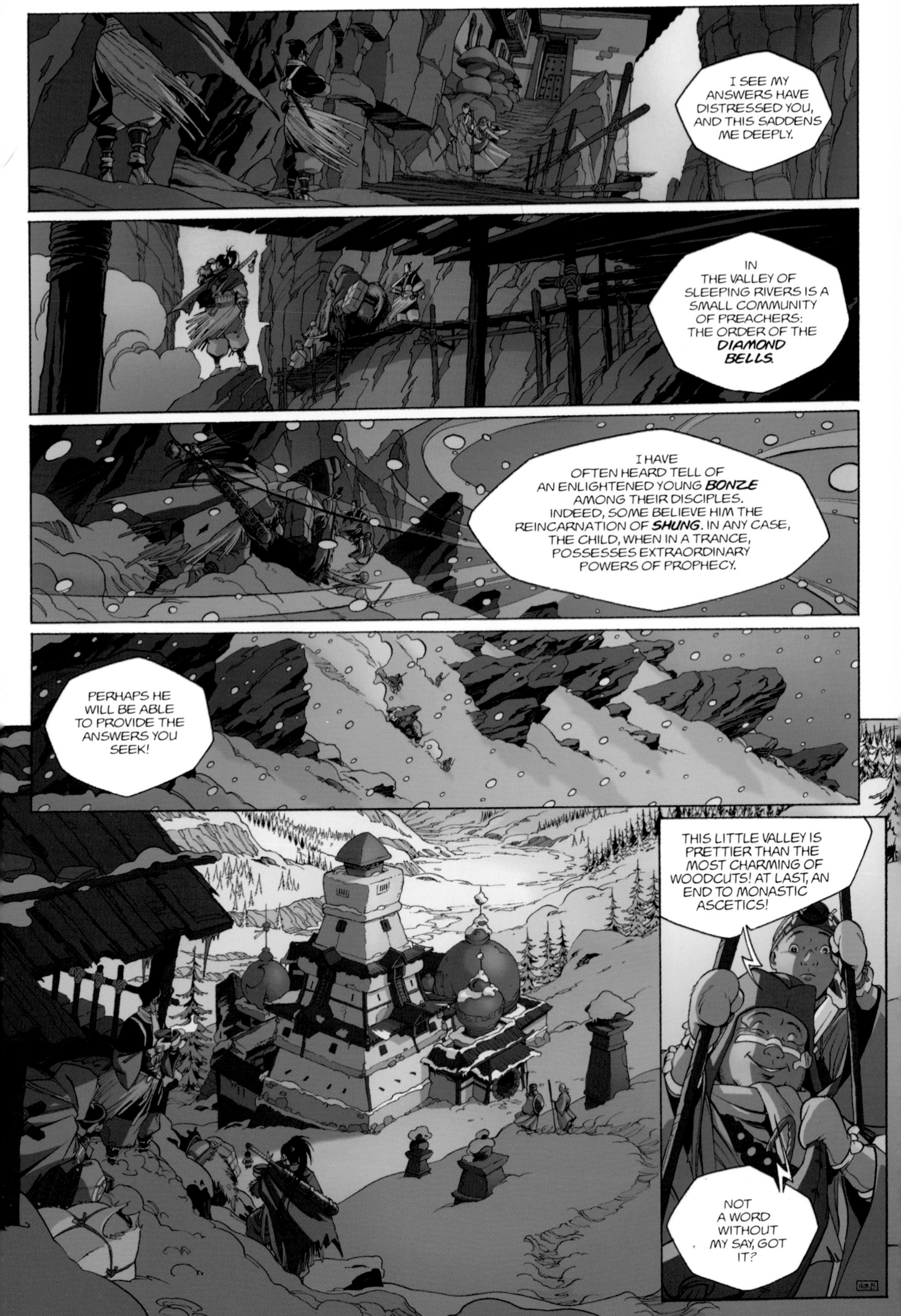
I SEE MY ANSWERS HAVE DISTRESSED YOU, AND THIS SADDENS ME DEEPLY.
IN THE VALLEY OF SLEEPING RIVERS IS A SMALL COMMUNITY OF PREACHERS: THE ORDER OF THE DIAMOND BELLS.
I HAVE OFTEN HEARD TELL OF AN ENLIGHTENED YOUNG BONZE AMONG THEIR DISCIPLES. INDEED, SOME BELIEVE HIM THE REINCARNATION OF SHUNG. IN ANY CASE, THE CHILD, WHEN IN A TRANCE, POSSESSES EXTRAORDINARY POWERS OF PROPHECY.
PERHAPS HE WILL BE ABLE TO PROVIDE THE ANSWERS YOU SEEK!
THIS LITTLE VALLEY IS PRETTIER THAN THE MOST CHARMING OF WOODCUTS! AT LAST, AN END TO MONASTIC ASCETICS!
NOT A WORD WITHOUT MY SAY, GOT IT?

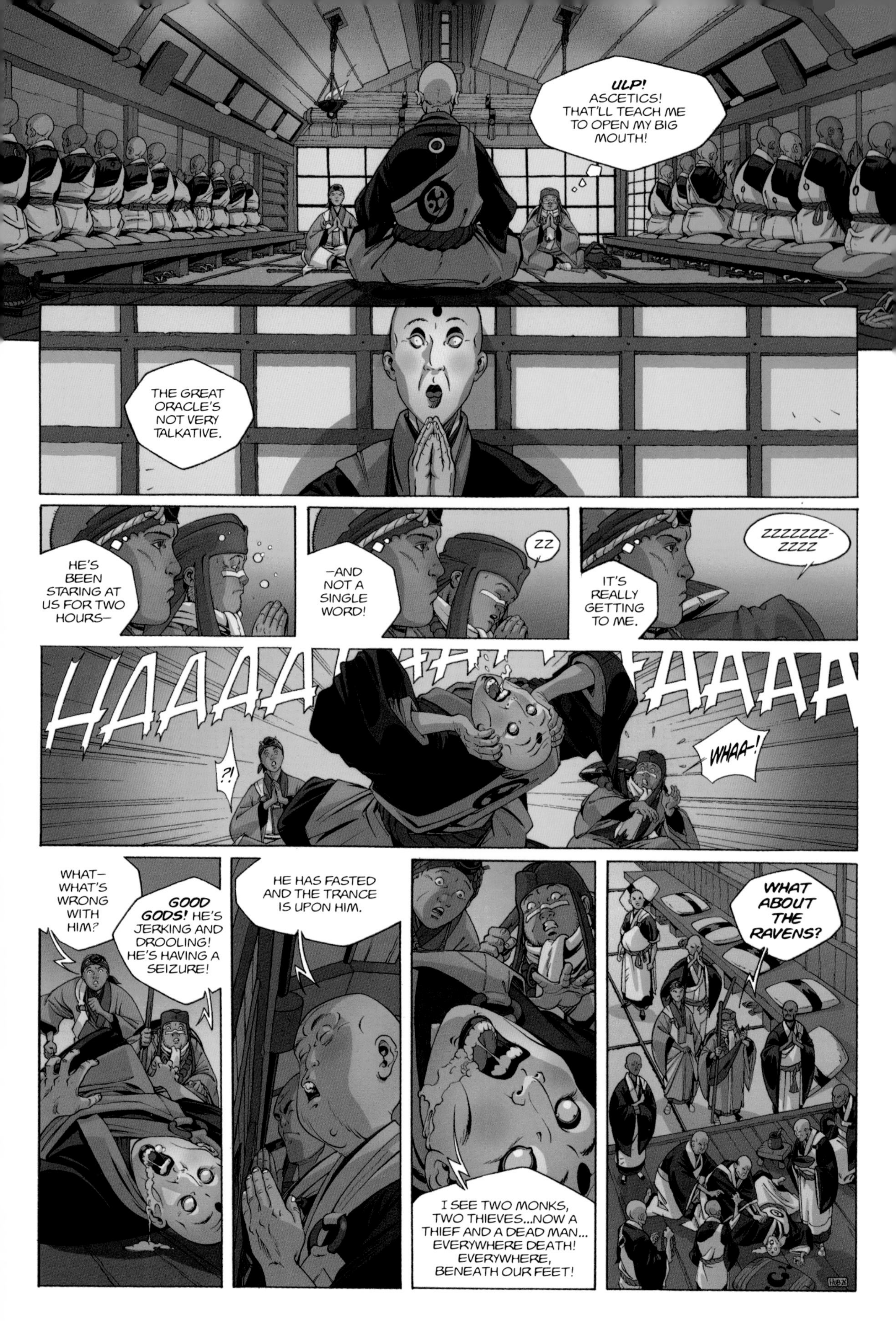
ULP! ASCETICS! THAT'LL TEACH ME TO OPEN MY BIG MOUTH!
THE GREAT ORACLE'S NOT VERY TALKATIVE.
HE'S BEEN STARING AT US FOR TWO HOURS—
—AND NOT A SINGLE WORD!
ZZ
IT'S REALLY GETTING TO ME.
ZZZZZZZ-ZZZZ
HAAAAAAAAAAAA
?!
WHAA-!
WHAT— WHAT'S WRONG WITH HIM?
GOOD GODS! HE'S JERKING AND DROOLING! HE'S HAVING A SEIZURE!
HE HAS FASTED AND THE TRANCE IS UPON HIM.
I SEE TWO MONKS, TWO THIEVES...NOW A THIEF AND A DEAD MAN... EVERYWHERE DEATH! EVERYWHERE, BENEATH OUR FEET!
WHAT ABOUT THE RAVENS?

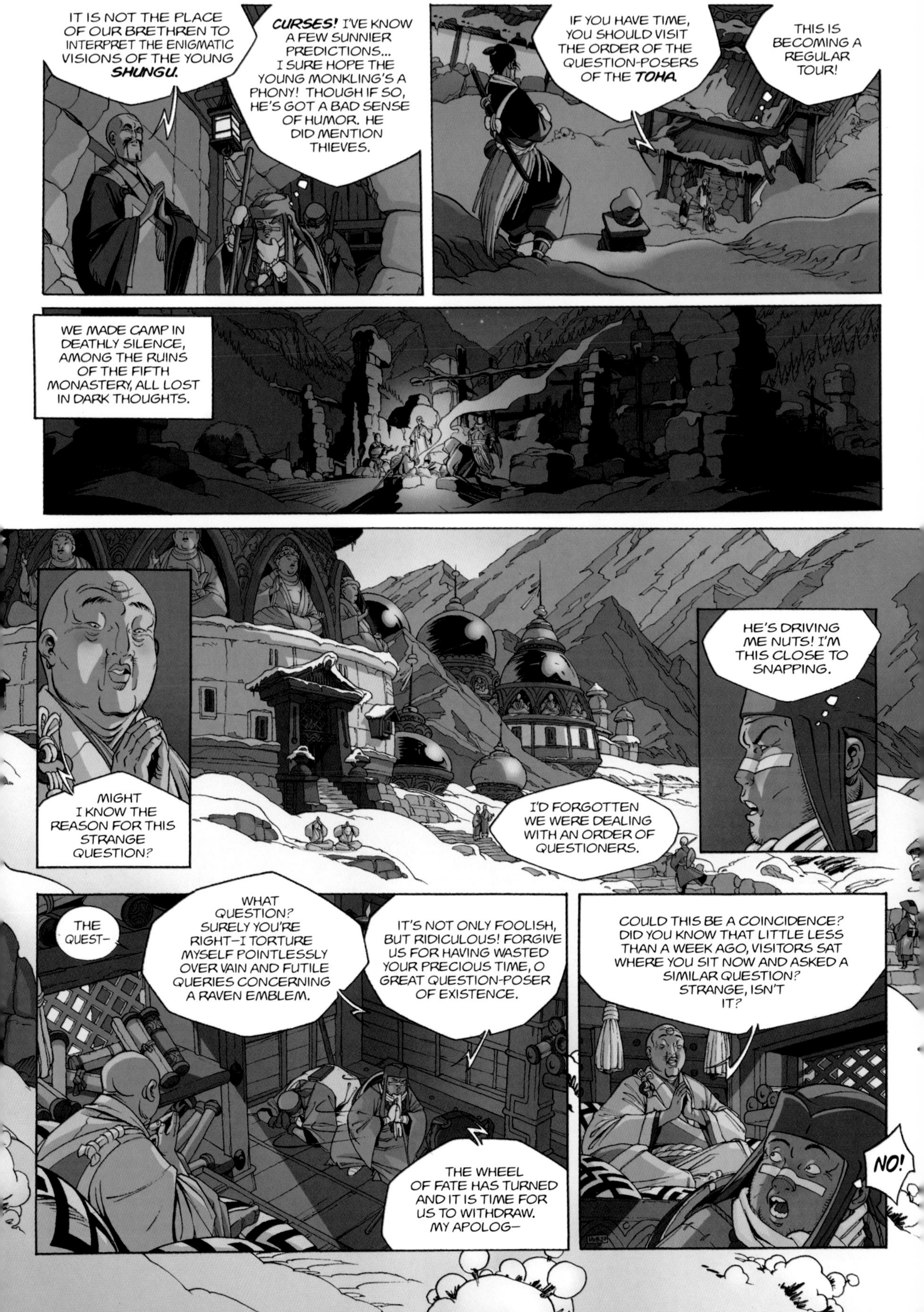
IT IS NOT THE PLACE OF OUR BRETHREN TO INTERPRET THE ENIGMATIC VISIONS OF THE YOUNG SHUNGU.
CURSES! I'VE KNOW A FEW SUNNIER PREDICTIONS... I SURE HOPE THE YOUNG MONKLING'S A PHONY! THOUGH IF SO, HE'S GOT A BAD SENSE OF HUMOR. HE DID MENTION THIEVES.
IF YOU HAVE TIME, YOU SHOULD VISIT THE ORDER OF THE QUESTION-POSERS OF THE TOHA.
THIS IS BECOMING A REGULAR TOUR!
WE MADE CAMP IN DEATHLY SILENCE, AMONG THE RUINS OF THE FIFTH MONASTERY, ALL LOST IN DARK THOUGHTS.
MIGHT I KNOW THE REASON FOR THIS STRANGE QUESTION?
I'D FORGOTTEN WE WERE DEALING WITH AN ORDER OF QUESTIONERS.
HE'S DRIVING ME NUTS! I'M THIS CLOSE TO SNAPPING.
THE QUEST–
WHAT QUESTION? SURELY YOU'RE RIGHT—I TORTURE MYSELF POINTLESSLY OVER VAIN AND FUTILE QUERIES CONCERNING A RAVEN EMBLEM.
IT'S NOT ONLY FOOLISH, BUT RIDICULOUS! FORGIVE US FOR HAVING WASTED YOUR PRECIOUS TIME, O GREAT QUESTION-POSER OF EXISTENCE.
THE WHEEL OF FATE HAS TURNED AND IT IS TIME FOR US TO WITHDRAW. MY APOLOG–
COULD THIS BE A COINCIDENCE? DID YOU KNOW THAT LITTLE LESS THAN A WEEK AGO, VISITORS SAT WHERE YOU SIT NOW AND ASKED A SIMILAR QUESTION? STRANGE, ISN'T IT?
NO!

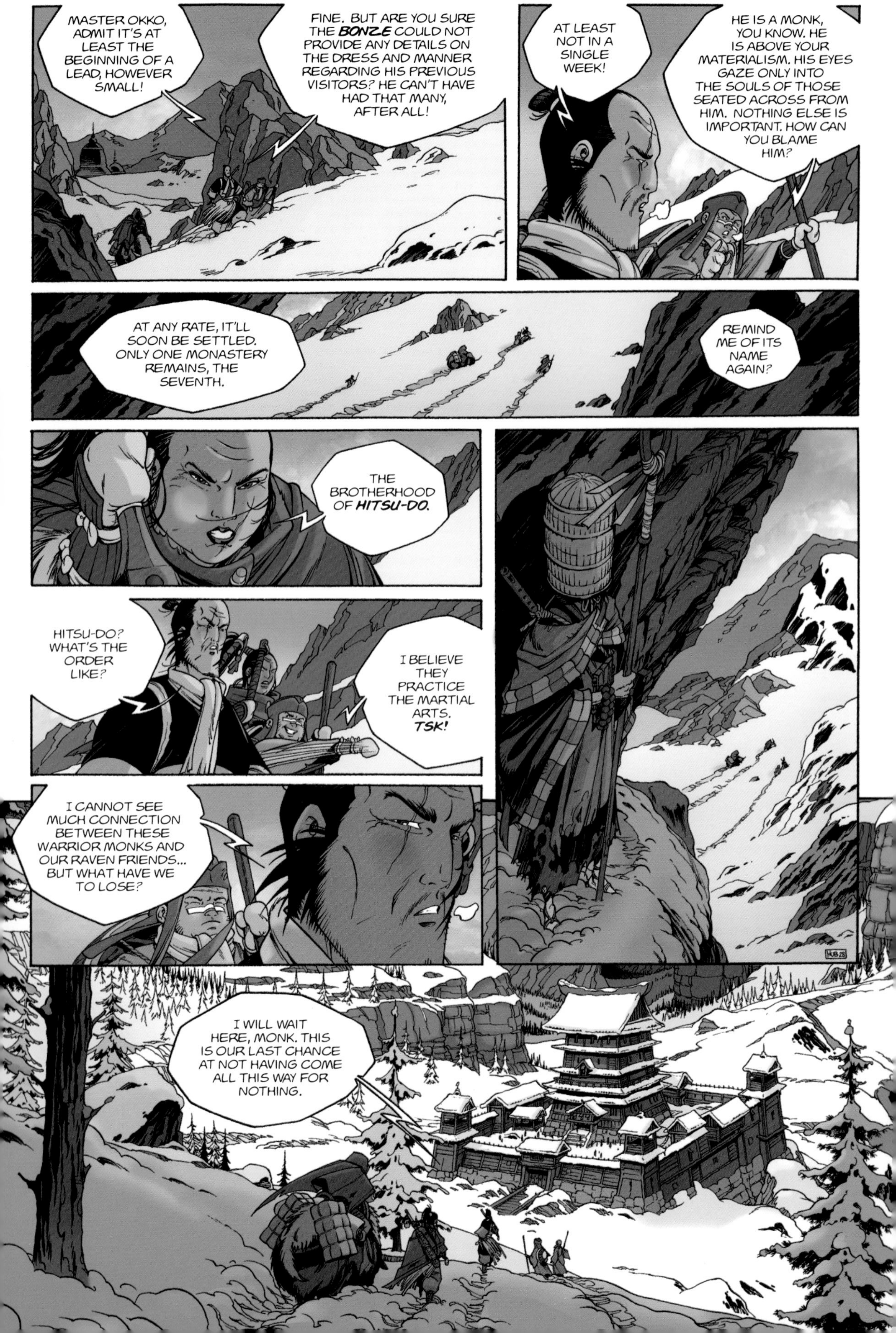
MASTER OKKO, ADMIT IT'S AT LEAST THE BEGINNING OF A LEAD, HOWEVER SMALL!
FINE. BUT ARE YOU SURE THE BONZE COULD NOT PROVIDE ANY DETAILS ON THE DRESS AND MANNER REGARDING HIS PREVIOUS VISITORS? HE CAN'T HAVE HAD THAT MANY, AFTER ALL!
AT LEAST NOT IN A SINGLE WEEK!
HE IS A MONK, YOU KNOW. HE IS ABOVE YOUR MATERIALISM. HIS EYES GAZE ONLY INTO THE SOULS OF THOSE SEATED ACROSS FROM HIM. NOTHING ELSE IS IMPORTANT. HOW CAN YOU BLAME HIM?
AT ANY RATE, IT'LL SOON BE SETTLED. ONLY ONE MONASTERY REMAINS, THE SEVENTH.
REMIND ME OF ITS NAME AGAIN?
THE BROTHERHOOD OF HITSU-DO.
HITSU-DO? WHAT'S THE ORDER LIKE?
I BELIEVE THEY PRACTICE THE MARTIAL ARTS. TSK!
I CANNOT SEE MUCH CONNECTION BETWEEN THESE WARRIOR MONKS AND OUR RAVEN FRIENDS... BUT WHAT HAVE WE TO LOSE?
HUB 28
I WILL WAIT HERE, MONK. THIS IS OUR LAST CHANCE AT NOT HAVING COME ALL THIS WAY FOR NOTHING.

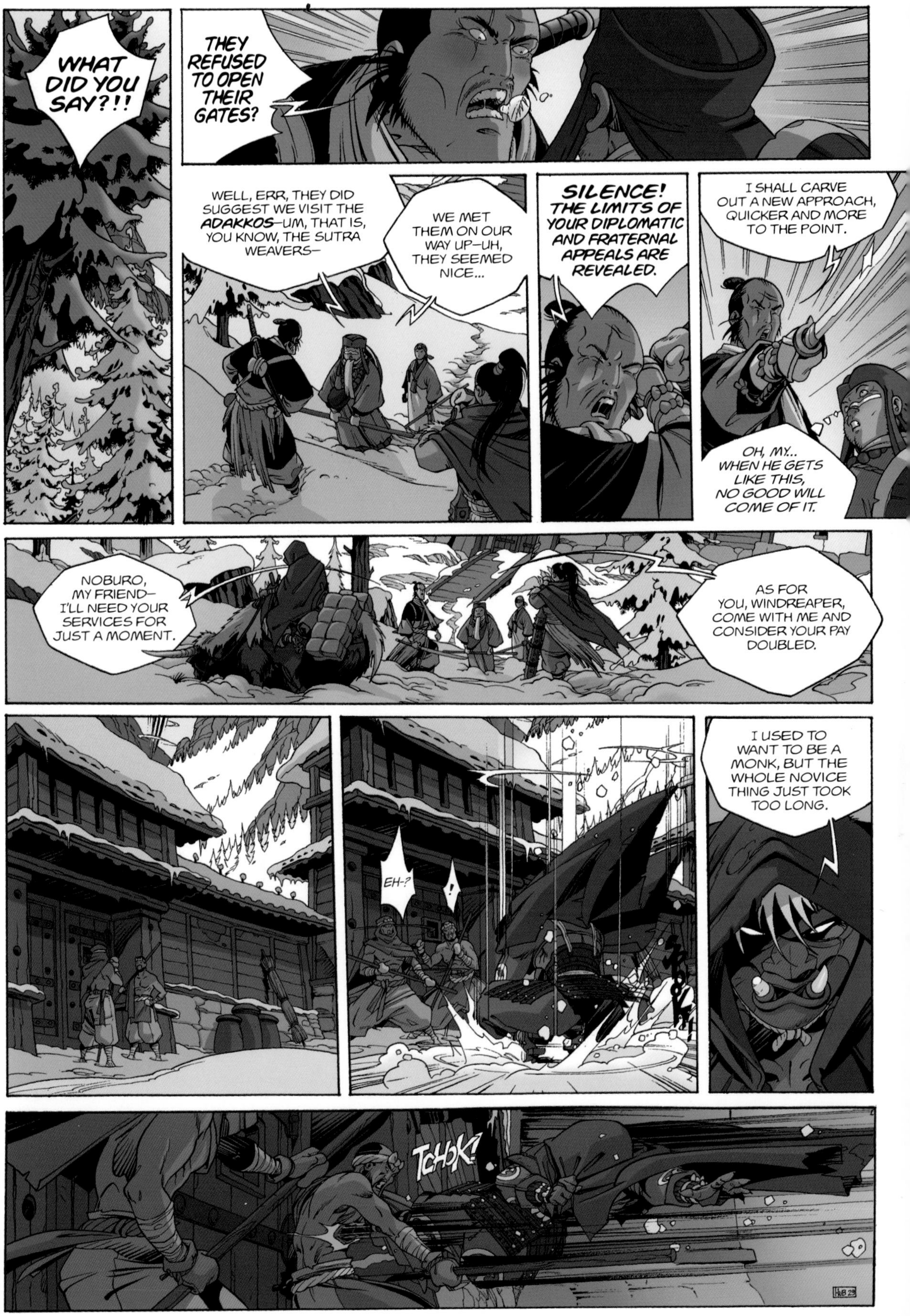
WHAT DID YOU SAY?!!
THEY REFUSED TO OPEN THEIR GATES?
WELL, ERR, THEY DID SUGGEST WE VISIT THE ADAKKOS—UM, THAT IS, YOU KNOW, THE SUTRA WEAVERS—
WE MET THEM ON OUR WAY UP—UH, THEY SEEMED NICE...
SILENCE! THE LIMITS OF YOUR DIPLOMATIC AND FRATERNAL APPEALS ARE REVEALED.
I SHALL CARVE OUT A NEW APPROACH, QUICKER AND MORE TO THE POINT.
OH, MY... WHEN HE GETS LIKE THIS, NO GOOD WILL COME OF IT.
NOBURO, MY FRIEND— I'LL NEED YOUR SERVICES FOR JUST A MOMENT.
AS FOR YOU, WINDREAPER, COME WITH ME AND CONSIDER YOUR PAY DOUBLED.
EH-?
!
I USED TO WANT TO BE A MONK, BUT THE WHOLE NOVICE THING JUST TOOK TOO LONG.
TCHOK!

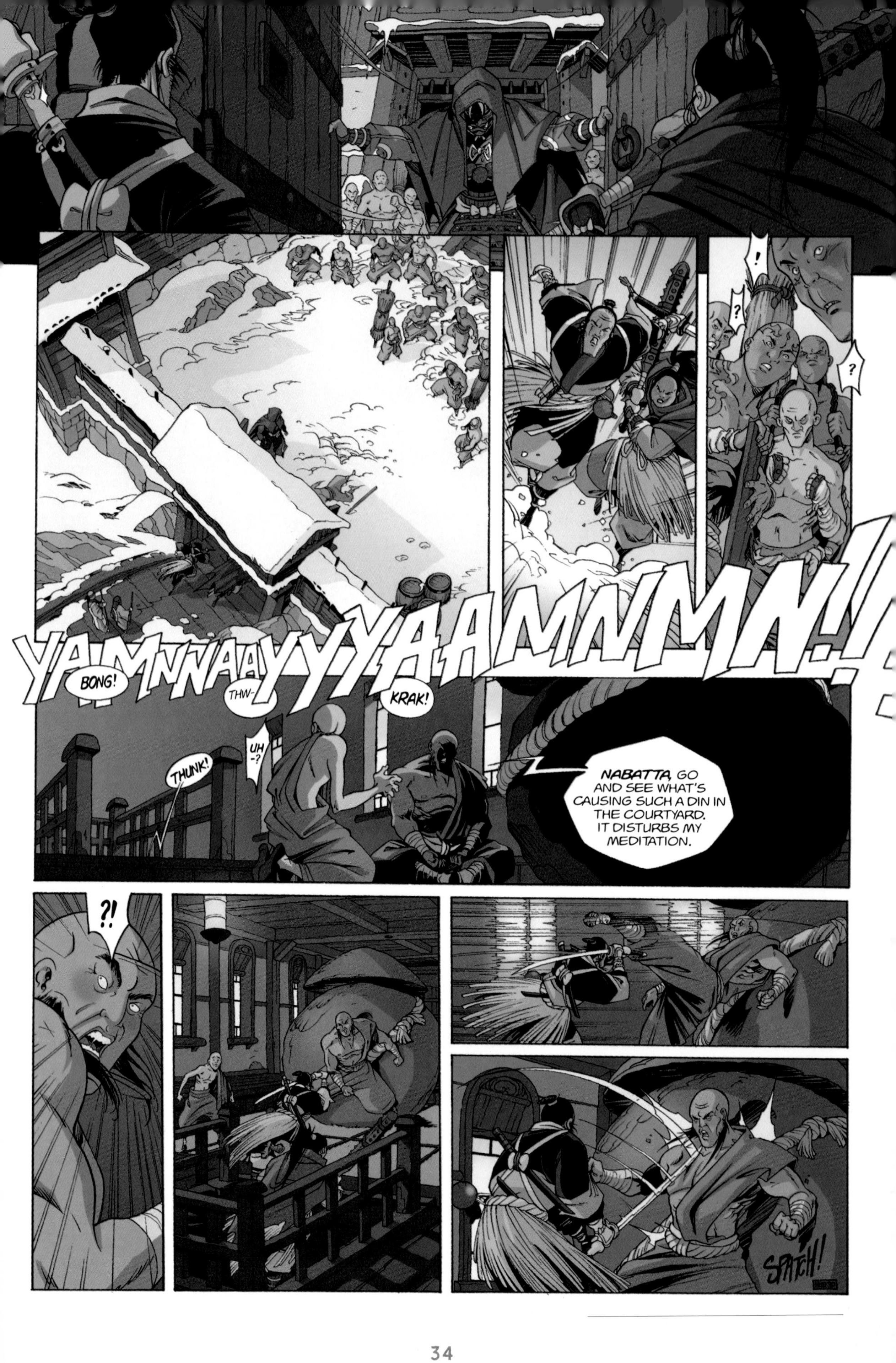
!
?
?
YAMNNAAYYYAAMNMA!!
BONG!
THW-
KRAK!
THUNK!
UH -?
NABATTA, GO AND SEE WHAT'S CAUSING SUCH A DIN IN THE COURTYARD. IT DISTURBS MY MEDITATION.
?!
SPATCH!

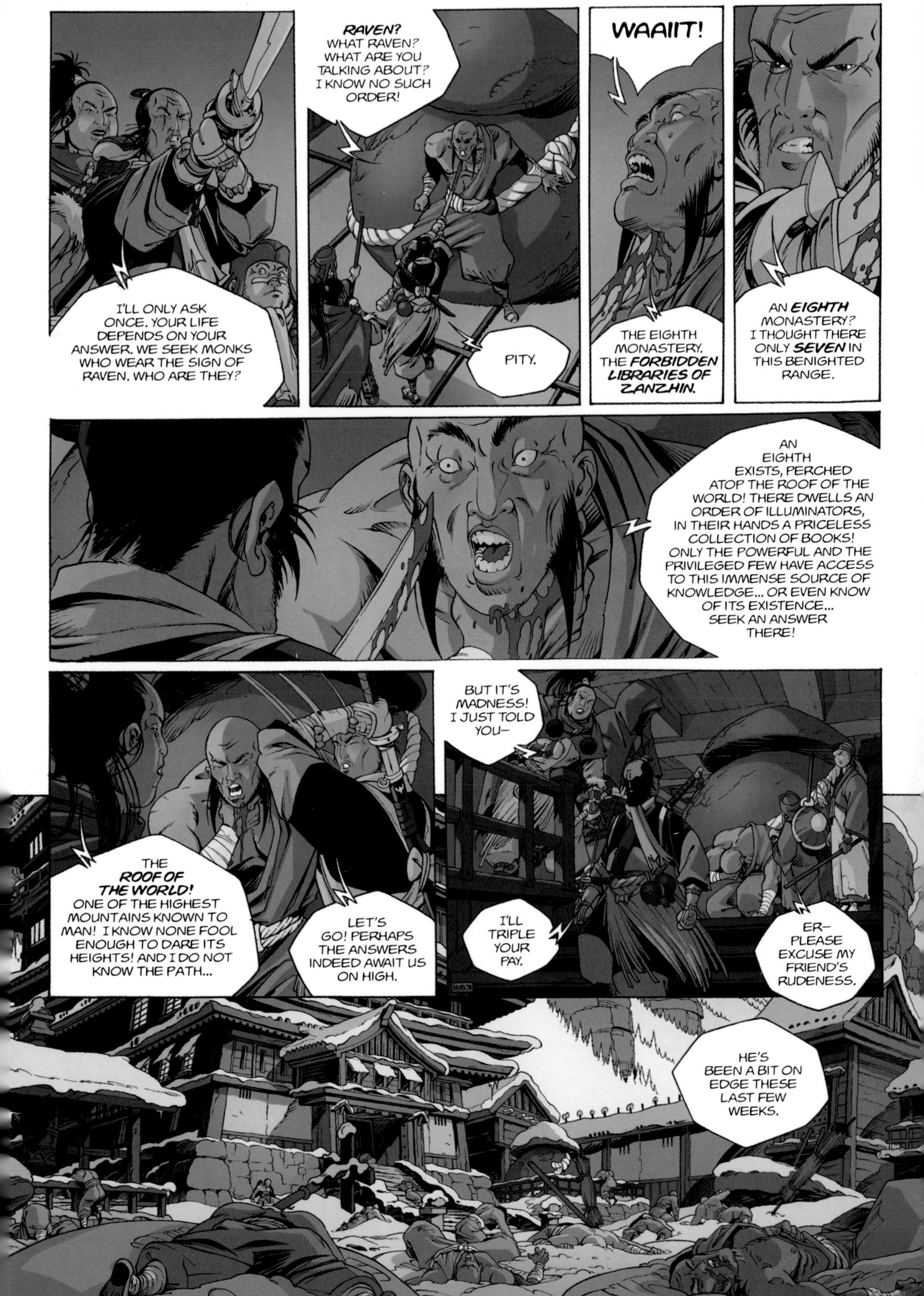
I'LL ONLY ASK ONCE. YOUR LIFE DEPENDS ON YOUR ANSWER. WE SEEK MONKS WHO WEAR THE SIGN OF RAVEN. WHO ARE THEY?
RAVEN? WHAT RAVEN? WHAT ARE YOU TALKING ABOUT? I KNOW NO SUCH ORDER!
PITY.
WAAIIT!
THE EIGHTH MONASTERY. THE FORBIDDEN LIBRARIES OF ZANZHIN.
AN EIGHTH MONASTERY? I THOUGHT THERE ONLY SEVEN IN THIS BENIGHTED RANGE.
AN EIGHTH EXISTS, PERCHED ATOP THE ROOF OF THE WORLD! THERE DWELLS AN ORDER OF ILLUMINATORS, IN THEIR HANDS A PRICELESS COLLECTION OF BOOKS! ONLY THE POWERFUL AND THE PRIVILEGED FEW HAVE ACCESS TO THIS IMMENSE SOURCE OF KNOWLEDGE... OR EVEN KNOW OF ITS EXISTENCE... SEEK AN ANSWER THERE!
THE ROOF OF THE WORLD! ONE OF THE HIGHEST MOUNTAINS KNOWN TO MAN! I KNOW NONE FOOL ENOUGH TO DARE ITS HEIGHTS! AND I DO NOT KNOW THE PATH...
LET'S GO! PERHAPS THE ANSWERS INDEED AWAIT US ON HIGH.
BUT IT'S MADNESS! I JUST TOLD YOU—
I'LL TRIPLE YOUR PAY.
ER— PLEASE EXCUSE MY FRIEND'S RUDENESS.
HE'S BEEN A BIT ON EDGE THESE LAST FEW WEEKS.

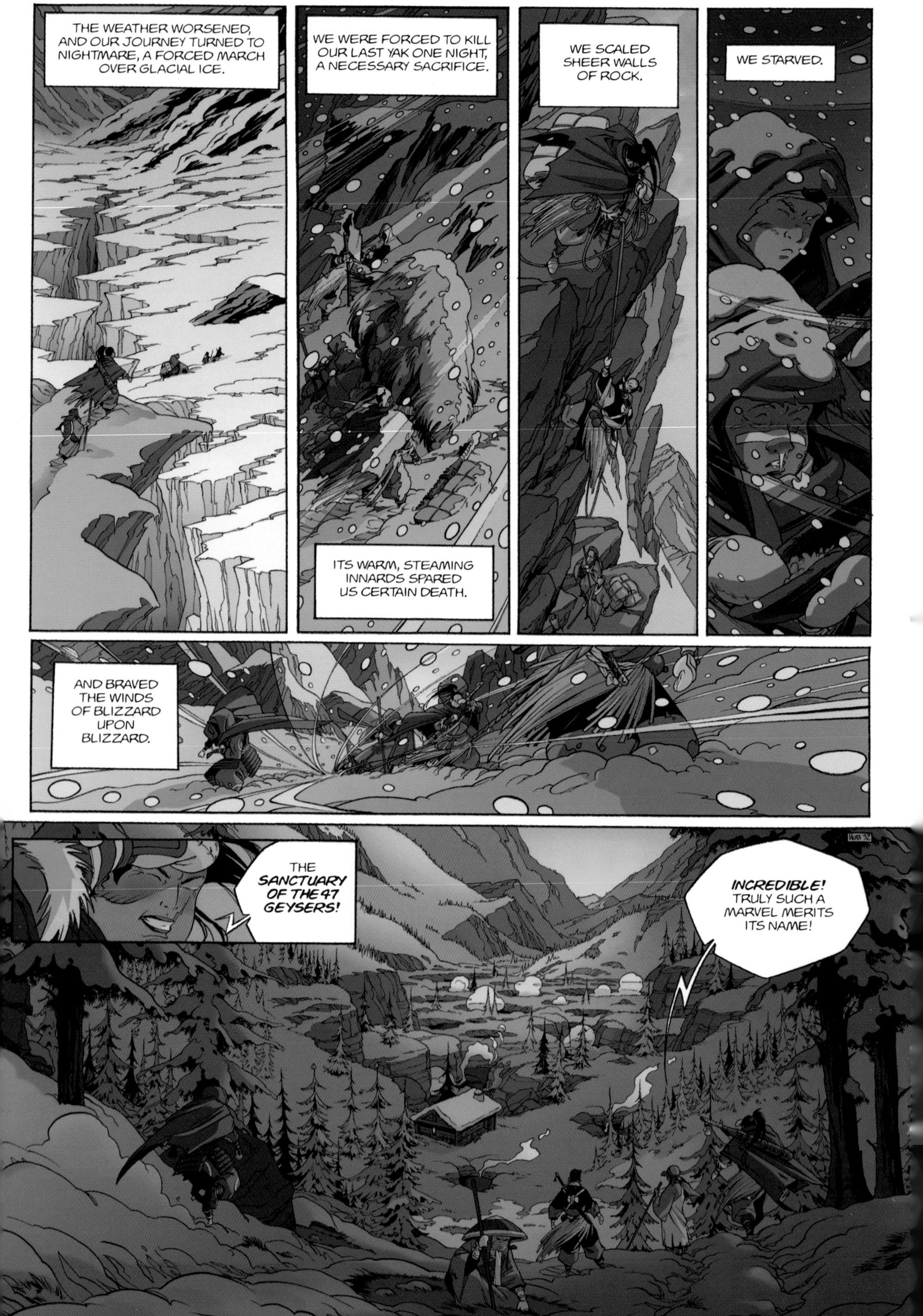
THE WEATHER WORSENED, AND OUR JOURNEY TURNED TO NIGHTMARE, A FORCED MARCH OVER GLACIAL ICE.
WE WERE FORCED TO KILL OUR LAST YAK ONE NIGHT, A NECESSARY SACRIFICE.
ITS WARM, STEAMING INNARDS SPARED US CERTAIN DEATH.
WE SCALED SHEER WALLS OF ROCK.
WE STARVED.
AND BRAVED THE WINDS OF BLIZZARD UPON BLIZZARD.
THE SANCTUARY OF THE 47 GEYSERS!
INCREDIBLE! TRULY SUCH A MARVEL MERITS ITS NAME!

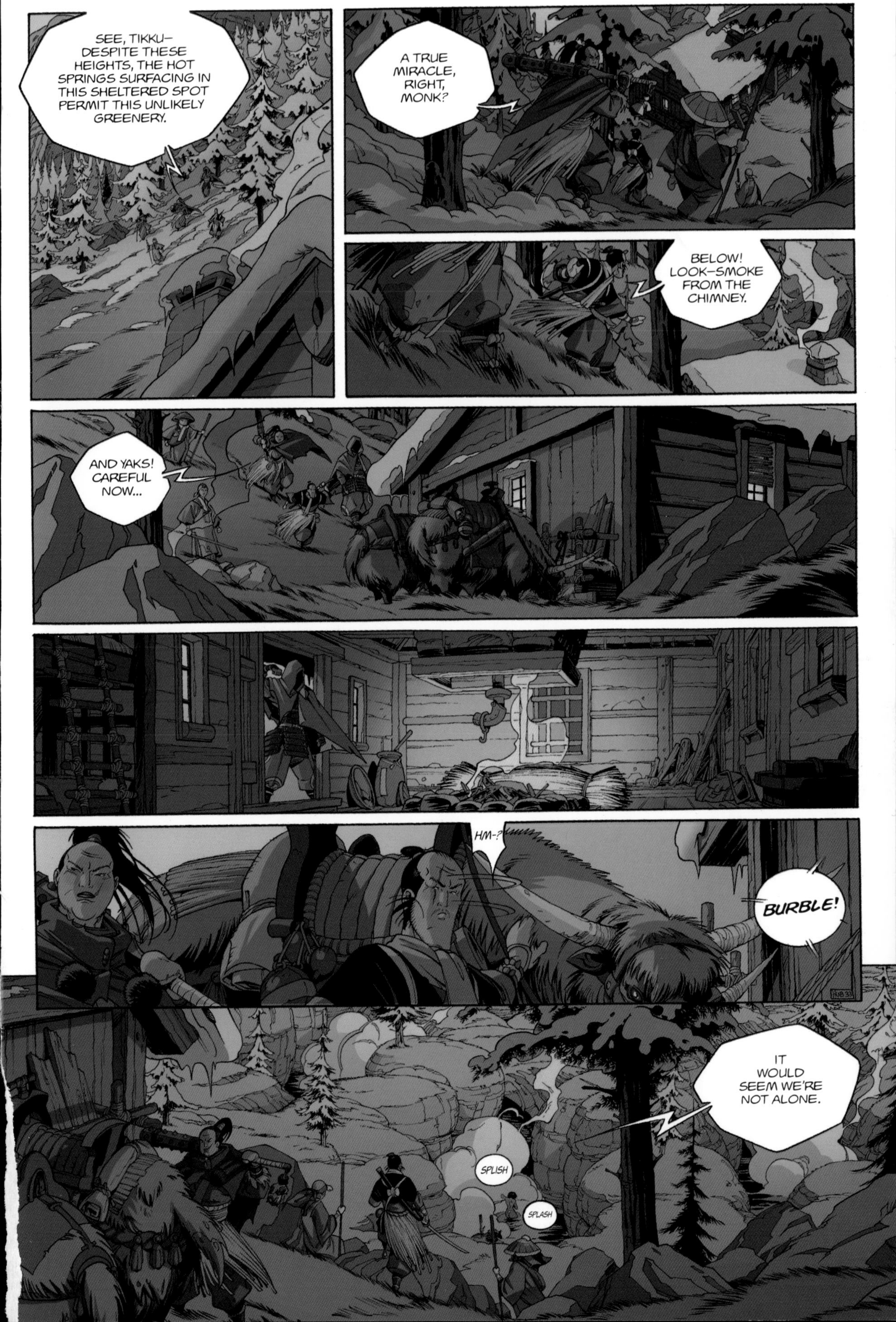
SEE, TIKKU— DESPITE THESE HEIGHTS, THE HOT SPRINGS SURFACING IN THIS SHELTERED SPOT PERMIT THIS UNLIKELY GREENERY.
A TRUE MIRACLE, RIGHT, MONK?
BELOW! LOOK—SMOKE FROM THE CHIMNEY.
AND YAKS! CAREFUL NOW...
HM-?
BURBLE!
IT WOULD SEEM WE'RE NOT ALONE.
SPLISH
SPLASH

SAINTS OF TAHO! SHE'S BEAUTIFUL! PITY SHE'S MISSING AN ARM.

SNIF!

SNIF!

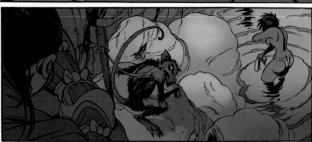

A NEZUMI*!

SNIF!

SNIF!

SNIF!

I HATE THOSE CREATURES! *PTUI!* THEY'VE BUT ONE IDEA IN THEIR HEADS: *PLUNDER*

WH -?!

EH -!

POW

* JAPANESE FOR "RAT".

38

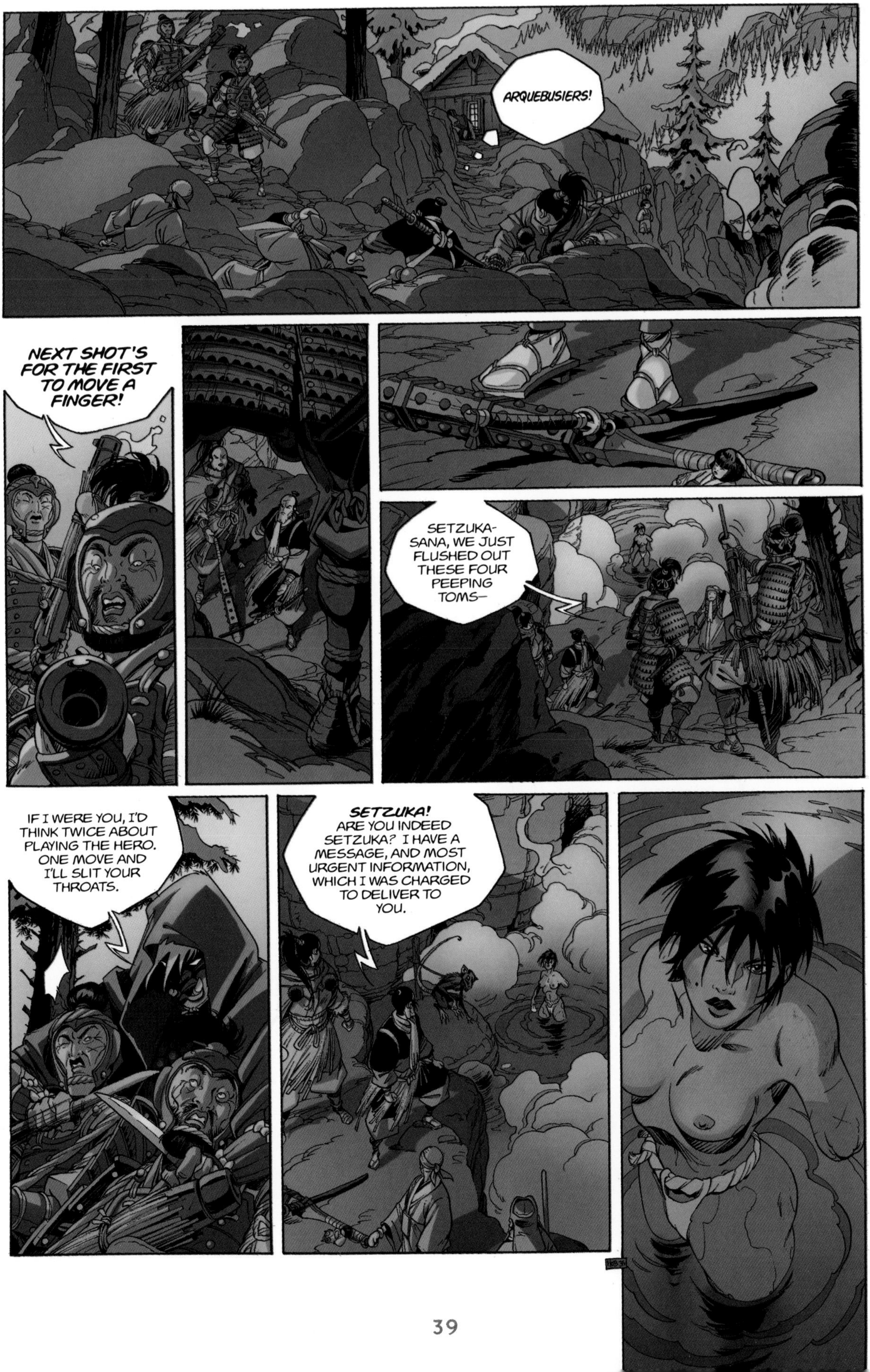
ARQUEBUSIERS!
NEXT SHOT'S FOR THE FIRST TO MOVE A FINGER!
SETZUKA-SANA, WE JUST FLUSHED OUT THESE FOUR PEEPING TOMS—
IF I WERE YOU, I'D THINK TWICE ABOUT PLAYING THE HERO. ONE MOVE AND I'LL SLIT YOUR THROATS.
SETZUKA! ARE YOU INDEED SETZUKA? I HAVE A MESSAGE, AND MOST URGENT INFORMATION, WHICH I WAS CHARGED TO DELIVER TO YOU.

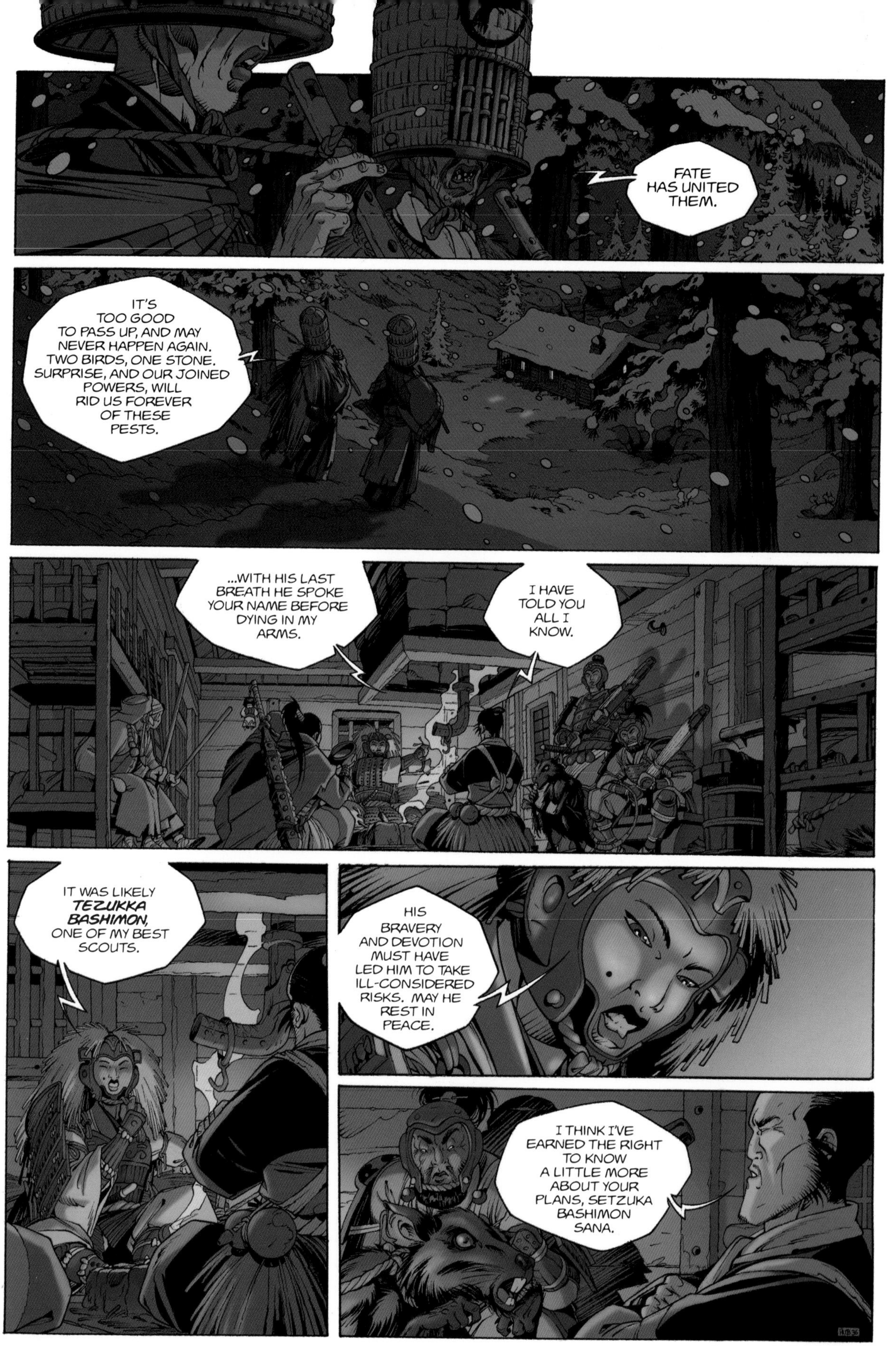
FATE HAS UNITED THEM.
IT'S TOO GOOD TO PASS UP, AND MAY NEVER HAPPEN AGAIN. TWO BIRDS, ONE STONE. SURPRISE, AND OUR JOINED POWERS, WILL RID US FOREVER OF THESE PESTS.
...WITH HIS LAST BREATH HE SPOKE YOUR NAME BEFORE DYING IN MY ARMS.
I HAVE TOLD YOU ALL I KNOW.
IT WAS LIKELY ***TEZUKKA BASHIMON***, ONE OF MY BEST SCOUTS.
HIS BRAVERY AND DEVOTION MUST HAVE LED HIM TO TAKE ILL-CONSIDERED RISKS. MAY HE REST IN PEACE.
I THINK I'VE EARNED THE RIGHT TO KNOW A LITTLE MORE ABOUT YOUR PLANS, SETZUKA BASHIMON SANA.

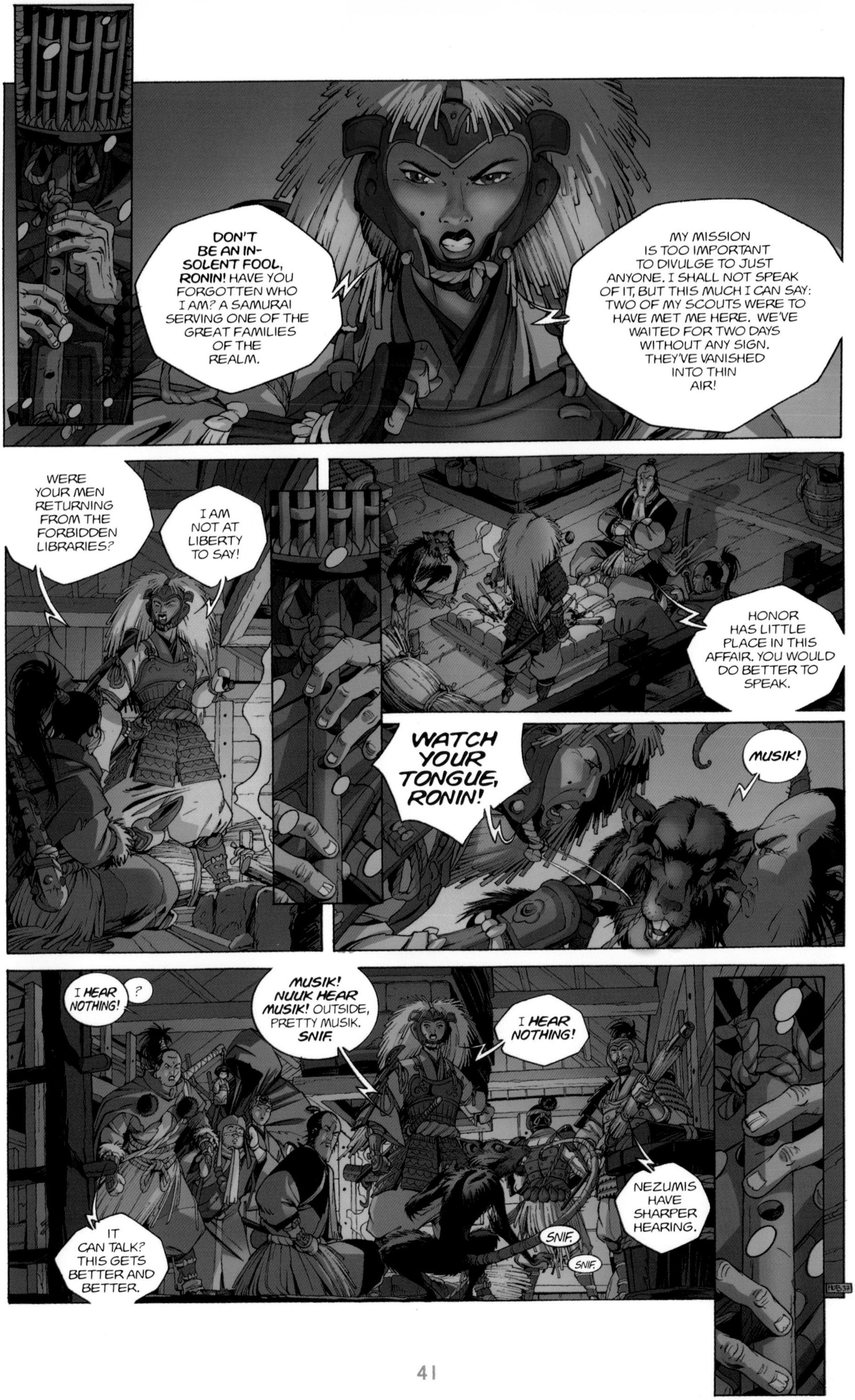

DON'T BE AN IN-SOLENT FOOL, RONIN! HAVE YOU FORGOTTEN WHO I AM? A SAMURAI SERVING ONE OF THE GREAT FAMILIES OF THE REALM.
MY MISSION IS TOO IMPORTANT TO DIVULGE TO JUST ANYONE. I SHALL NOT SPEAK OF IT, BUT THIS MUCH I CAN SAY: TWO OF MY SCOUTS WERE TO HAVE MET ME HERE. WE'VE WAITED FOR TWO DAYS WITHOUT ANY SIGN. THEY'VE VANISHED INTO THIN AIR!
WERE YOUR MEN RETURNING FROM THE FORBIDDEN LIBRARIES?
I AM NOT AT LIBERTY TO SAY!
HONOR HAS LITTLE PLACE IN THIS AFFAIR. YOU WOULD DO BETTER TO SPEAK.
WATCH YOUR TONGUE, RONIN!
MUSIK!
I HEAR NOTHING!
?
MUSIK! NUUK HEAR MUSIK! OUTSIDE, PRETTY MUSIK. SNIF.
I HEAR NOTHING!
NEZUMIS HAVE SHARPER HEARING.
IT CAN TALK? THIS GETS BETTER AND BETTER.
SNIF.
SNIF.

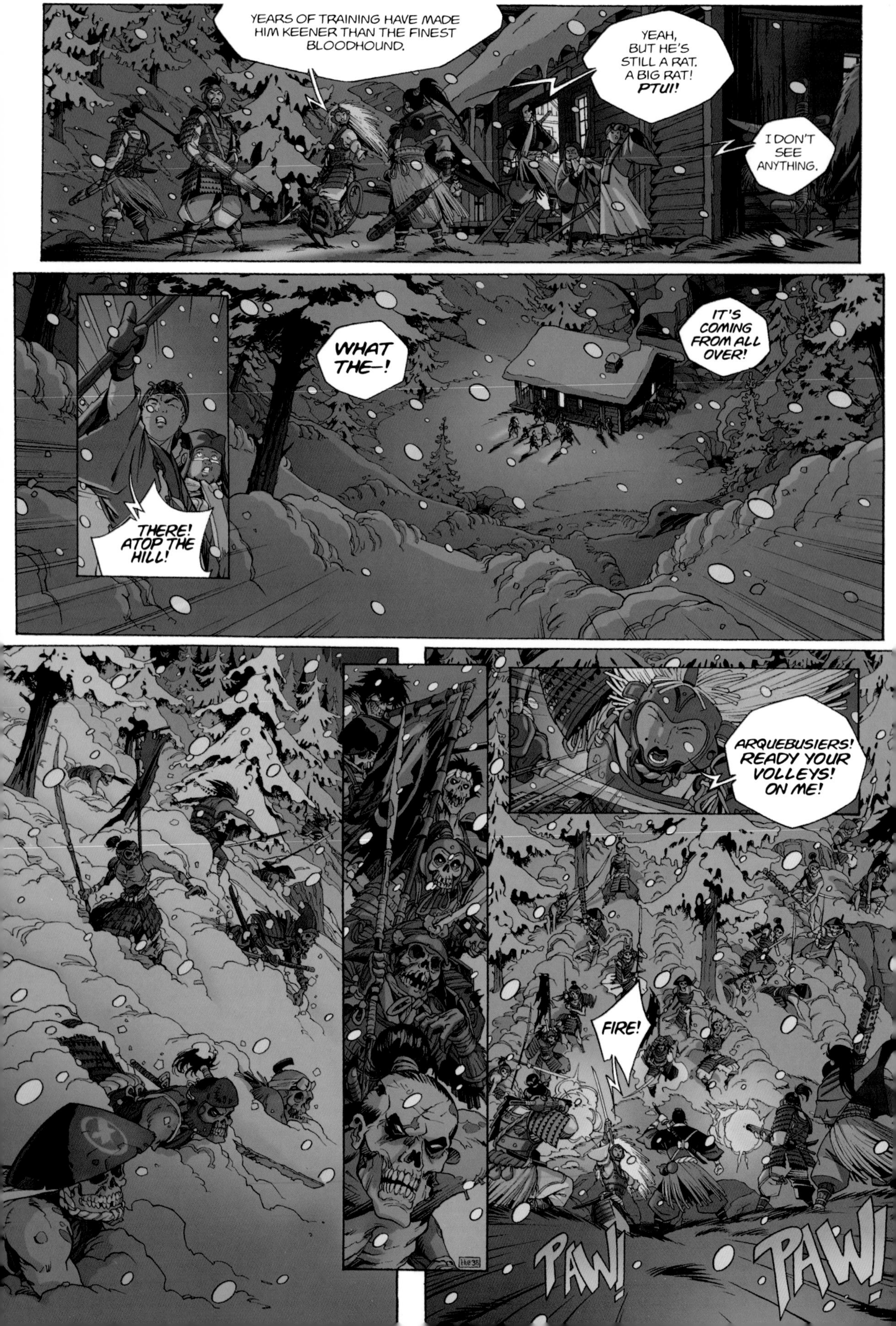

YEARS OF TRAINING HAVE MADE HIM KEENER THAN THE FINEST BLOODHOUND.
YEAH, BUT HE'S STILL A RAT. A BIG RAT! PTUI!
I DON'T SEE ANYTHING.
WHAT THE—!
IT'S COMING FROM ALL OVER!
THERE! ATOP THE HILL!
ARQUEBUSIERS! READY YOUR VOLLEYS! ON ME!
FIRE!
PAW!
PAW!

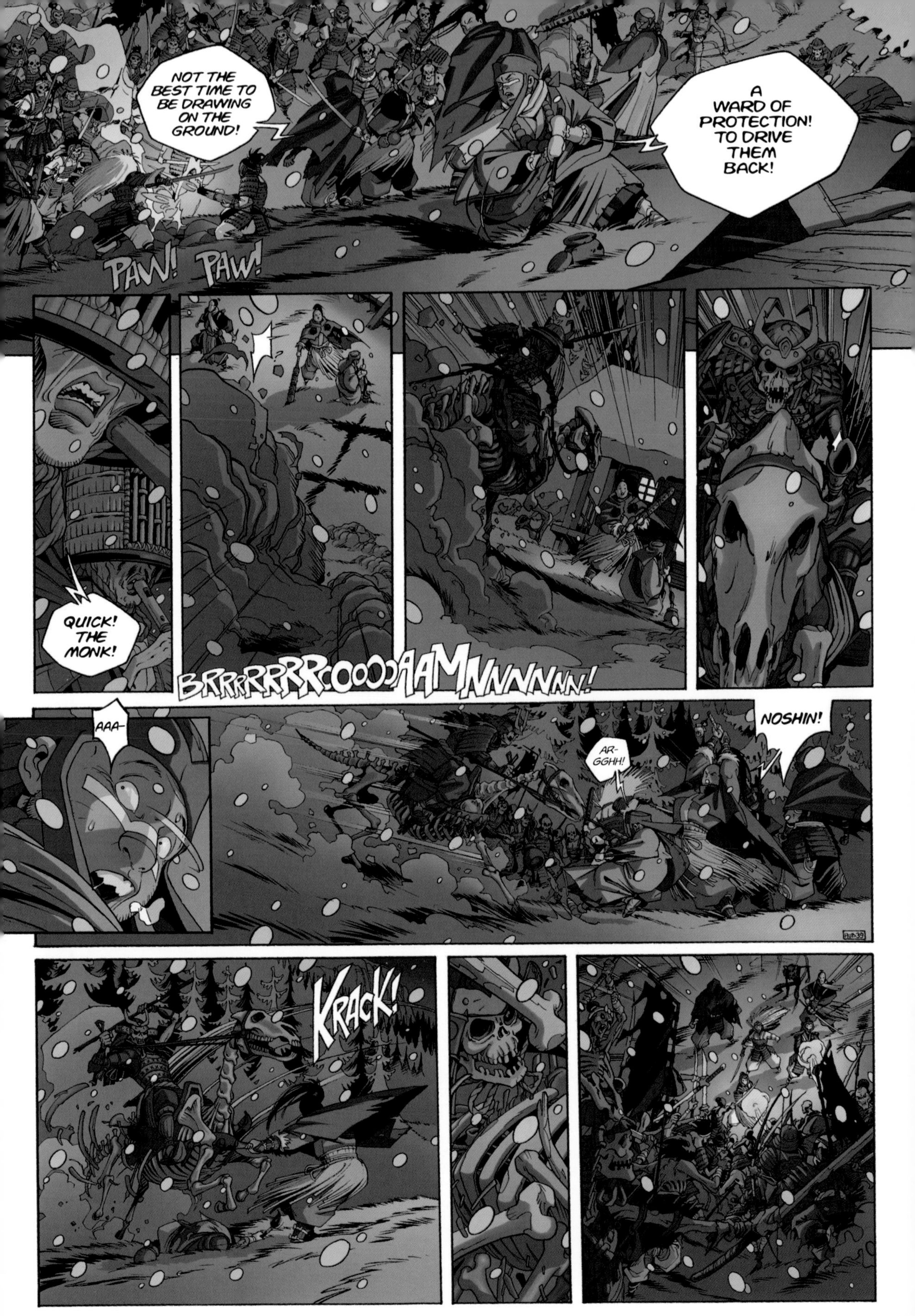
NOT THE BEST TIME TO BE DRAWING ON THE GROUND!
A WARD OF PROTECTION! TO DRIVE THEM BACK!
PAW! PAW!
QUICK! THE MONK!
BRRRRRRRCOOOOAAMNNNNNNN!
AAA-
AR-GGHH!
NOSHIN!
KRACK!

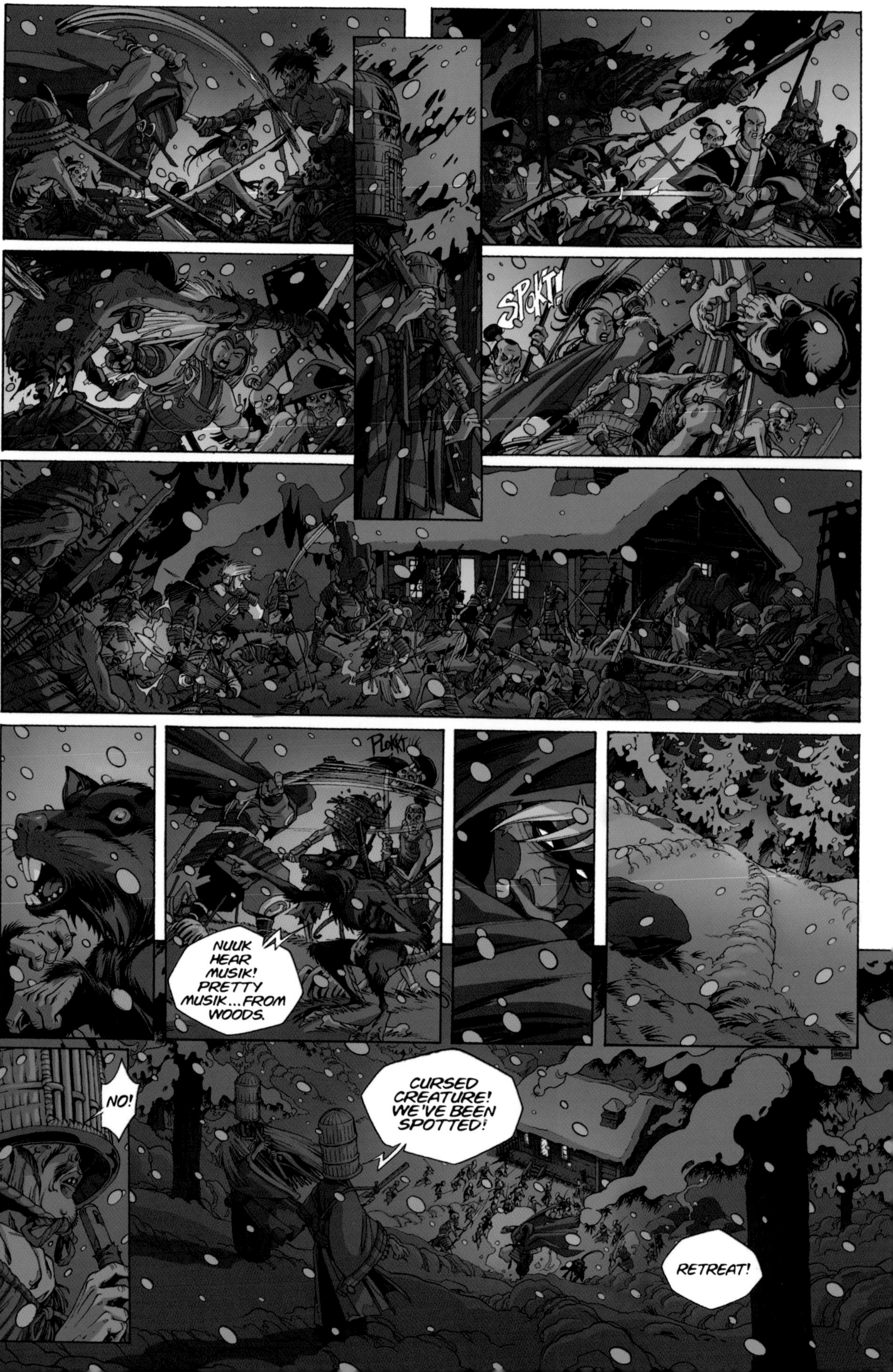
SPOKT!
PLOKKT
NUUK HEAR MUSIK! PRETTY MUSIK... FROM WOODS.
NO!
CURSED CREATURE! WE'VE BEEN SPOTTED!
RETREAT!

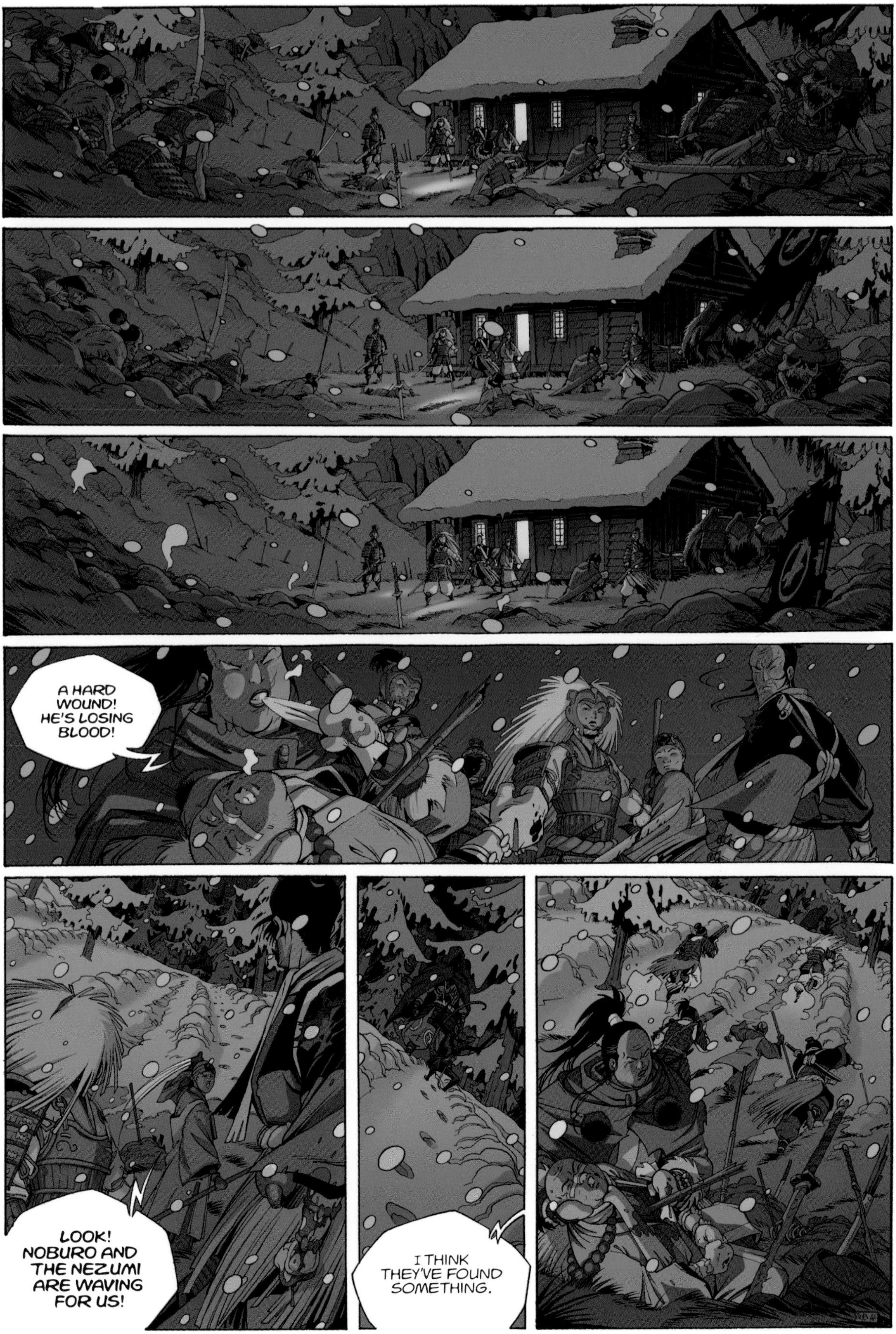
A HARD WOUND! HE'S LOSING BLOOD!
LOOK! NOBURO AND THE NEZUMI ARE WAVING FOR US!
I THINK THEY'VE FOUND SOMETHING.

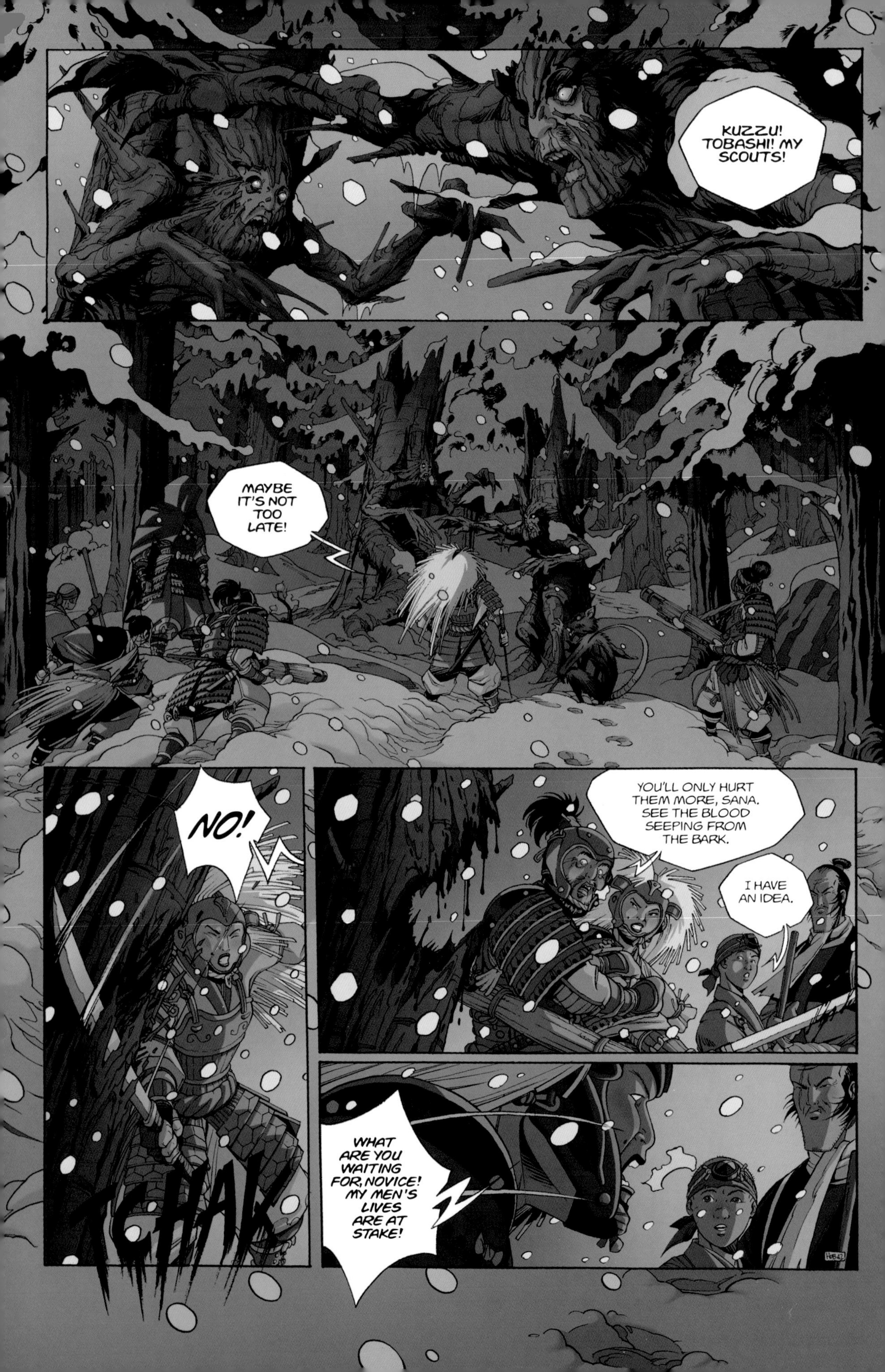
KUZZU! TOBASHI! MY SCOUTS!
MAYBE IT'S NOT TOO LATE!
NO!
TCHAK
YOU'LL ONLY HURT THEM MORE, SANA. SEE THE BLOOD SEEPING FROM THE BARK.
I HAVE AN IDEA.
WHAT ARE YOU WAITING FOR, NOVICE! MY MEN'S LIVES ARE AT STAKE!

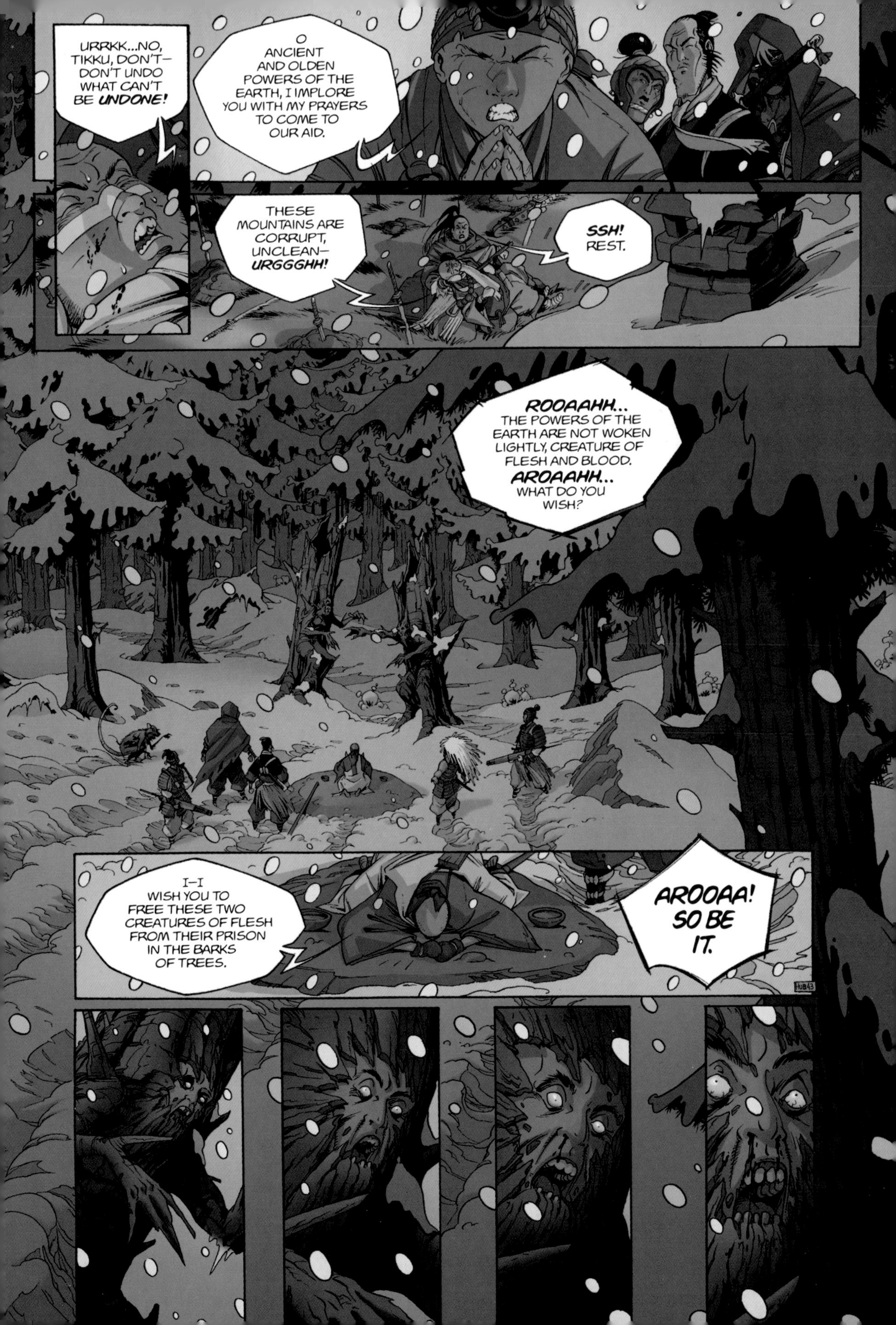
URRKK...NO, TIKKU, DON'T— DON'T UNDO WHAT CAN'T BE UNDONE!
O ANCIENT AND OLDEN POWERS OF THE EARTH, I IMPLORE YOU WITH MY PRAYERS TO COME TO OUR AID.
THESE MOUNTAINS ARE CORRUPT, UNCLEAN— URGGGHH!
SSH! REST.
ROOAAHH... THE POWERS OF THE EARTH ARE NOT WOKEN LIGHTLY, CREATURE OF FLESH AND BLOOD. AROAAHH... WHAT DO YOU WISH?
I—I WISH YOU TO FREE THESE TWO CREATURES OF FLESH FROM THEIR PRISON IN THE BARKS OF TREES.
AROOAA! SO BE IT.
HUB 43

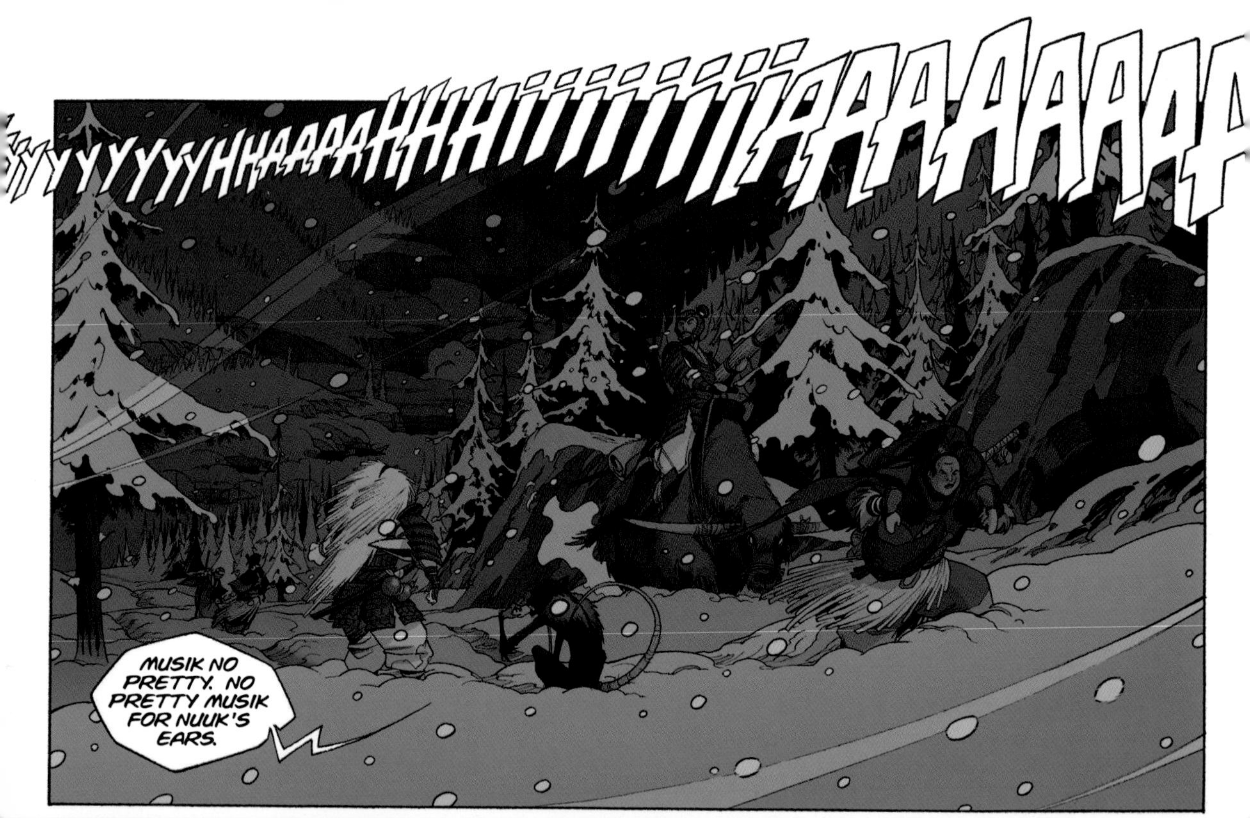
YYYYYYYHHAAAAHHHHIIIIIIIIIIIIIIRRAAAAAA
MUSIK NO PRETTY. NO PRETTY MUSIK FOR NUUK'S EARS.

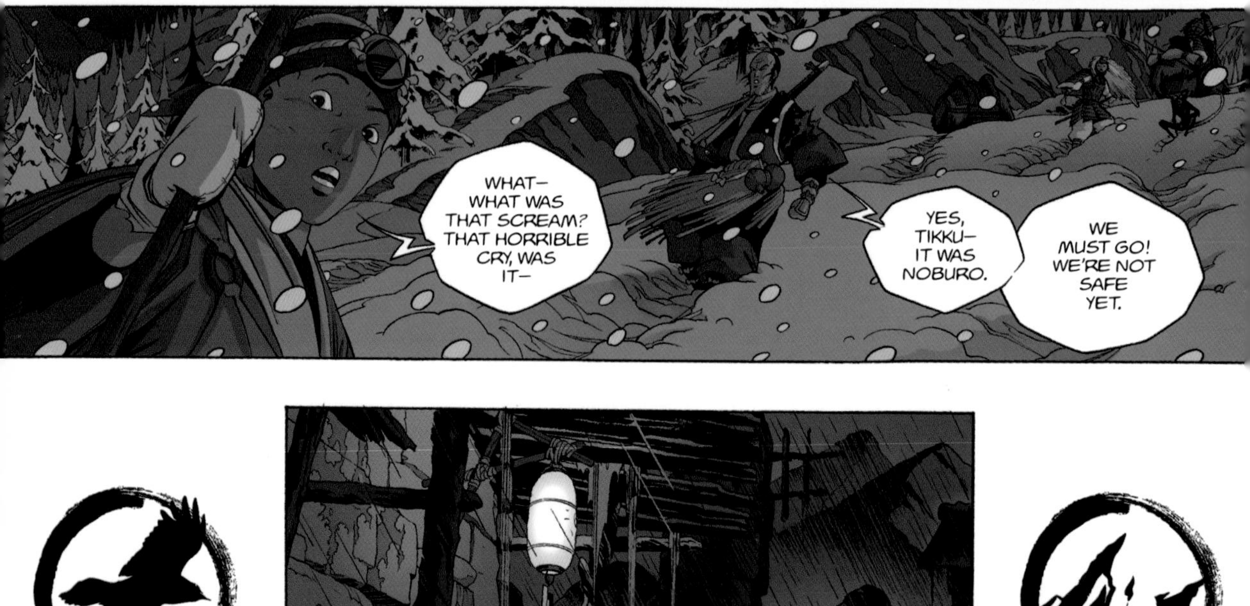
WHAT— WHAT WAS THAT SCREAM? THAT HORRIBLE CRY, WAS IT—
YES, TIKKU— IT WAS NOBURO.
WE MUST GO! WE'RE NOT SAFE YET.

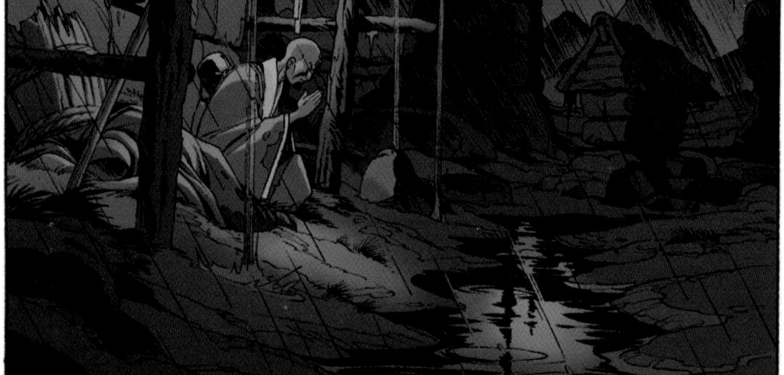

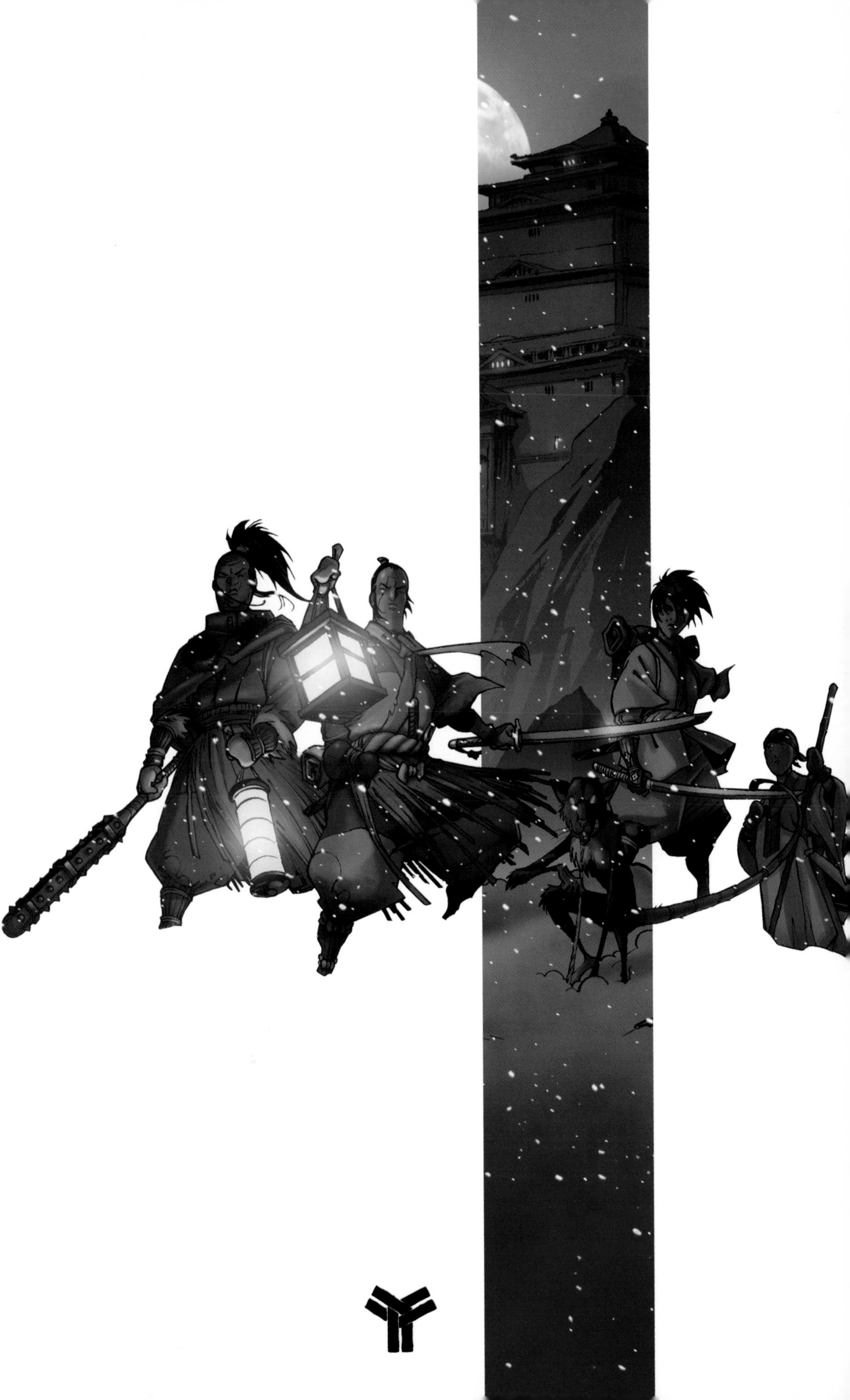

THE CYCLE OF EARTH

Part Two

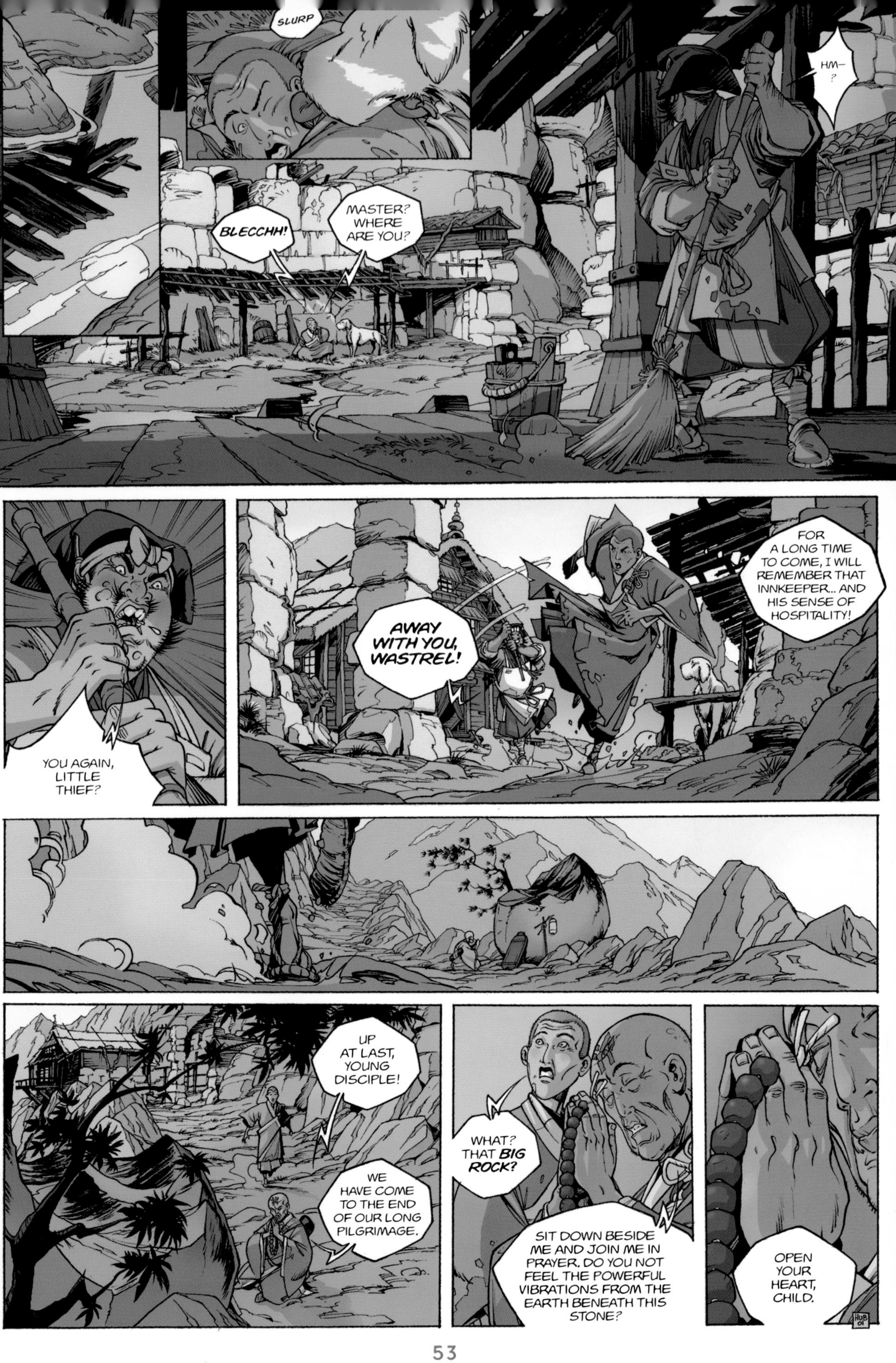

SLURP
HM—?
BLECCHH!
MASTER? WHERE ARE YOU?
YOU AGAIN, LITTLE THIEF?
AWAY WITH YOU, WASTREL!
FOR A LONG TIME TO COME, I WILL REMEMBER THAT INNKEEPER... AND HIS SENSE OF HOSPITALITY!
UP AT LAST, YOUNG DISCIPLE!
WE HAVE COME TO THE END OF OUR LONG PILGRIMAGE.
WHAT? THAT BIG ROCK?
SIT DOWN BESIDE ME AND JOIN ME IN PRAYER. DO YOU NOT FEEL THE POWERFUL VIBRATIONS FROM THE EARTH BENEATH THIS STONE?
OPEN YOUR HEART, CHILD.
HUB 01

54

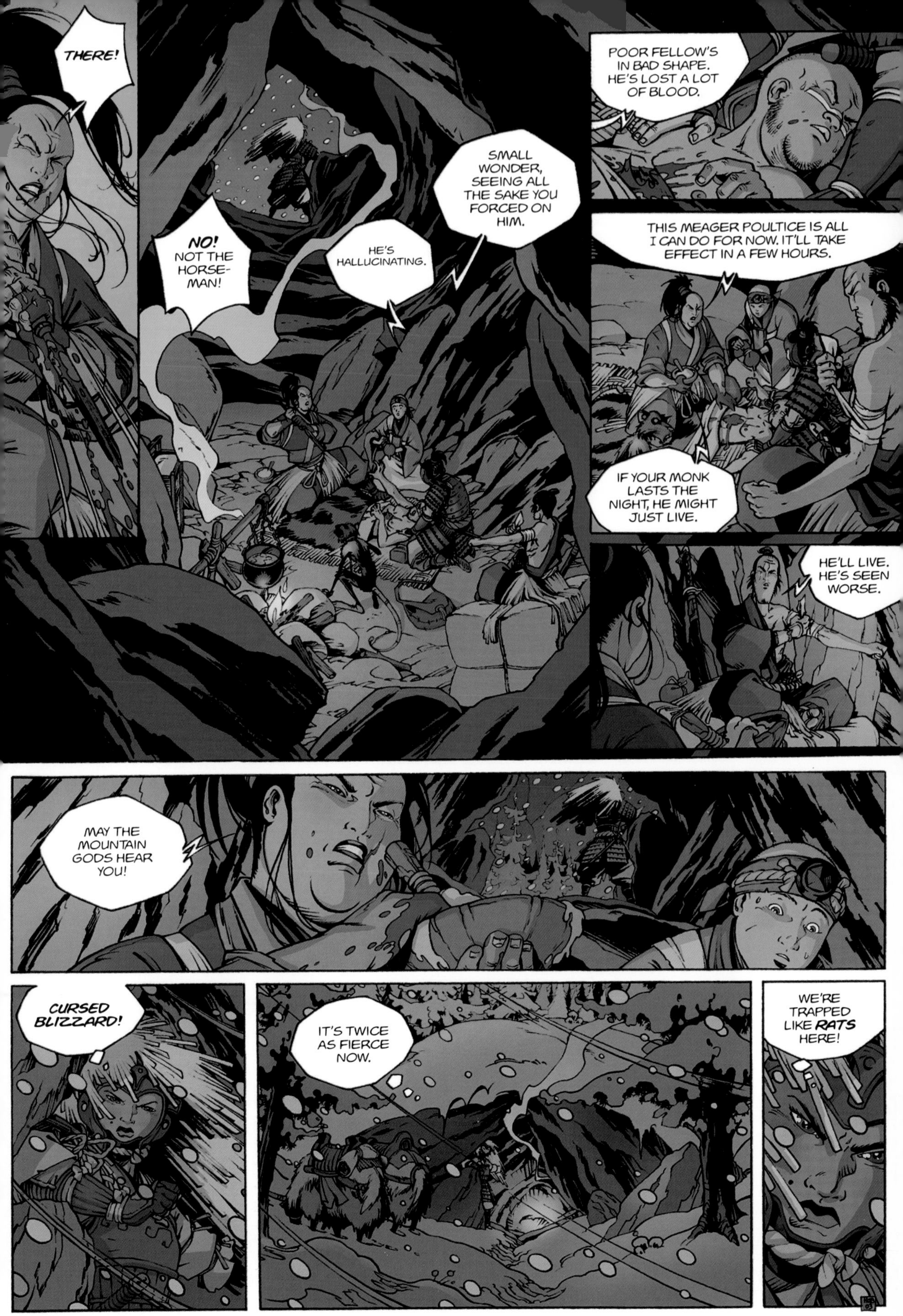
THERE!
NO! NOT THE HORSE-MAN!
HE'S HALLUCINATING.
SMALL WONDER, SEEING ALL THE SAKE YOU FORCED ON HIM.
POOR FELLOW'S IN BAD SHAPE. HE'S LOST A LOT OF BLOOD.
THIS MEAGER POULTICE IS ALL I CAN DO FOR NOW. IT'LL TAKE EFFECT IN A FEW HOURS.
IF YOUR MONK LASTS THE NIGHT, HE MIGHT JUST LIVE.
HE'LL LIVE. HE'S SEEN WORSE.
MAY THE MOUNTAIN GODS HEAR YOU!
CURSED BLIZZARD!
IT'S TWICE AS FIERCE NOW.
WE'RE TRAPPED LIKE RATS HERE!

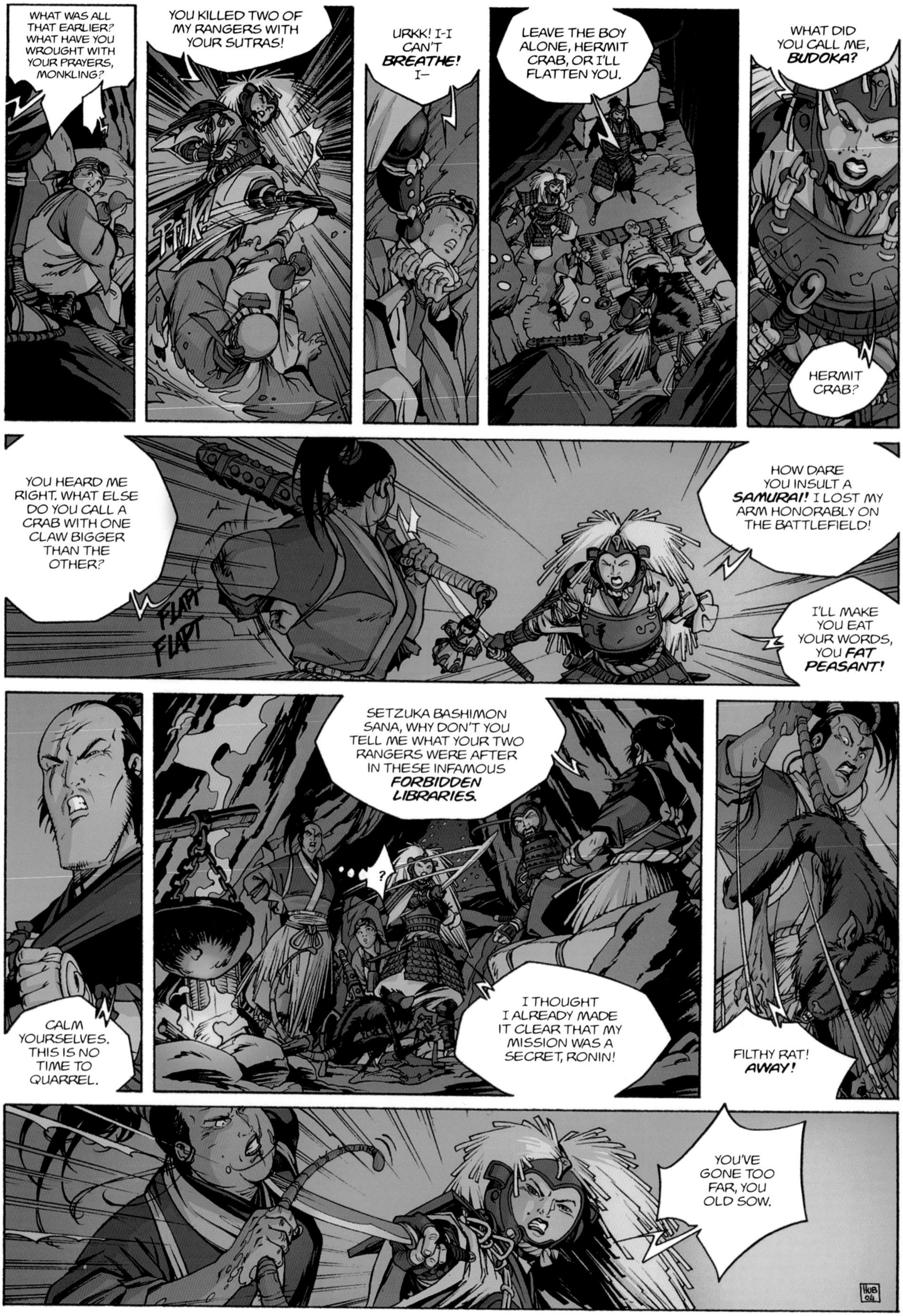
WHAT WAS ALL THAT EARLIER? WHAT HAVE YOU WROUGHT WITH YOUR PRAYERS, MONKLING?
YOU KILLED TWO OF MY RANGERS WITH YOUR SUTRAS!
PTTK!
URKK! I-I CAN'T BREATHE! I–
LEAVE THE BOY ALONE, HERMIT CRAB, OR I'LL FLATTEN YOU.
WHAT DID YOU CALL ME, BUDOKA?
HERMIT CRAB?
YOU HEARD ME RIGHT. WHAT ELSE DO YOU CALL A CRAB WITH ONE CLAW BIGGER THAN THE OTHER?
FLAP FLAP
HOW DARE YOU INSULT A SAMURAI! I LOST MY ARM HONORABLY ON THE BATTLEFIELD!
I'LL MAKE YOU EAT YOUR WORDS, YOU FAT PEASANT!
CALM YOURSELVES. THIS IS NO TIME TO QUARREL.
SETZUKA BASHIMON SANA, WHY DON'T YOU TELL ME WHAT YOUR TWO RANGERS WERE AFTER IN THESE INFAMOUS FORBIDDEN LIBRARIES.
?
I THOUGHT I ALREADY MADE IT CLEAR THAT MY MISSION WAS A SECRET, RONIN!
FILTHY RAT! AWAY!
YOU'VE GONE TOO FAR, YOU OLD SOW.
HUB 04

YOUR CHILDISH OUTBURST IS A CONFESSION OF WEAKNESS, SETZUKA BASHIMON.

?!

SOLIDER, I WOULD ADVISE AGAINST ANY HEROICS. THE LIFE OF YOUR IMPETUOUS YOUNG *SENSEI** HANGS IN THE BALANCE.

!

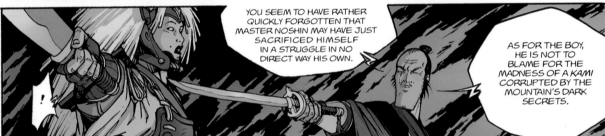

YOU SEEM TO HAVE RATHER QUICKLY FORGOTTEN THAT MASTER NOSHIN MAY HAVE JUST SACRIFICED HIMSELF IN A STRUGGLE IN NO DIRECT WAY HIS OWN.

!

AS FOR THE BOY, HE IS NOT TO BLAME FOR THE MADNESS OF A *KAMI* CORRUPTED BY THE MOUNTAIN'S DARK SECRETS.

THE STORM SEEMS TO HAVE CAUGHT YOU UNPREPARED. I'VE NO WISH TO OFFEND, BUT IN LIGHT OF RECENT EVENTS, I CONSIDER YOU TOO YOUNG AND INEXPERIENCED TO COMPLETE YOUR MISSION ALONE.

I GIVE YOU ONE LAST CHANCE TO TELL ME WHY I SHOULD JOIN MY CAUSE TO YOURS.

...I'M LISTENING.

* SENSEI: MASTER.

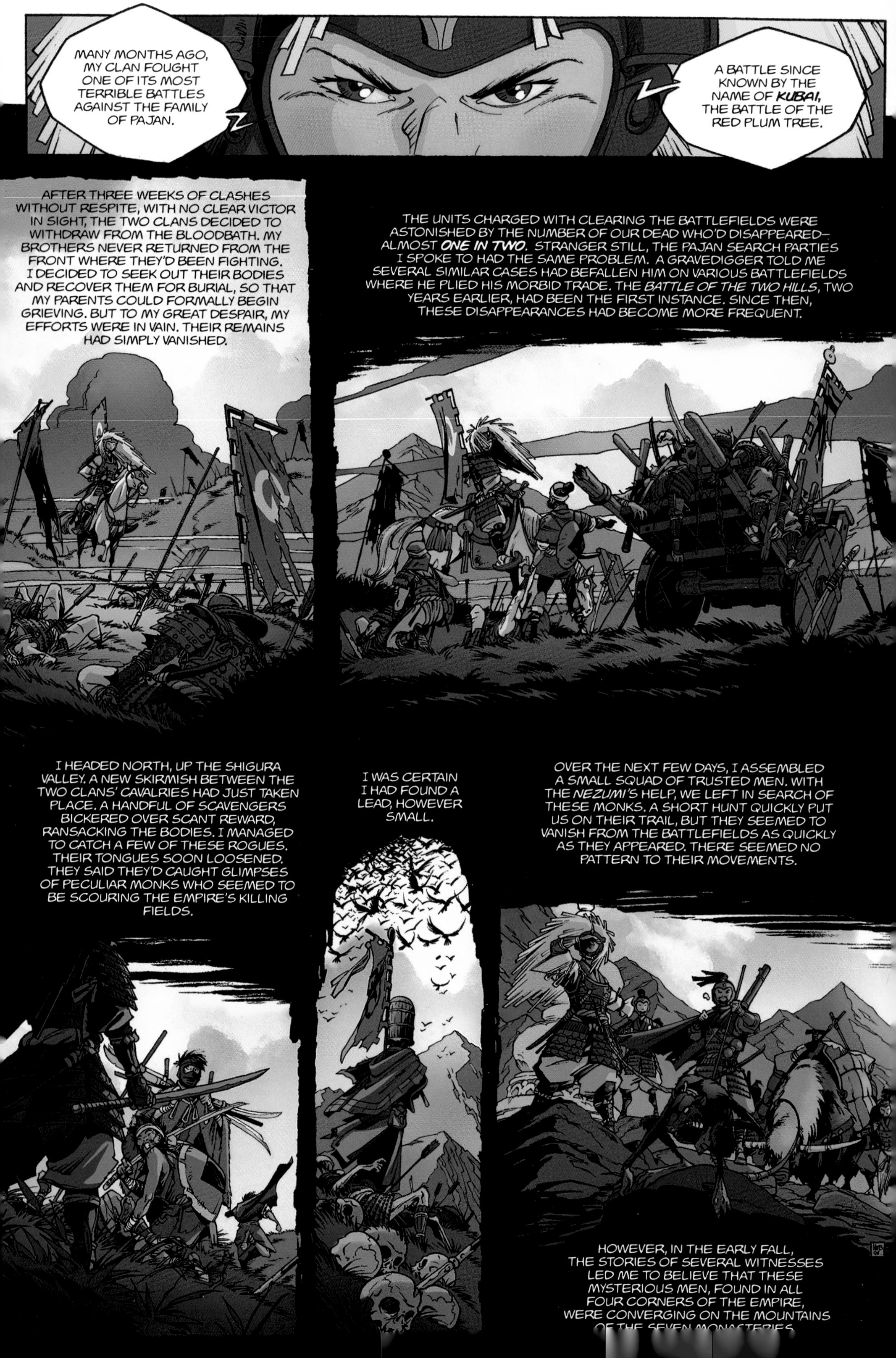
MANY MONTHS AGO, MY CLAN FOUGHT ONE OF ITS MOST TERRIBLE BATTLES AGAINST THE FAMILY OF PAJAN.
A BATTLE SINCE KNOWN BY THE NAME OF KUBAI, THE BATTLE OF THE RED PLUM TREE.
AFTER THREE WEEKS OF CLASHES WITHOUT RESPITE, WITH NO CLEAR VICTOR IN SIGHT, THE TWO CLANS DECIDED TO WITHDRAW FROM THE BLOODBATH. MY BROTHERS NEVER RETURNED FROM THE FRONT WHERE THEY'D BEEN FIGHTING. I DECIDED TO SEEK OUT THEIR BODIES AND RECOVER THEM FOR BURIAL, SO THAT MY PARENTS COULD FORMALLY BEGIN GRIEVING. BUT TO MY GREAT DESPAIR, MY EFFORTS WERE IN VAIN. THEIR REMAINS HAD SIMPLY VANISHED.
THE UNITS CHARGED WITH CLEARING THE BATTLEFIELDS WERE ASTONISHED BY THE NUMBER OF OUR DEAD WHO'D DISAPPEARED— ALMOST ONE IN TWO. STRANGER STILL, THE PAJAN SEARCH PARTIES I SPOKE TO HAD THE SAME PROBLEM. A GRAVEDIGGER TOLD ME SEVERAL SIMILAR CASES HAD BEFALLEN HIM ON VARIOUS BATTLEFIELDS WHERE HE PLIED HIS MORBID TRADE. THE BATTLE OF THE TWO HILLS, TWO YEARS EARLIER, HAD BEEN THE FIRST INSTANCE. SINCE THEN, THESE DISAPPEARANCES HAD BECOME MORE FREQUENT.
I HEADED NORTH, UP THE SHIGURA VALLEY. A NEW SKIRMISH BETWEEN THE TWO CLANS' CAVALRIES HAD JUST TAKEN PLACE. A HANDFUL OF SCAVENGERS BICKERED OVER SCANT REWARD, RANSACKING THE BODIES. I MANAGED TO CATCH A FEW OF THESE ROGUES. THEIR TONGUES SOON LOOSENED. THEY SAID THEY'D CAUGHT GLIMPSES OF PECULIAR MONKS WHO SEEMED TO BE SCOURING THE EMPIRE'S KILLING FIELDS.
I WAS CERTAIN I HAD FOUND A LEAD, HOWEVER SMALL.
OVER THE NEXT FEW DAYS, I ASSEMBLED A SMALL SQUAD OF TRUSTED MEN. WITH THE NEZUMI'S HELP, WE LEFT IN SEARCH OF THESE MONKS. A SHORT HUNT QUICKLY PUT US ON THEIR TRAIL, BUT THEY SEEMED TO VANISH FROM THE BATTLEFIELDS AS QUICKLY AS THEY APPEARED. THERE SEEMED NO PATTERN TO THEIR MOVEMENTS.
HOWEVER, IN THE EARLY FALL, THE STORIES OF SEVERAL WITNESSES LED ME TO BELIEVE THAT THESE MYSTERIOUS MEN, FOUND IN ALL FOUR CORNERS OF THE EMPIRE, WERE CONVERGING ON THE MOUNTAINS OF THE SEVEN MONASTERIES.

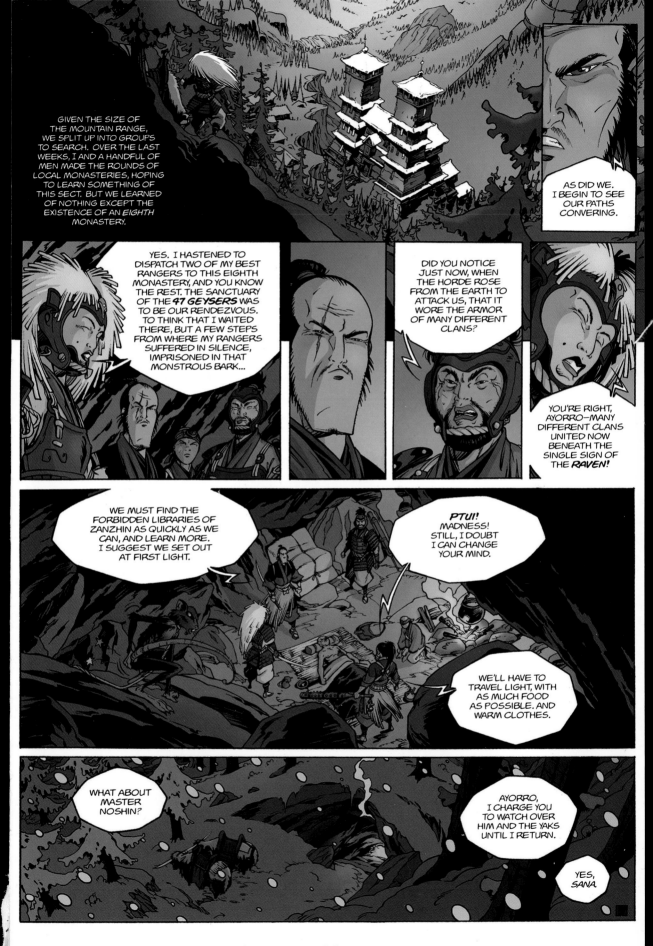

GIVEN THE SIZE OF THE MOUNTAIN RANGE, WE SPLIT UP INTO GROUPS TO SEARCH. OVER THE LAST WEEKS, I AND A HANDFUL OF MEN MADE THE ROUNDS OF LOCAL MONASTERIES, HOPING TO LEARN SOMETHING OF THIS SECT. BUT WE LEARNED OF NOTHING EXCEPT THE EXISTENCE OF AN *EIGHTH* MONASTERY.

AS DID WE. I BEGIN TO SEE OUR PATHS CONVERING.

YES. I HASTENED TO DISPATCH TWO OF MY BEST RANGERS TO THIS EIGHTH MONASTERY, AND YOU KNOW THE REST. THE SANCTUARY OF THE **47 GEYSERS** WAS TO BE OUR RENDEZVOUS. TO THINK THAT I WAITED THERE, BUT A FEW STEPS FROM WHERE MY RANGERS SUFFERED IN SILENCE, IMPRISONED IN THAT MONSTROUS BARK...

DID YOU NOTICE JUST NOW, WHEN THE HORDE ROSE FROM THE EARTH TO ATTACK US, THAT IT WORE THE ARMOR OF MANY DIFFERENT CLANS?

YOU'RE RIGHT, AYORRO—MANY DIFFERENT CLANS UNITED NOW BENEATH THE SINGLE SIGN OF THE **RAVEN!**

WE MUST FIND THE FORBIDDEN LIBRARIES OF ZANZHIN AS QUICKLY AS WE CAN, AND LEARN MORE. I SUGGEST WE SET OUT AT FIRST LIGHT.

PTUI! MADNESS! STILL, I DOUBT I CAN CHANGE YOUR MIND.

WE'LL HAVE TO TRAVEL LIGHT, WITH AS MUCH FOOD AS POSSIBLE. AND WARM CLOTHES.

WHAT ABOUT MASTER NOSHIN?

AYORRO, I CHARGE YOU TO WATCH OVER HIM AND THE YAKS UNTIL I RETURN.

YES, SANA.

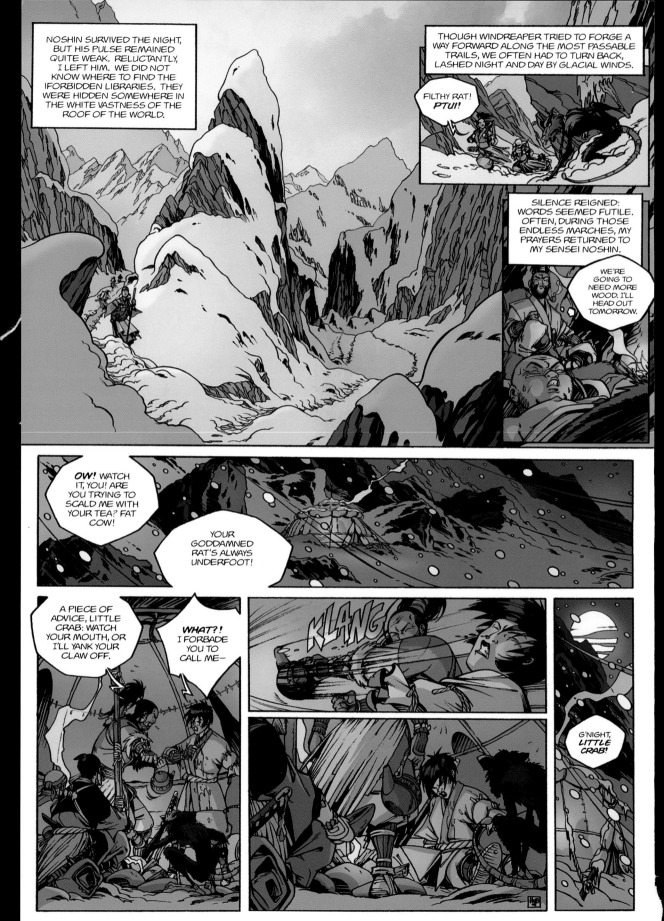

NOSHIN SURVIVED THE NIGHT, BUT HIS PULSE REMAINED QUITE WEAK. RELUCTANTLY, I LEFT HIM. WE DID NOT KNOW WHERE TO FIND THE IFORBIDDEN LIBRARIES. THEY WERE HIDDEN SOMEWHERE IN THE WHITE VASTNESS OF THE ROOF OF THE WORLD.

THOUGH WINDREAPER TRIED TO FORGE A WAY FORWARD ALONG THE MOST PASSABLE TRAILS, WE OFTEN HAD TO TURN BACK, LASHED NIGHT AND DAY BY GLACIAL WINDS.

FILTHY RAT! *PTUI!*

SILENCE REIGNED: WORDS SEEMED FUTILE. OFTEN, DURING THOSE ENDLESS MARCHES, MY PRAYERS RETURNED TO MY SENSEI NOSHIN.

WE'RE GOING TO NEED MORE WOOD. I'LL HEAD OUT TOMORROW.

OW! WATCH IT, YOU! ARE YOU TRYING TO SCALD ME WITH YOUR TEA? FAT COW!

YOUR GODDAMNED RAT'S ALWAYS UNDERFOOT!

A PIECE OF ADVICE, LITTLE CRAB: WATCH YOUR MOUTH, OR I'LL YANK YOUR CLAW OFF.

WHAT?! I FORBADE YOU TO CALL ME—

KLANG

G'NIGHT, *LITTLE CRAB!*

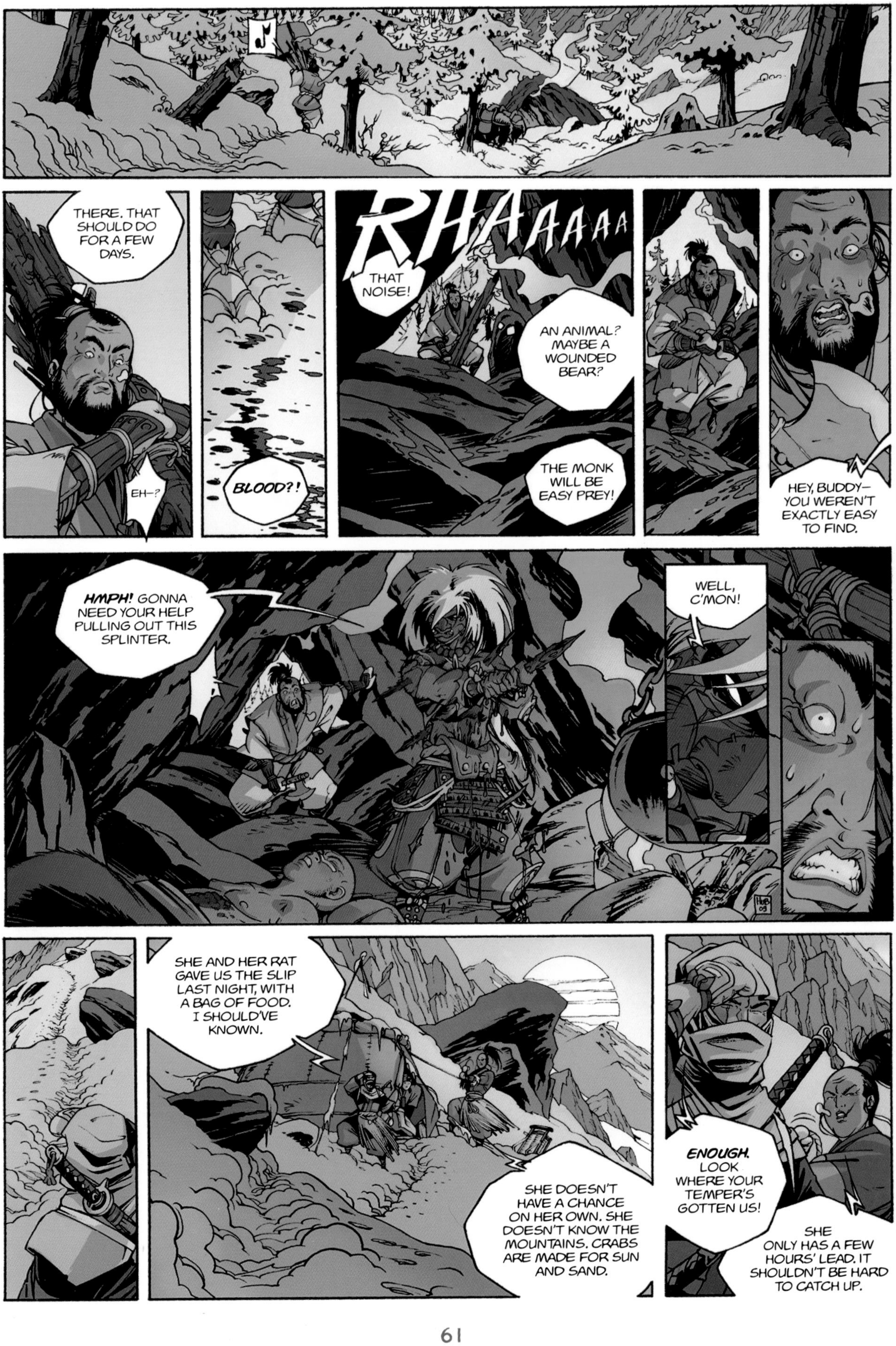
THERE. THAT SHOULD DO FOR A FEW DAYS.
EH–?
BLOOD?!
RHAAAAA
THAT NOISE!
AN ANIMAL? MAYBE A WOUNDED BEAR?
THE MONK WILL BE EASY PREY!
HEY, BUDDY– YOU WEREN'T EXACTLY EASY TO FIND.
HMPH! GONNA NEED YOUR HELP PULLING OUT THIS SPLINTER.
WELL, C'MON!
SHE AND HER RAT GAVE US THE SLIP LAST NIGHT, WITH A BAG OF FOOD. I SHOULD'VE KNOWN.
SHE DOESN'T HAVE A CHANCE ON HER OWN. SHE DOESN'T KNOW THE MOUNTAINS. CRABS ARE MADE FOR SUN AND SAND.
ENOUGH. LOOK WHERE YOUR TEMPER'S GOTTEN US!
SHE ONLY HAS A FEW HOURS' LEAD. IT SHOULDN'T BE HARD TO CATCH UP.

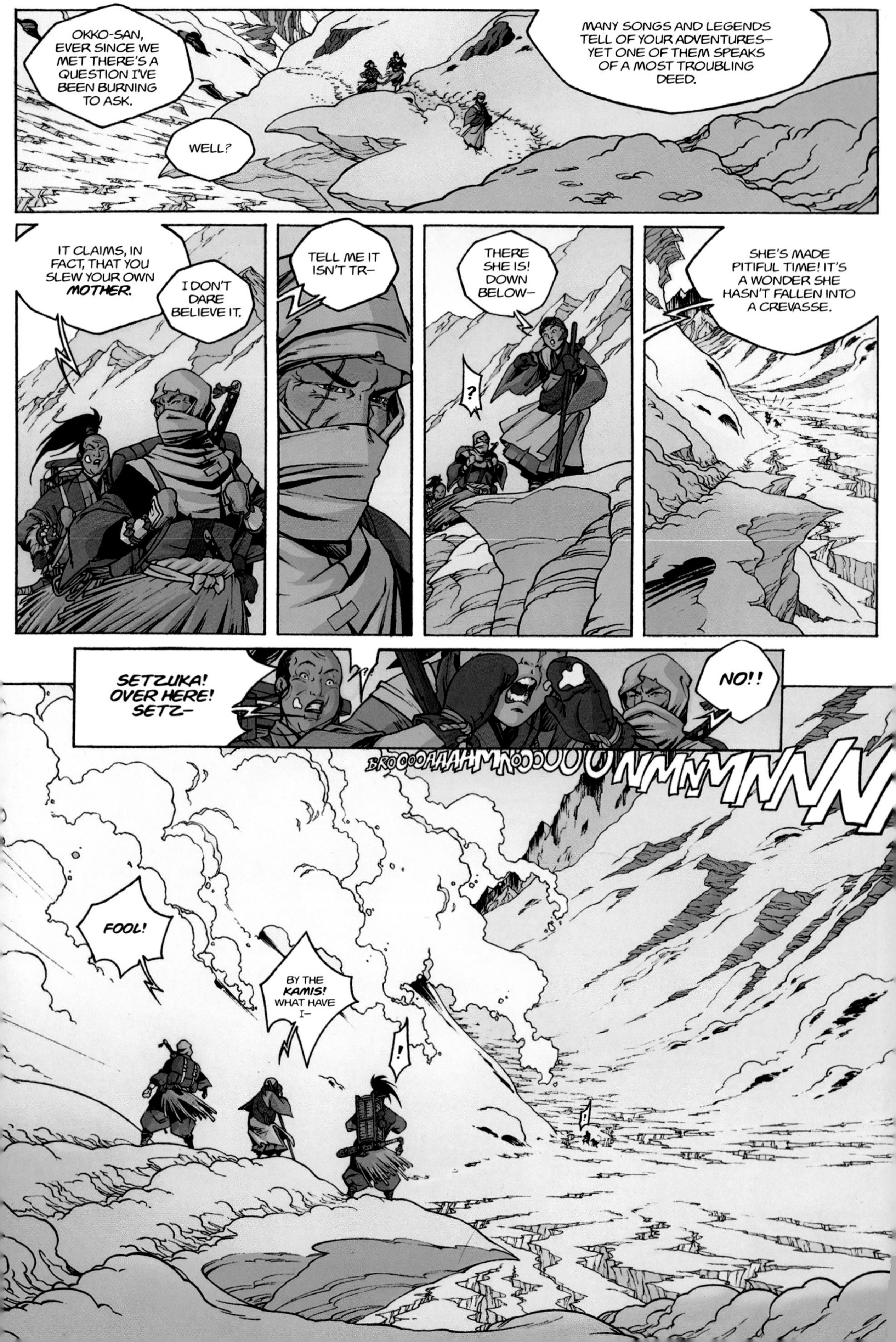
OKKO-SAN, EVER SINCE WE MET THERE'S A QUESTION I'VE BEEN BURNING TO ASK.
WELL?
MANY SONGS AND LEGENDS TELL OF YOUR ADVENTURES— YET ONE OF THEM SPEAKS OF A MOST TROUBLING DEED.
IT CLAIMS, IN FACT, THAT YOU SLEW YOUR OWN MOTHER.
I DON'T DARE BELIEVE IT.
TELL ME IT ISN'T TR—
THERE SHE IS! DOWN BELOW—
?
SHE'S MADE PITIFUL TIME! IT'S A WONDER SHE HASN'T FALLEN INTO A CREVASSE.
SETZUKA! OVER HERE! SETZ—
NO!!
FOOL!
BY THE KAMIS! WHAT HAVE I—
!

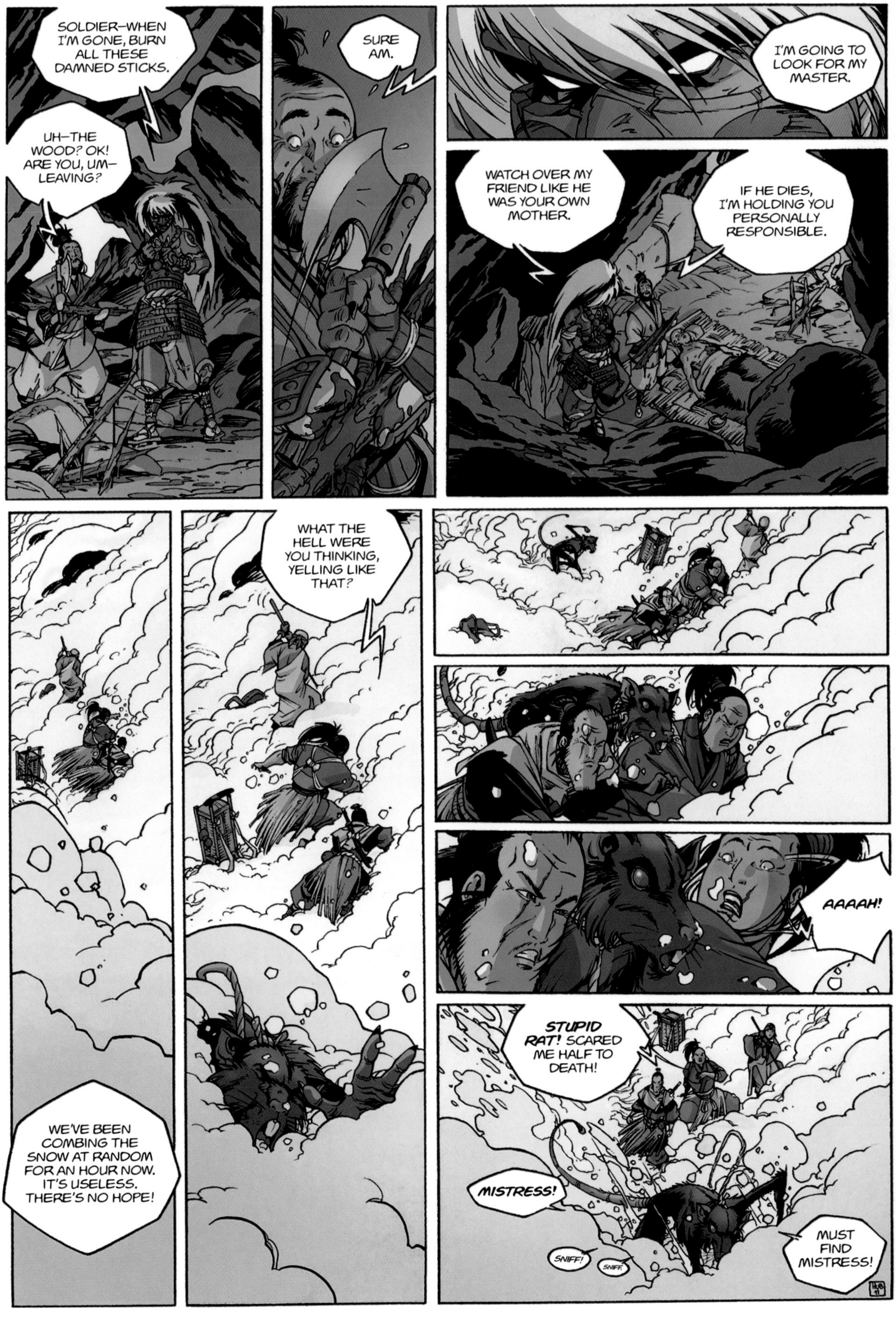

SOLDIER—WHEN I'M GONE, BURN ALL THESE DAMNED STICKS.
UH—THE WOOD? OK! ARE YOU, UM—LEAVING?
SURE AM.
I'M GOING TO LOOK FOR MY MASTER.
WATCH OVER MY FRIEND LIKE HE WAS YOUR OWN MOTHER.
IF HE DIES, I'M HOLDING YOU PERSONALLY RESPONSIBLE.
WE'VE BEEN COMBING THE SNOW AT RANDOM FOR AN HOUR NOW. IT'S USELESS. THERE'S NO HOPE!
WHAT THE HELL WERE YOU THINKING, YELLING LIKE THAT?
AAAAH!
STUPID RAT! SCARED ME HALF TO DEATH!
MISTRESS!
SNIFF!
SNIFF.
MUST FIND MISTRESS!

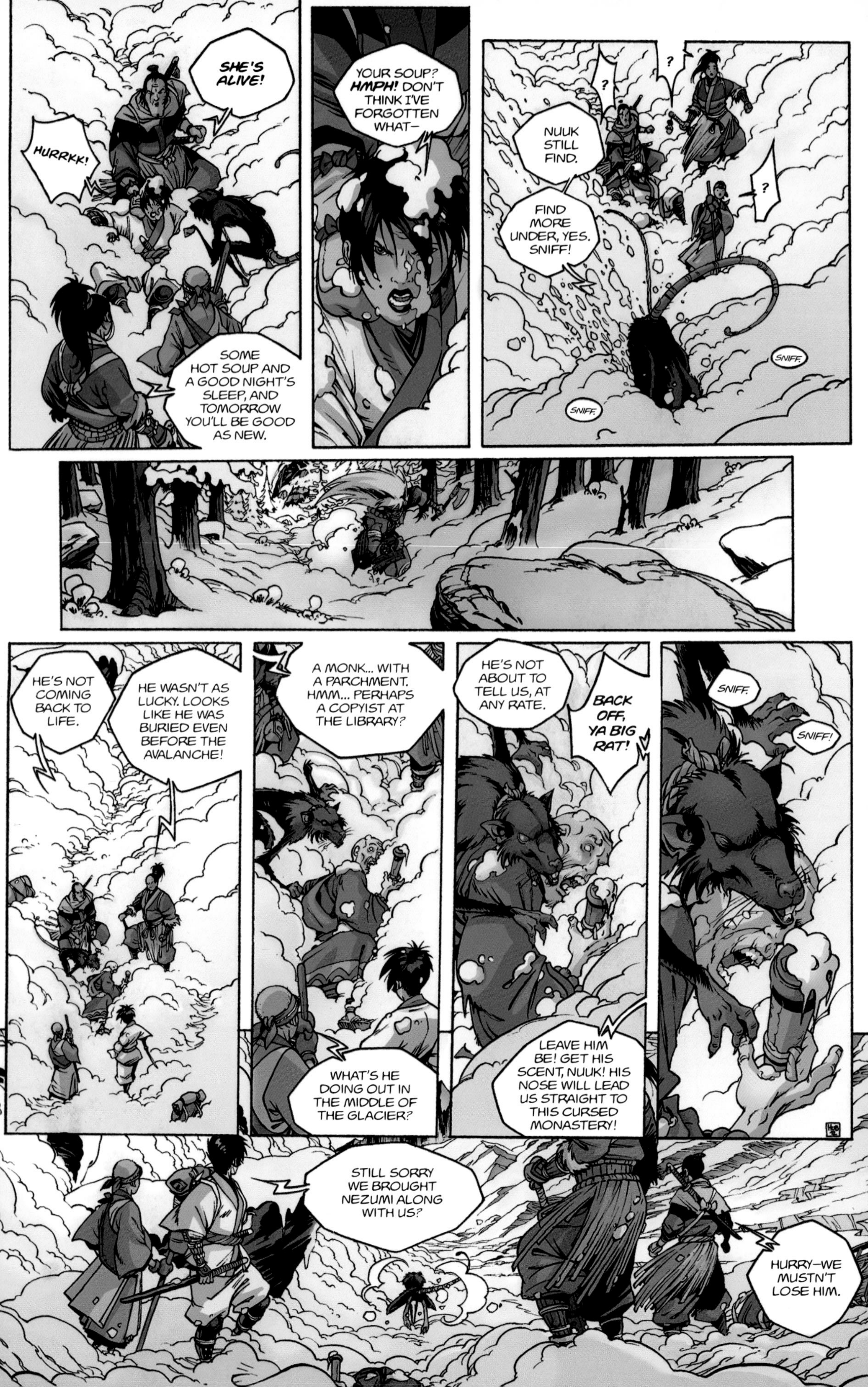
HURRKK!
SHE'S ALIVE!
SOME HOT SOUP AND A GOOD NIGHT'S SLEEP, AND TOMORROW YOU'LL BE GOOD AS NEW.
YOUR SOUP? HMPH! DON'T THINK I'VE FORGOTTEN WHAT—
?
?
NUUK STILL FIND.
FIND MORE UNDER, YES. SNIFF!
?
SNIFF.
SNIFF.
HE'S NOT COMING BACK TO LIFE.
HE WASN'T AS LUCKY. LOOKS LIKE HE WAS BURIED EVEN BEFORE THE AVALANCHE!
A MONK... WITH A PARCHMENT. HMM... PERHAPS A COPYIST AT THE LIBRARY?
WHAT'S HE DOING OUT IN THE MIDDLE OF THE GLACIER?
HE'S NOT ABOUT TO TELL US, AT ANY RATE.
BACK OFF, YA BIG RAT!
LEAVE HIM BE! GET HIS SCENT, NUUK! HIS NOSE WILL LEAD US STRAIGHT TO THIS CURSED MONASTERY!
SNIFF.
SNIFF!
STILL SORRY WE BROUGHT NEZUMI ALONG WITH US?
HURRY—WE MUSTN'T LOSE HIM.

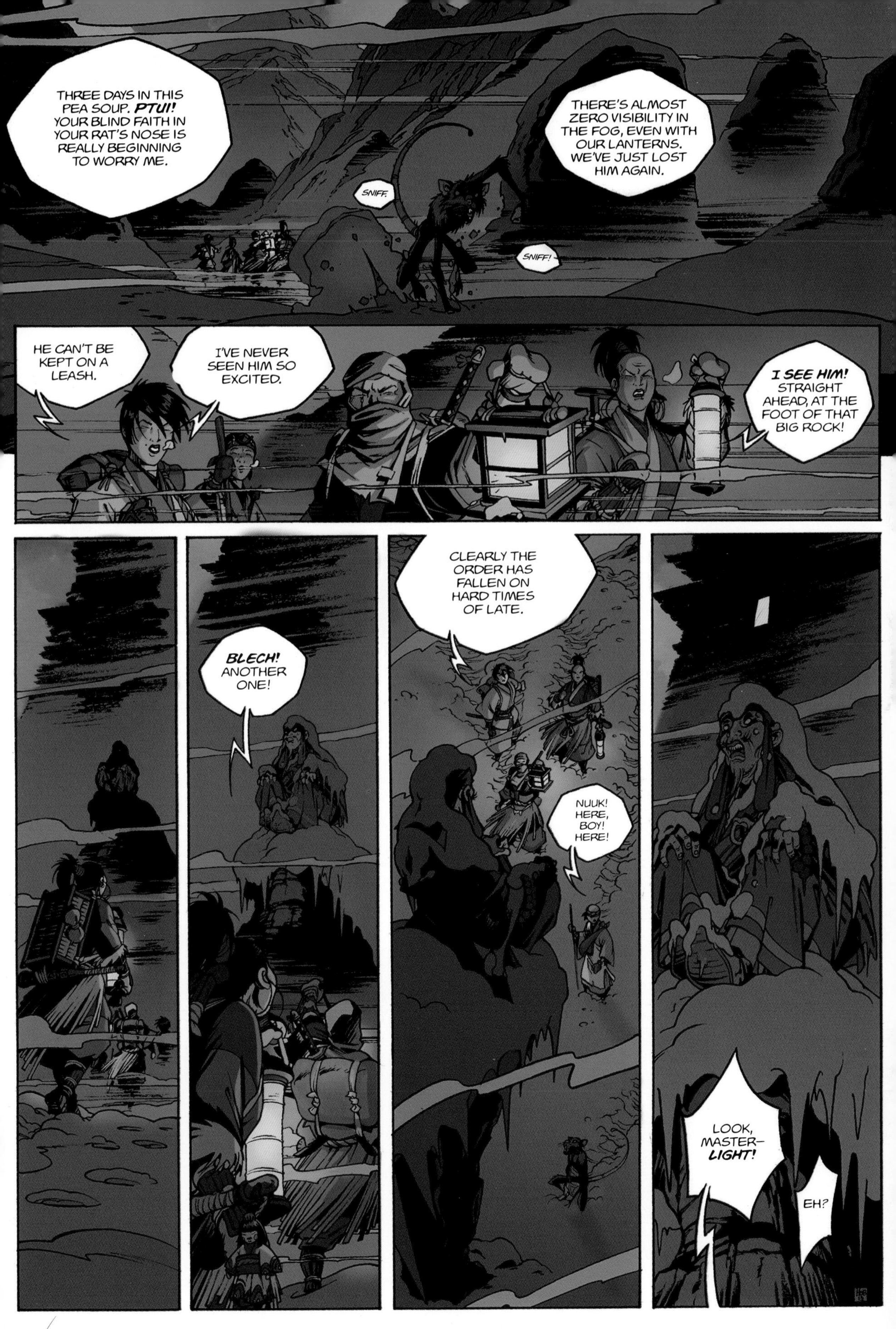
THREE DAYS IN THIS PEA SOUP. PTUI! YOUR BLIND FAITH IN YOUR RAT'S NOSE IS REALLY BEGINNING TO WORRY ME.
SNIFF.
THERE'S ALMOST ZERO VISIBILITY IN THE FOG, EVEN WITH OUR LANTERNS. WE'VE JUST LOST HIM AGAIN.
SNIFF!
HE CAN'T BE KEPT ON A LEASH.
I'VE NEVER SEEN HIM SO EXCITED.
I SEE HIM! STRAIGHT AHEAD, AT THE FOOT OF THAT BIG ROCK!
BLECH! ANOTHER ONE!
CLEARLY THE ORDER HAS FALLEN ON HARD TIMES OF LATE.
NUUK! HERE, BOY! HERE!
LOOK, MASTER— LIGHT!
EH?

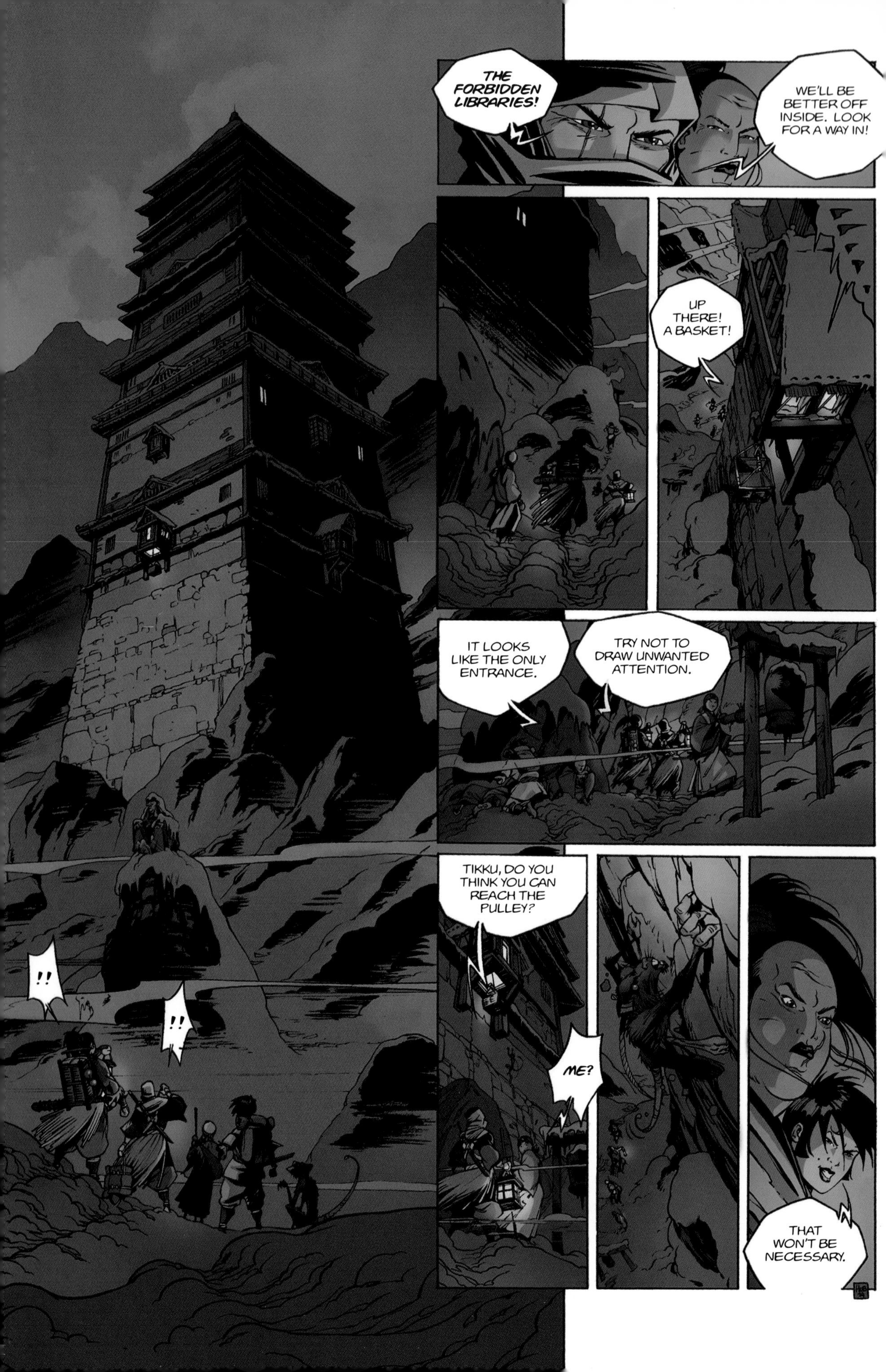
THE FORBIDDEN LIBRARIES!
WE'LL BE BETTER OFF INSIDE. LOOK FOR A WAY IN!
UP THERE! A BASKET!
IT LOOKS LIKE THE ONLY ENTRANCE.
TRY NOT TO DRAW UNWANTED ATTENTION.
!!
!!
TIKKU, DO YOU THINK YOU CAN REACH THE PULLEY?
ME?
THAT WON'T BE NECESSARY.

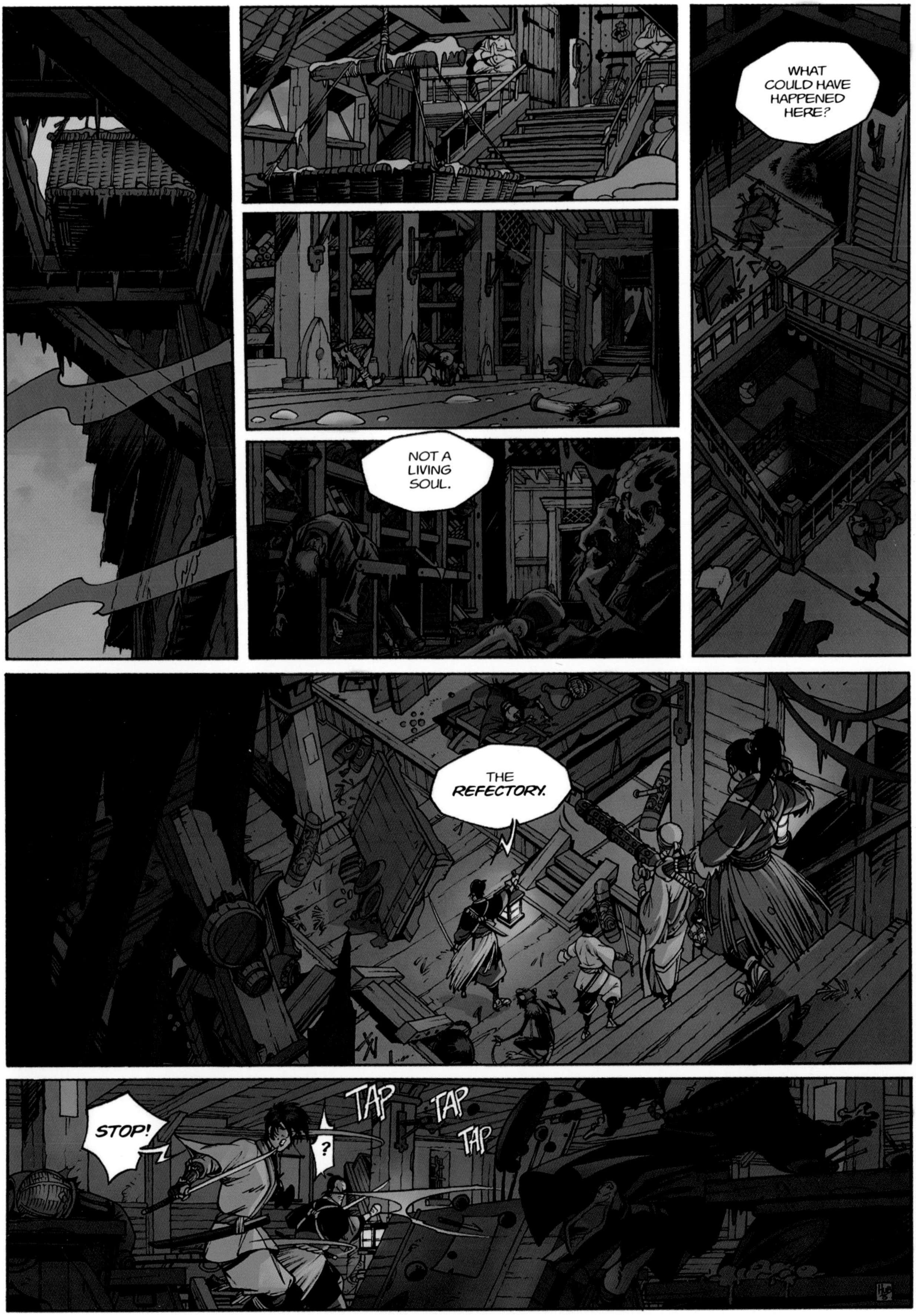
WHAT COULD HAVE HAPPENED HERE?
NOT A LIVING SOUL.
THE REFECTORY.
STOP!
?
TAP
TAP
TAP

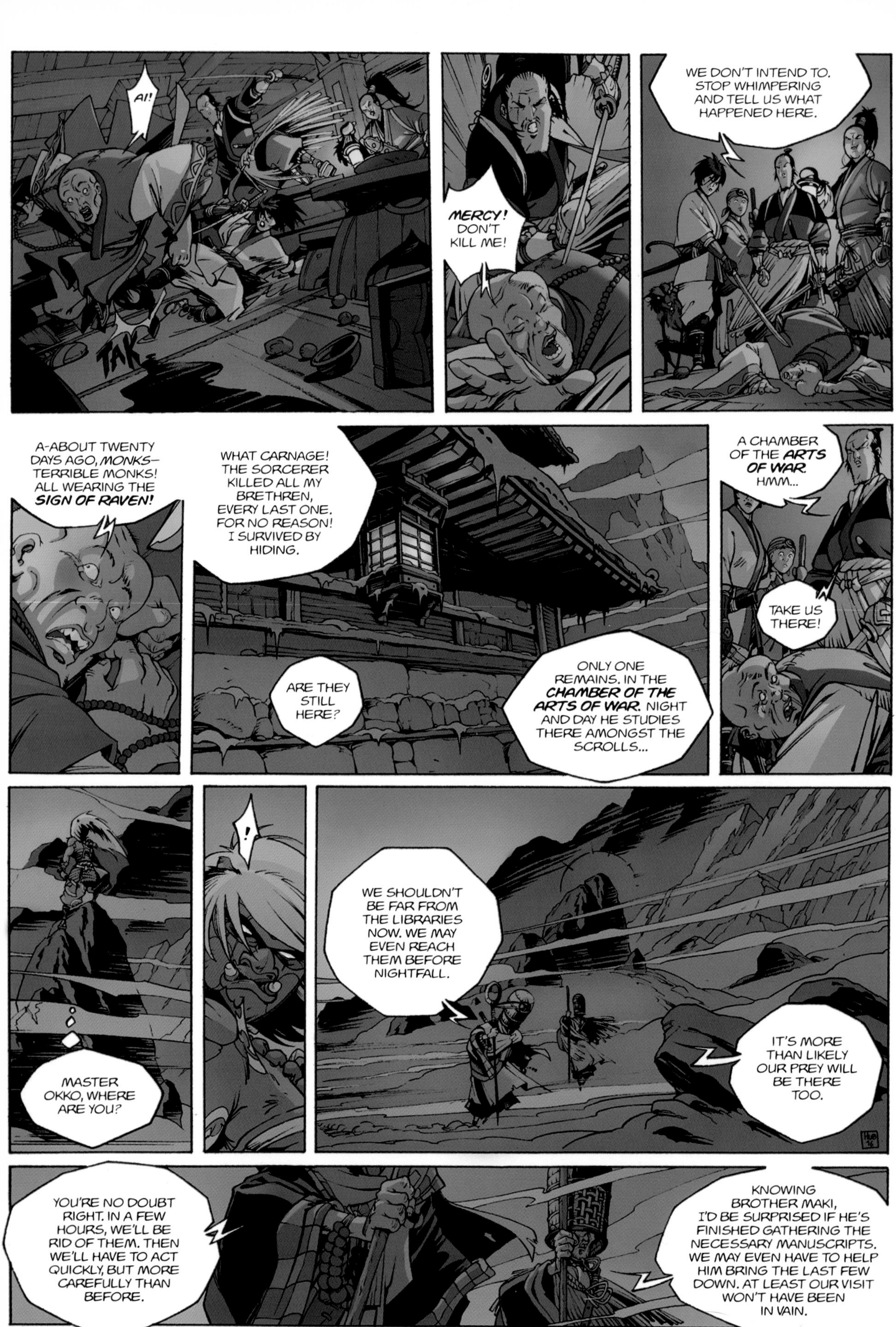
AI!
TAK
MERCY! DON'T KILL ME!
WE DON'T INTEND TO. STOP WHIMPERING AND TELL US WHAT HAPPENED HERE.
A-ABOUT TWENTY DAYS AGO, MONKS— TERRIBLE MONKS! ALL WEARING THE SIGN OF RAVEN!
WHAT CARNAGE! THE SORCERER KILLED ALL MY BRETHREN, EVERY LAST ONE. FOR NO REASON! I SURVIVED BY HIDING.
ARE THEY STILL HERE?
ONLY ONE REMAINS. IN THE CHAMBER OF THE ARTS OF WAR. NIGHT AND DAY HE STUDIES THERE AMONGST THE SCROLLS...
A CHAMBER OF THE ARTS OF WAR. HMM...
TAKE US THERE!
MASTER OKKO, WHERE ARE YOU?
!
WE SHOULDN'T BE FAR FROM THE LIBRARIES NOW. WE MAY EVEN REACH THEM BEFORE NIGHTFALL.
IT'S MORE THAN LIKELY OUR PREY WILL BE THERE TOO.
YOU'RE NO DOUBT RIGHT. IN A FEW HOURS, WE'LL BE RID OF THEM. THEN WE'LL HAVE TO ACT QUICKLY, BUT MORE CAREFULLY THAN BEFORE.
KNOWING BROTHER MAKI, I'D BE SURPRISED IF HE'S FINISHED GATHERING THE NECESSARY MANUSCRIPTS. WE MAY EVEN HAVE TO HELP HIM BRING THE LAST FEW DOWN. AT LEAST OUR VISIT WON'T HAVE BEEN IN VAIN.

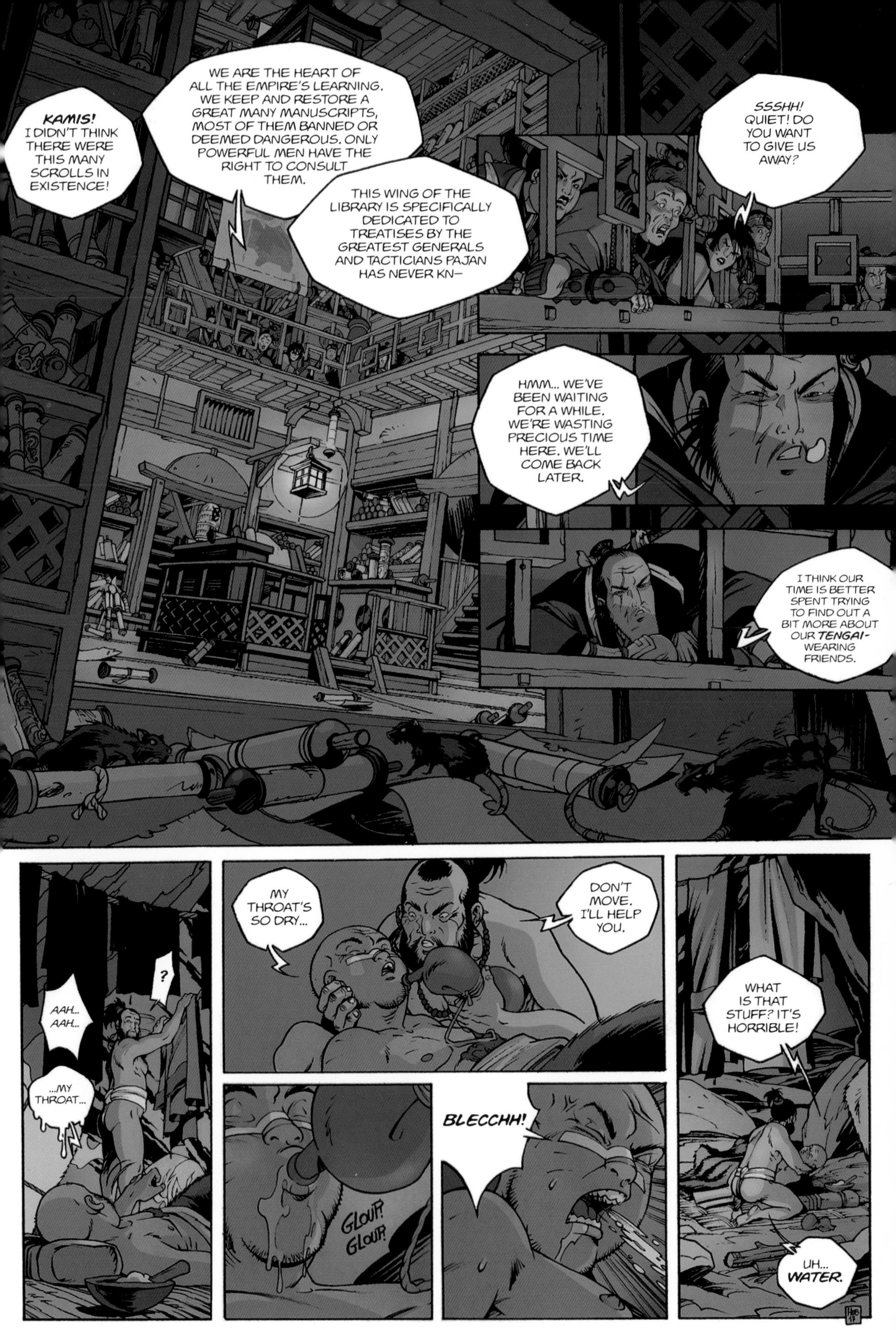
KAMIS! I DIDN'T THINK THERE WERE THIS MANY SCROLLS IN EXISTENCE!
WE ARE THE HEART OF ALL THE EMPIRE'S LEARNING. WE KEEP AND RESTORE A GREAT MANY MANUSCRIPTS, MOST OF THEM BANNED OR DEEMED DANGEROUS. ONLY POWERFUL MEN HAVE THE RIGHT TO CONSULT THEM.
THIS WING OF THE LIBRARY IS SPECIFICALLY DEDICATED TO TREATISES BY THE GREATEST GENERALS AND TACTICIANS PAJAN HAS NEVER KN–
SSSHH! QUIET! DO YOU WANT TO GIVE US AWAY?
HMM... WE'VE BEEN WAITING FOR A WHILE. WE'RE WASTING PRECIOUS TIME HERE. WE'LL COME BACK LATER.
I THINK OUR TIME IS BETTER SPENT TRYING TO FIND OUT A BIT MORE ABOUT OUR TENGAI-WEARING FRIENDS.
AAH... AAH...
?
...MY THROAT...
MY THROAT'S SO DRY...
DON'T MOVE. I'LL HELP YOU.
GLOUP! GLOUP!
BLECCHH!
WHAT IS THAT STUFF? IT'S HORRIBLE!
UH... WATER.

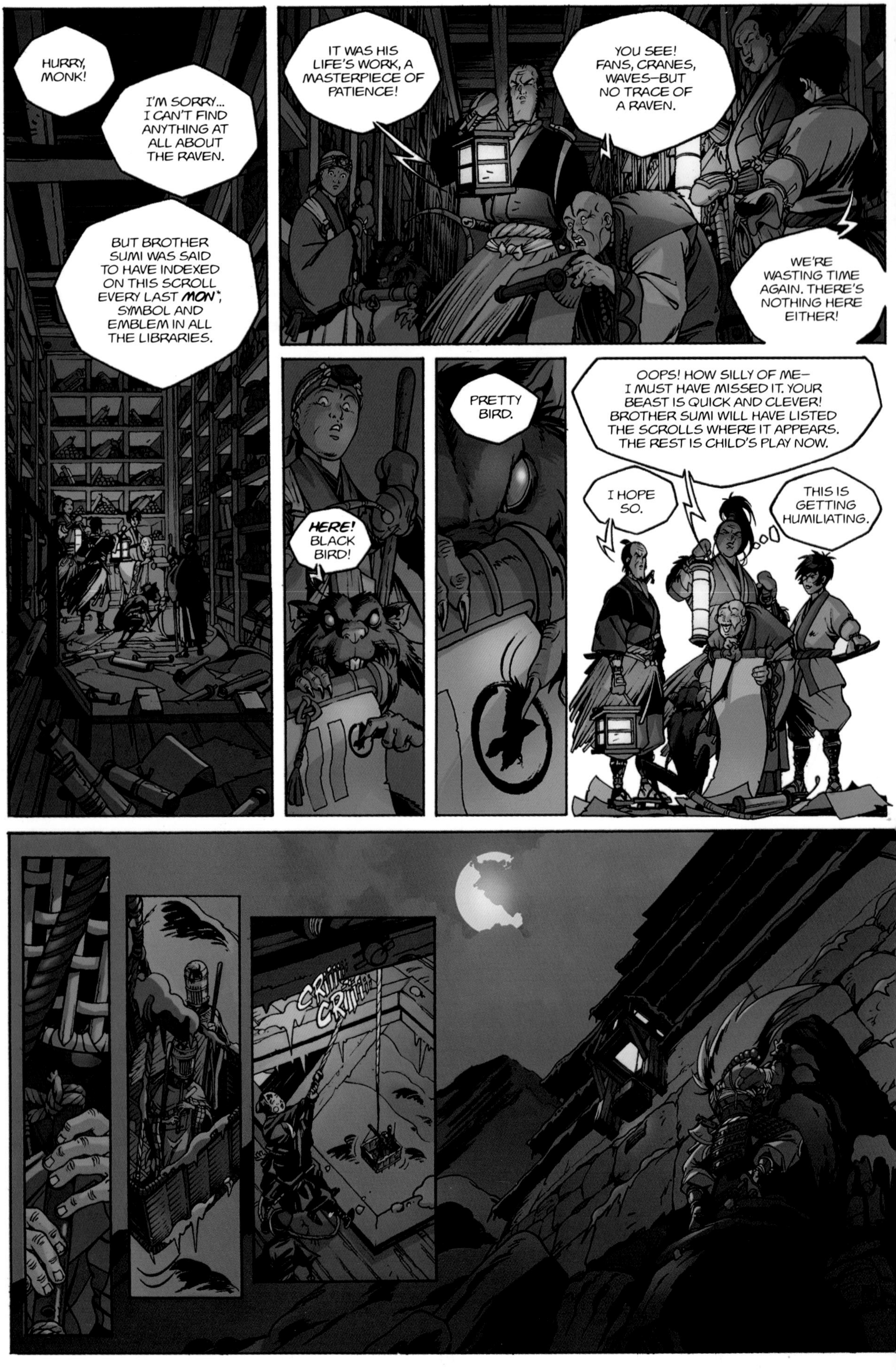
HURRY, MONK!
I'M SORRY... I CAN'T FIND ANYTHING AT ALL ABOUT THE RAVEN.
BUT BROTHER SUMI WAS SAID TO HAVE INDEXED ON THIS SCROLL EVERY LAST **MON***, SYMBOL AND EMBLEM IN ALL THE LIBRARIES.
IT WAS HIS LIFE'S WORK, A MASTERPIECE OF PATIENCE!
YOU SEE! FANS, CRANES, WAVES—BUT NO TRACE OF A RAVEN.
WE'RE WASTING TIME AGAIN. THERE'S NOTHING HERE EITHER!
HERE! BLACK BIRD!
PRETTY BIRD.
OOPS! HOW SILLY OF ME— I MUST HAVE MISSED IT. YOUR BEAST IS QUICK AND CLEVER! BROTHER SUMI WILL HAVE LISTED THE SCROLLS WHERE IT APPEARS. THE REST IS CHILD'S PLAY NOW.
I HOPE SO.
THIS IS GETTING HUMILIATING.
CRiiii CRiiii

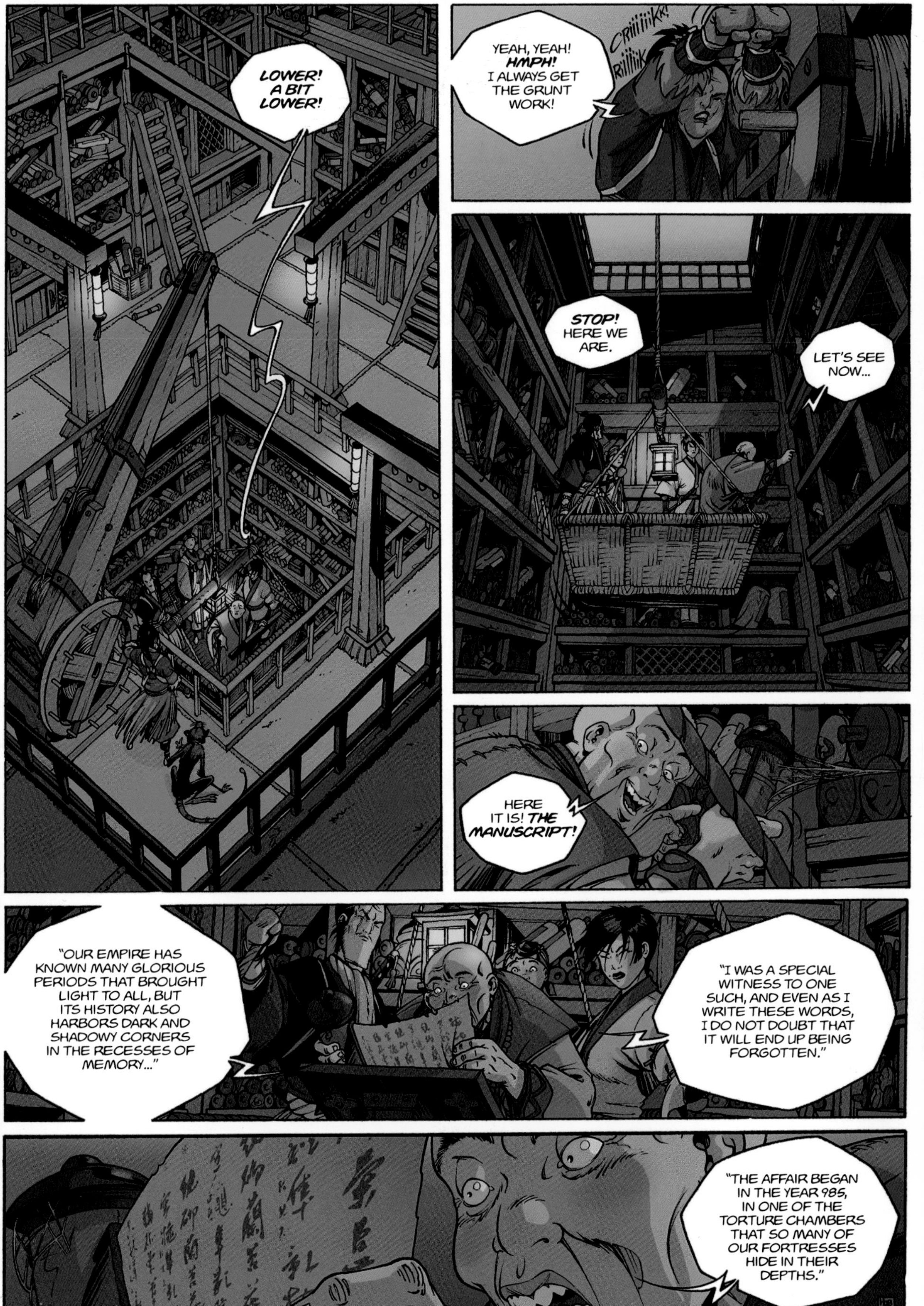
LOWER! A BIT LOWER!
YEAH, YEAH! HMPH! I ALWAYS GET THE GRUNT WORK!
CRIIIIIIKK! RIIIIIK
STOP! HERE WE ARE.
LET'S SEE NOW...
HERE IT IS! THE MANUSCRIPT!
"OUR EMPIRE HAS KNOWN MANY GLORIOUS PERIODS THAT BROUGHT LIGHT TO ALL, BUT ITS HISTORY ALSO HARBORS DARK AND SHADOWY CORNERS IN THE RECESSES OF MEMORY..."
"I WAS A SPECIAL WITNESS TO ONE SUCH, AND EVEN AS I WRITE THESE WORDS, I DO NOT DOUBT THAT IT WILL END UP BEING FORGOTTEN."
"THE AFFAIR BEGAN IN THE YEAR 985, IN ONE OF THE TORTURE CHAMBERS THAT SO MANY OF OUR FORTRESSES HIDE IN THEIR DEPTHS."

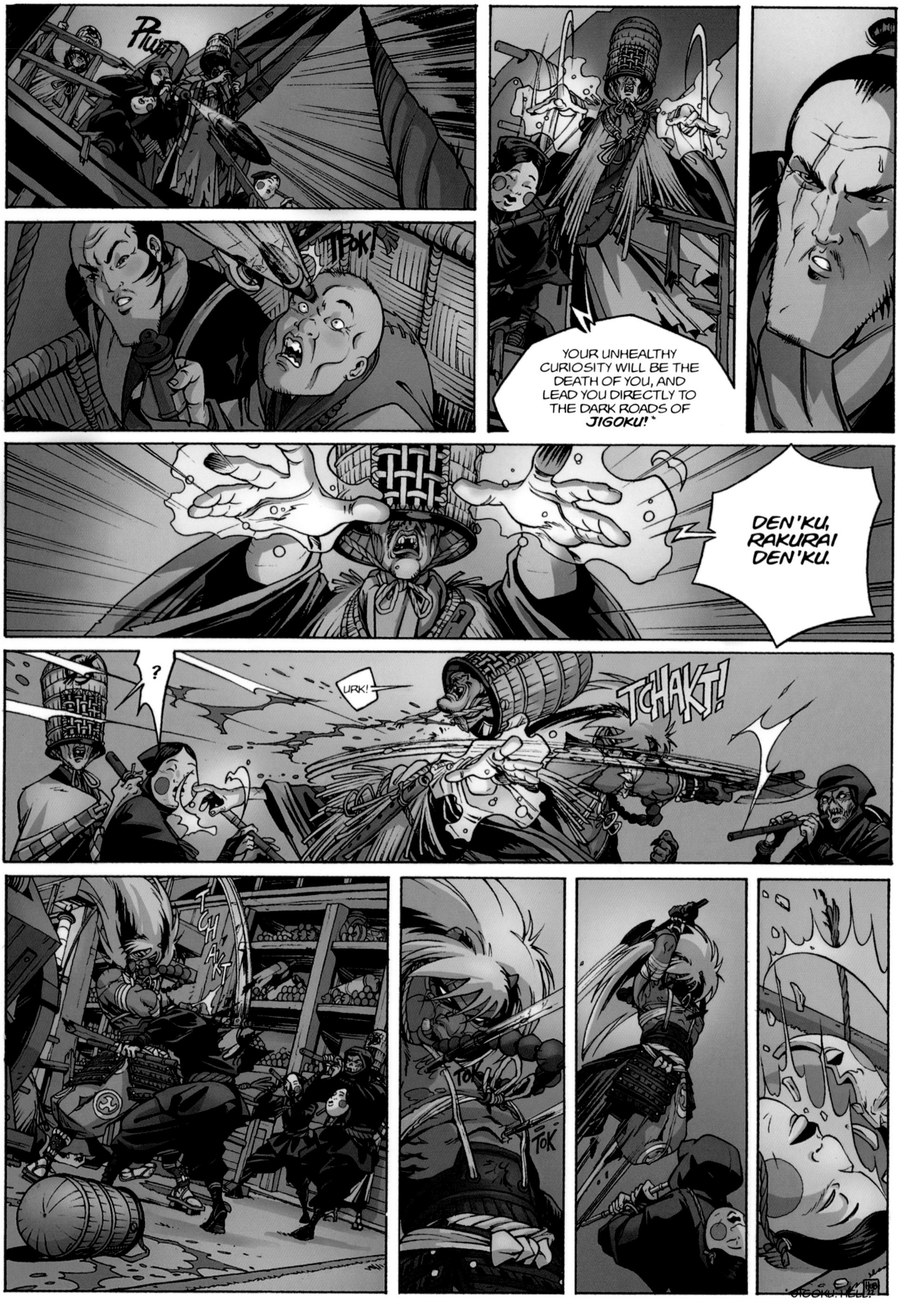
PFUFF
TPOK!
YOUR UNHEALTHY CURIOSITY WILL BE THE DEATH OF YOU, AND LEAD YOU DIRECTLY TO THE DARK ROADS OF JIGOKU!*
DEN'KU, RAKURAI DEN'KU.
?
URK!
TCHAKT!
TCHAKT
TOK
TOK
*JIGOKU: HELL.

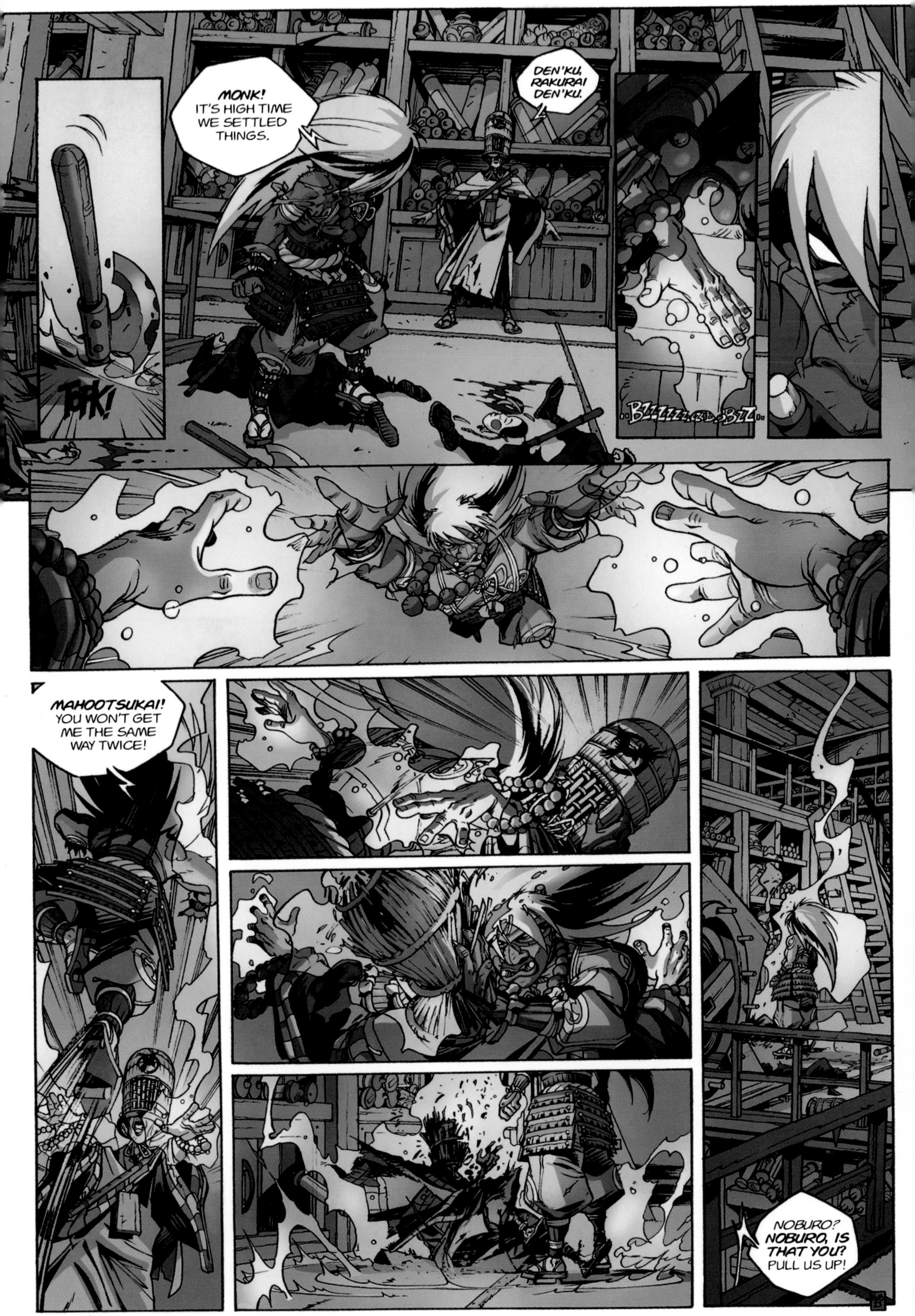
TORK!
MONK! IT'S HIGH TIME WE SETTLED THINGS.
DEN'KU, RAKURAI DEN'KU.
..BZZZZZZZZZZZ..BZZ..
MAHOOTSUKAI! YOU WON'T GET ME THE SAME WAY TWICE!
NOBURO? NOBURO, IS THAT YOU? PULL US UP!

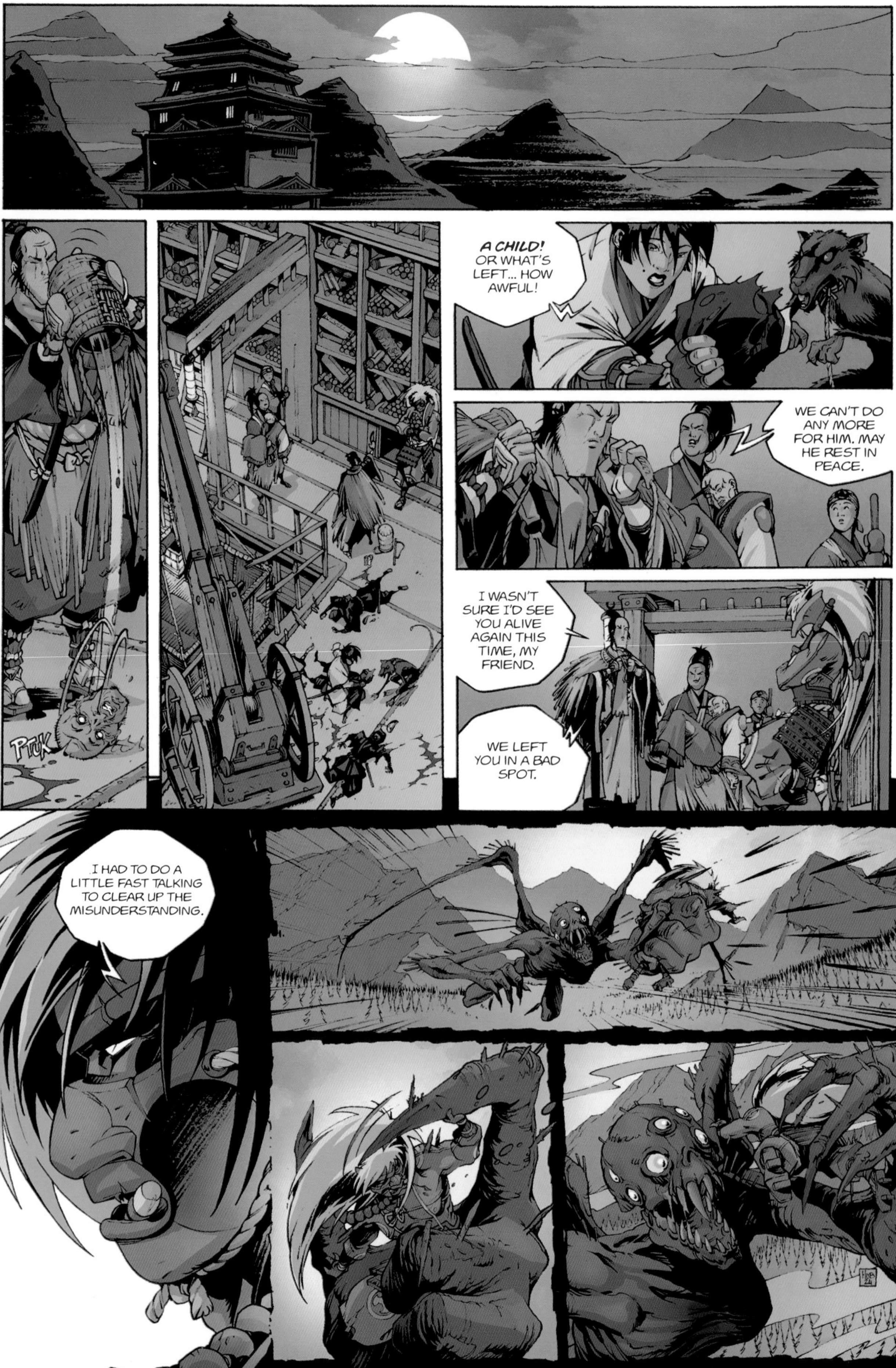
PTUK
A CHILD! OR WHAT'S LEFT... HOW AWFUL!
WE CAN'T DO ANY MORE FOR HIM. MAY HE REST IN PEACE.
I WASN'T SURE I'D SEE YOU ALIVE AGAIN THIS TIME, MY FRIEND.
WE LEFT YOU IN A BAD SPOT.
I HAD TO DO A LITTLE FAST TALKING TO CLEAR UP THE MISUNDERSTANDING.

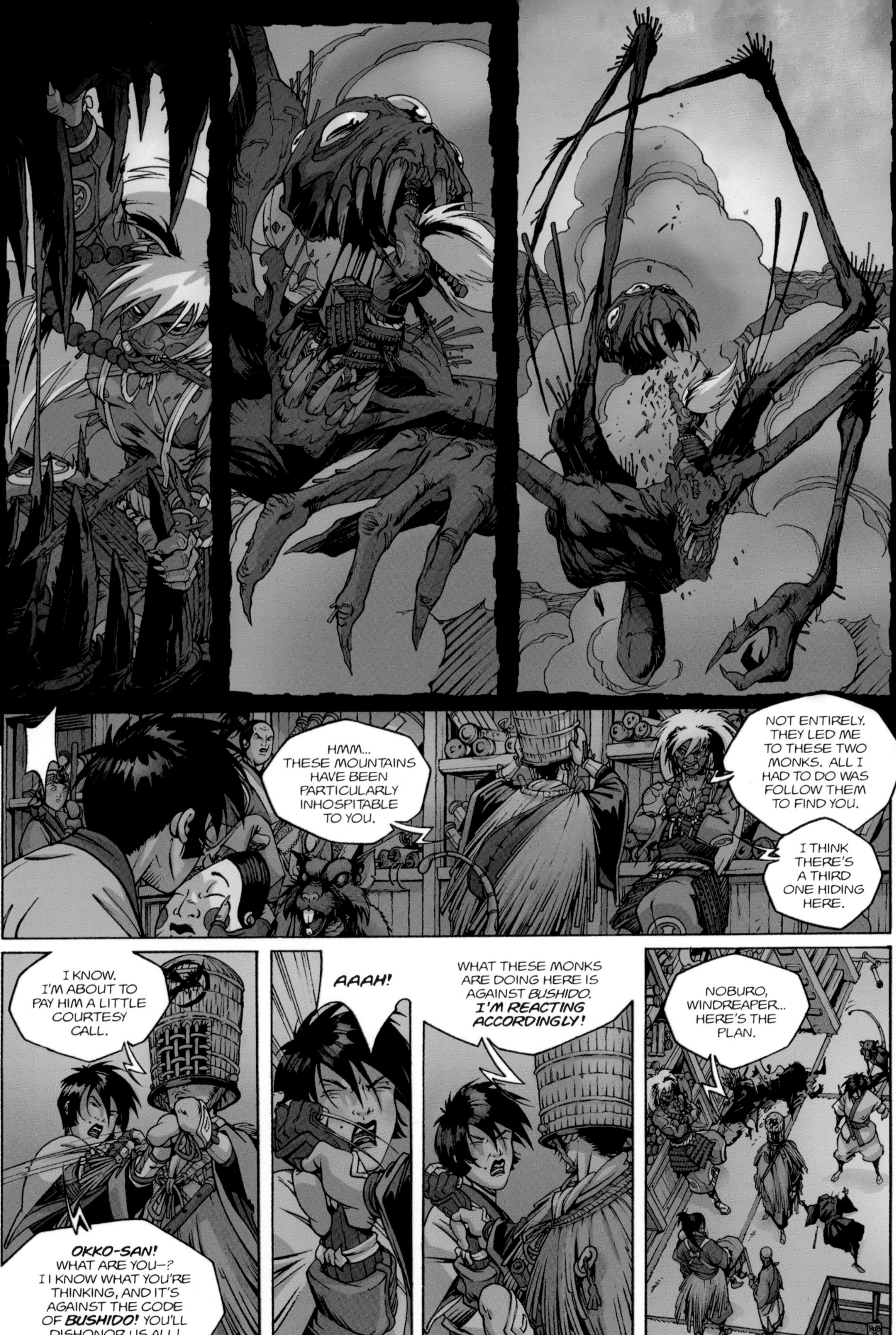
HMM... THESE MOUNTAINS HAVE BEEN PARTICULARLY INHOSPITABLE TO YOU.
NOT ENTIRELY. THEY LED ME TO THESE TWO MONKS. ALL I HAD TO DO WAS FOLLOW THEM TO FIND YOU.
I THINK THERE'S A THIRD ONE HIDING HERE.
I KNOW. I'M ABOUT TO PAY HIM A LITTLE COURTESY CALL.
OKKO-SAN! WHAT ARE YOU–? I I KNOW WHAT YOU'RE THINKING, AND IT'S AGAINST THE CODE OF BUSHIDO! YOU'LL DISHONOR US ALL!
AAAH!
WHAT THESE MONKS ARE DOING HERE IS AGAINST BUSHIDO. I'M REACTING ACCORDINGLY!
NOBURO, WINDREAPER... HERE'S THE PLAN.

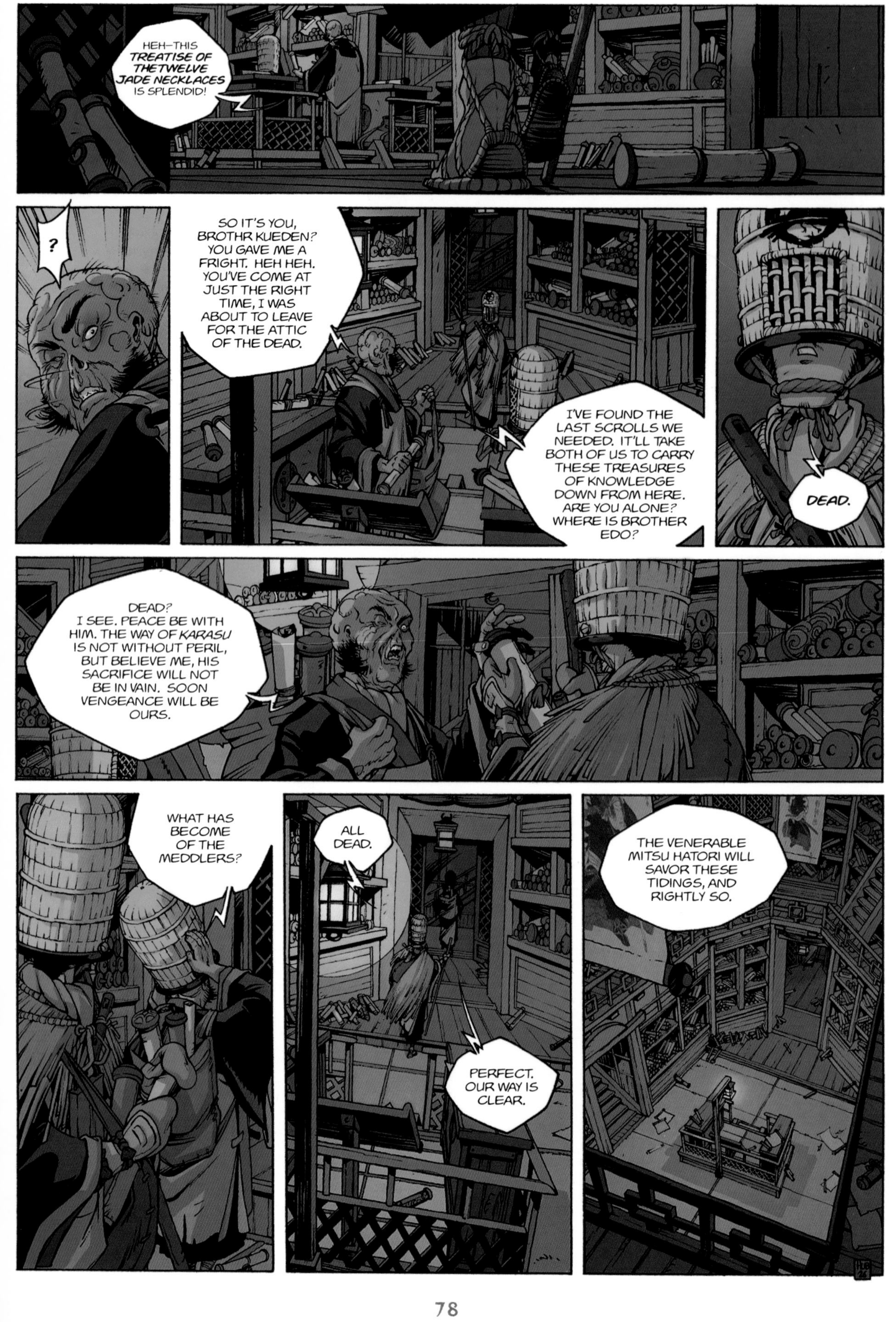
HEH—THIS *TREATISE OF THETWELVE JADE NECKLACES* IS SPLENDID!
?
SO IT'S YOU, BROTHR KUEDEN? YOU GAVE ME A FRIGHT. HEH HEH. YOU'VE COME AT JUST THE RIGHT TIME, I WAS ABOUT TO LEAVE FOR THE ATTIC OF THE DEAD.
I'VE FOUND THE LAST SCROLLS WE NEEDED. IT'LL TAKE BOTH OF US TO CARRY THESE TREASURES OF KNOWLEDGE DOWN FROM HERE. ARE YOU ALONE? WHERE IS BROTHER EDO?
DEAD.
DEAD? I SEE. PEACE BE WITH HIM. THE WAY OF *KARASU* IS NOT WITHOUT PERIL, BUT BELIEVE ME, HIS SACRIFICE WILL NOT BE IN VAIN. SOON VENGEANCE WILL BE OURS.
WHAT HAS BECOME OF THE MEDDLERS?
ALL DEAD.
PERFECT. OUR WAY IS CLEAR.
THE VENERABLE MITSU HATORI WILL SAVOR THESE TIDINGS, AND RIGHTLY SO.

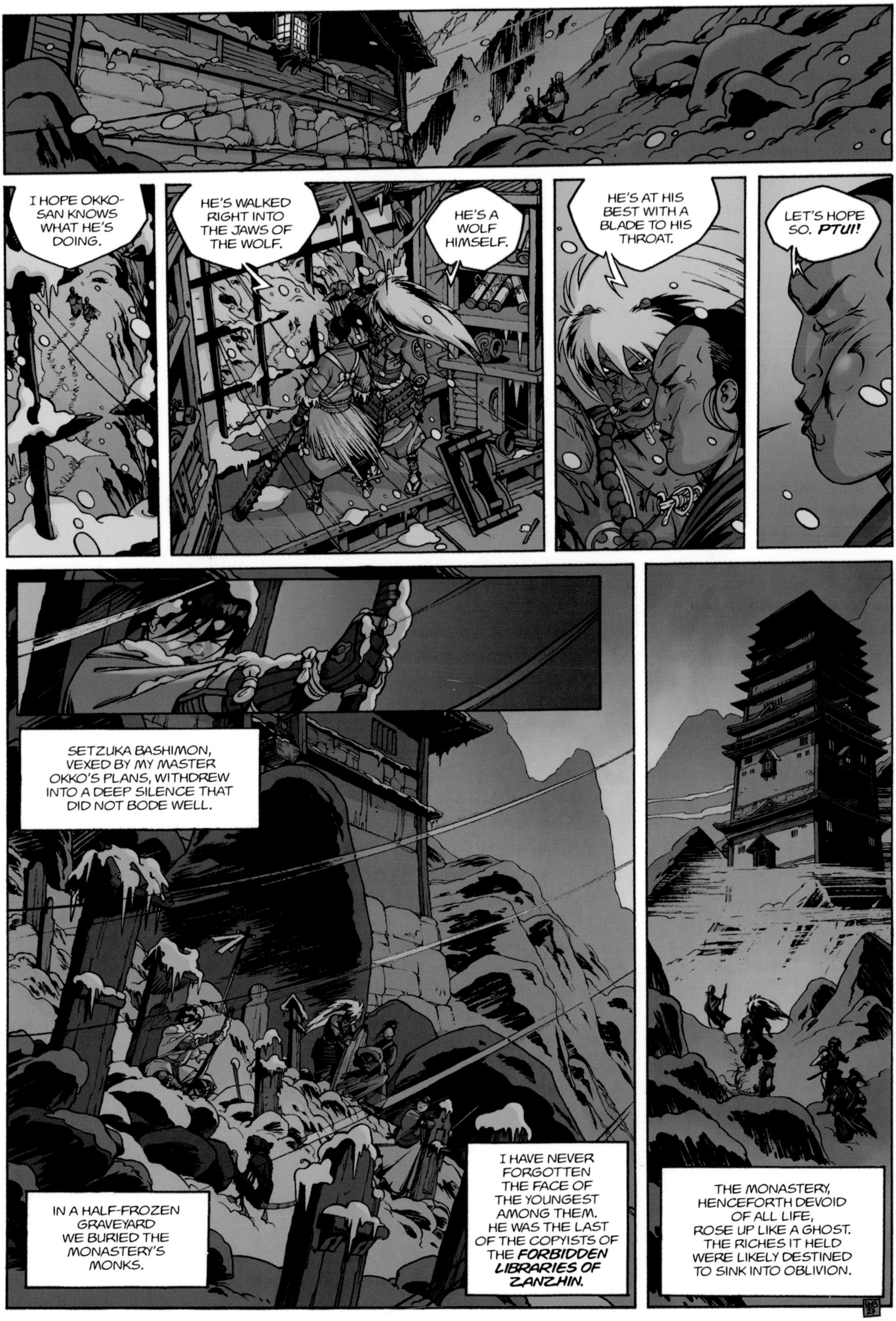

I HOPE OKKO-SAN KNOWS WHAT HE'S DOING.
HE'S WALKED RIGHT INTO THE JAWS OF THE WOLF.
HE'S A WOLF HIMSELF.
HE'S AT HIS BEST WITH A BLADE TO HIS THROAT.
LET'S HOPE SO. ***PTUI!***
SETZUKA BASHIMON, VEXED BY MY MASTER OKKO'S PLANS, WITHDREW INTO A DEEP SILENCE THAT DID NOT BODE WELL.
IN A HALF-FROZEN GRAVEYARD WE BURIED THE MONASTERY'S MONKS.
I HAVE NEVER FORGOTTEN THE FACE OF THE YOUNGEST AMONG THEM. HE WAS THE LAST OF THE COPYISTS OF THE ***FORBIDDEN LIBRARIES OF ZANZHIN.***
THE MONASTERY, HENCEFORTH DEVOID OF ALL LIFE, ROSE UP LIKE A GHOST. THE RICHES IT HELD WERE LIKELY DESTINED TO SINK INTO OBLIVION.

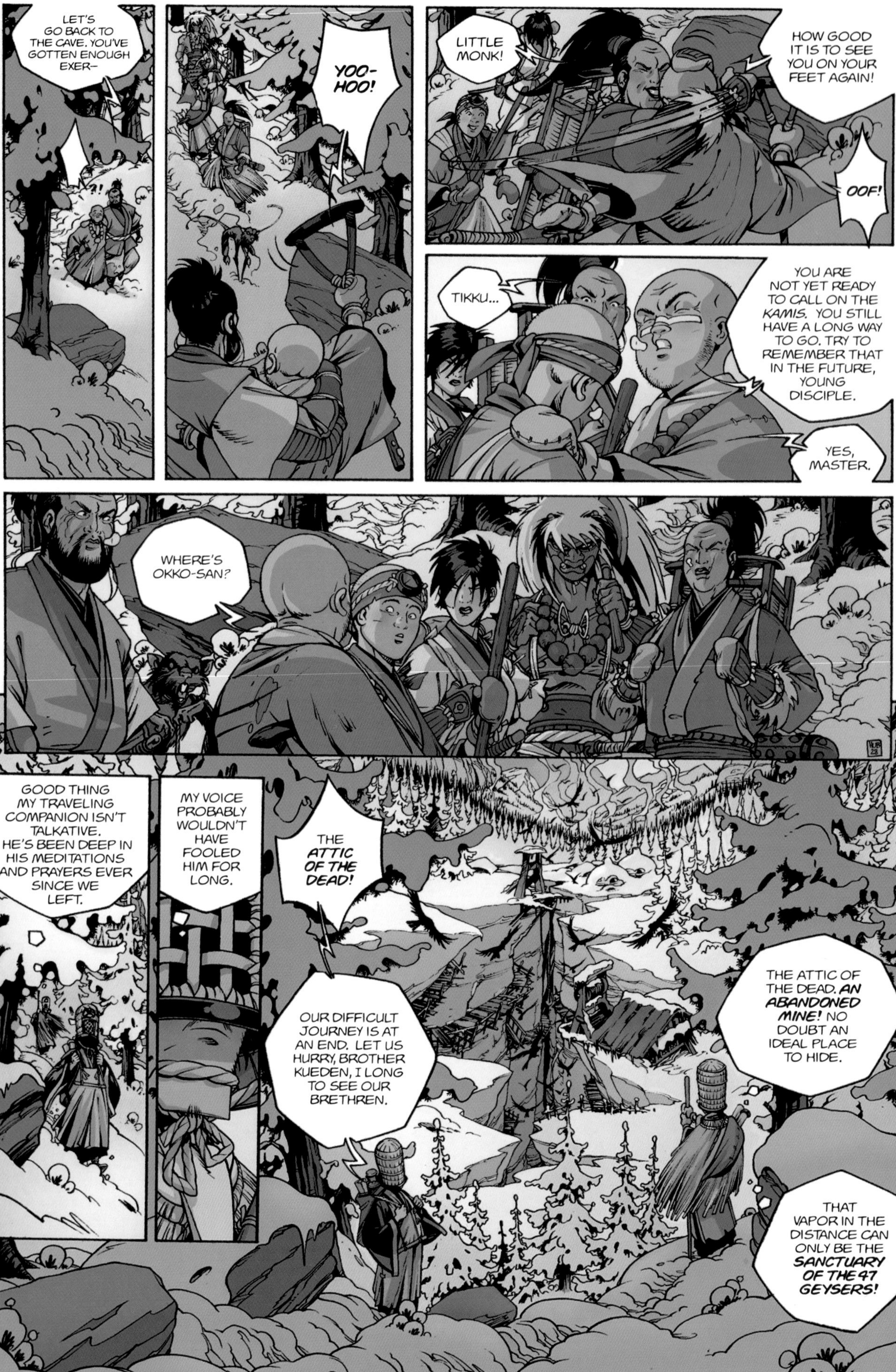
LET'S GO BACK TO THE CAVE. YOU'VE GOTTEN ENOUGH EXER–
YOO-HOO!
LITTLE MONK!
HOW GOOD IT IS TO SEE YOU ON YOUR FEET AGAIN!
OOF!
TIKKU...
YOU ARE NOT YET READY TO CALL ON THE KAMIS. YOU STILL HAVE A LONG WAY TO GO. TRY TO REMEMBER THAT IN THE FUTURE, YOUNG DISCIPLE.
YES, MASTER.
WHERE'S OKKO-SAN?
GOOD THING MY TRAVELING COMPANION ISN'T TALKATIVE. HE'S BEEN DEEP IN HIS MEDITATIONS AND PRAYERS EVER SINCE WE LEFT.
MY VOICE PROBABLY WOULDN'T HAVE FOOLED HIM FOR LONG.
THE ATTIC OF THE DEAD!
OUR DIFFICULT JOURNEY IS AT AN END. LET US HURRY, BROTHER KUEDEN, I LONG TO SEE OUR BRETHREN.
THE ATTIC OF THE DEAD. AN ABANDONED MINE! NO DOUBT AN IDEAL PLACE TO HIDE.
THAT VAPOR IN THE DISTANCE CAN ONLY BE THE SANCTUARY OF THE 47 GEYSERS!

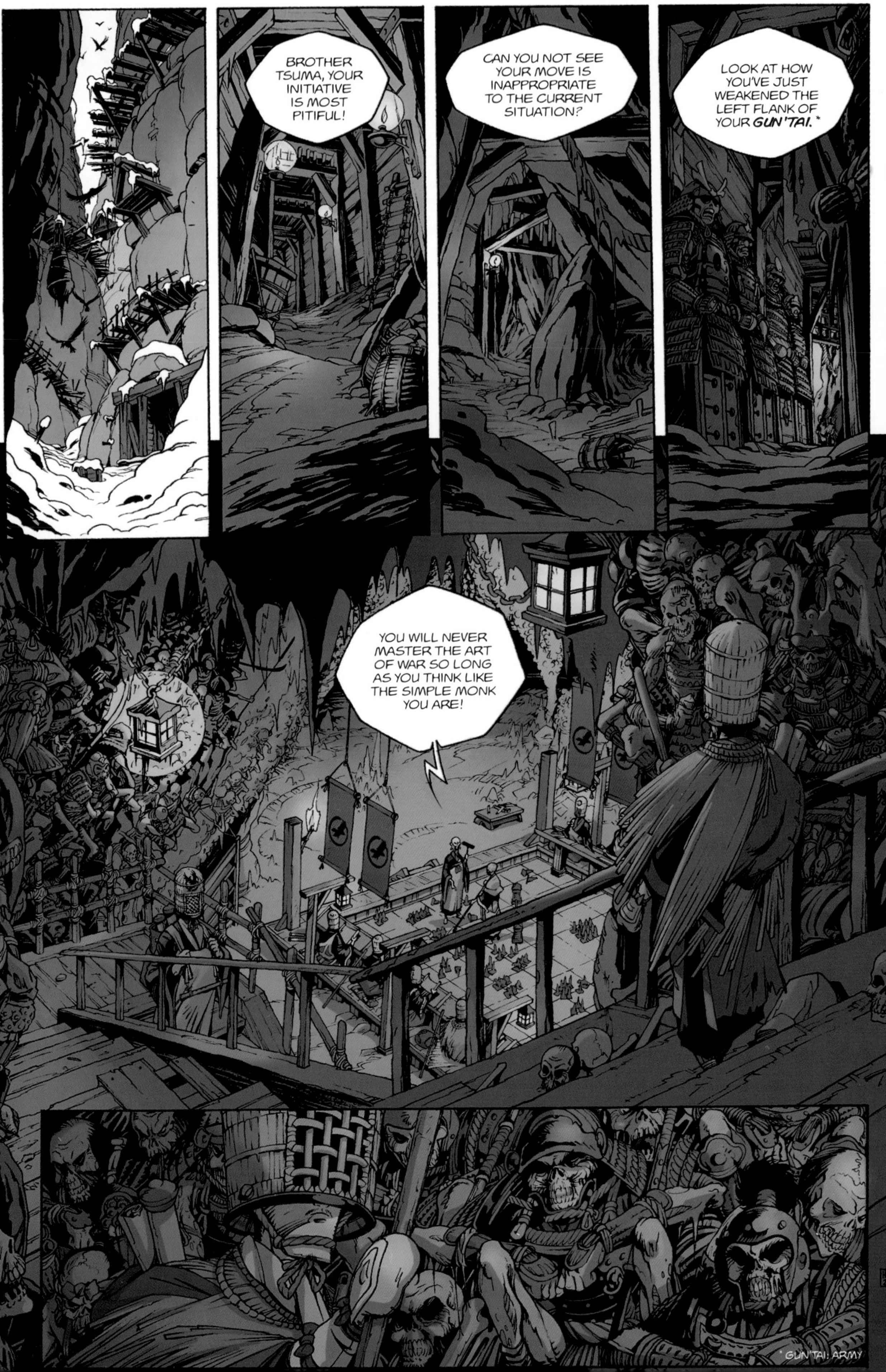
BROTHER TSUMA, YOUR INITIATIVE IS MOST PITIFUL!
CAN YOU NOT SEE YOUR MOVE IS INAPPROPRIATE TO THE CURRENT SITUATION?
LOOK AT HOW YOU'VE JUST WEAKENED THE LEFT FLANK OF YOUR GUN'TAI.*
YOU WILL NEVER MASTER THE ART OF WAR SO LONG AS YOU THINK LIKE THE SIMPLE MONK YOU ARE!
* GUN'TAI: ARMY

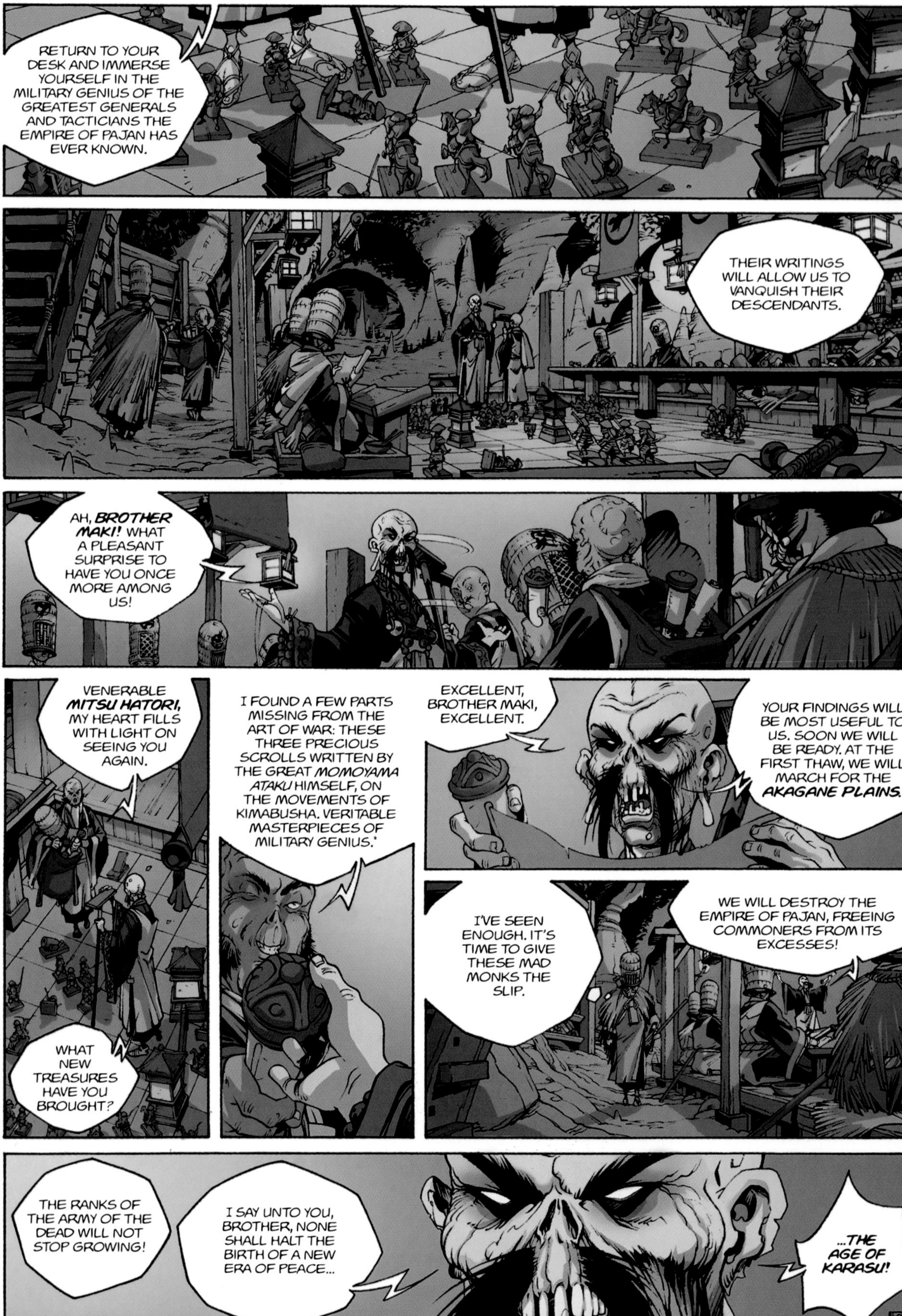

RETURN TO YOUR DESK AND IMMERSE YOURSELF IN THE MILITARY GENIUS OF THE GREATEST GENERALS AND TACTICIANS THE EMPIRE OF PAJAN HAS EVER KNOWN.
THEIR WRITINGS WILL ALLOW US TO VANQUISH THEIR DESCENDANTS.
AH, BROTHER MAKI! WHAT A PLEASANT SURPRISE TO HAVE YOU ONCE MORE AMONG US!
VENERABLE MITSU HATORI, MY HEART FILLS WITH LIGHT ON SEEING YOU AGAIN.
WHAT NEW TREASURES HAVE YOU BROUGHT?
I FOUND A FEW PARTS MISSING FROM THE ART OF WAR: THESE THREE PRECIOUS SCROLLS WRITTEN BY THE GREAT MOMOYAMA ATAKU HIMSELF, ON THE MOVEMENTS OF KIMABUSHA. VERITABLE MASTERPIECES OF MILITARY GENIUS.*
EXCELLENT, BROTHER MAKI, EXCELLENT.
YOUR FINDINGS WILL BE MOST USEFUL TO US. SOON WE WILL BE READY. AT THE FIRST THAW, WE WILL MARCH FOR THE AKAGANE PLAINS.
I'VE SEEN ENOUGH. IT'S TIME TO GIVE THESE MAD MONKS THE SLIP.
WE WILL DESTROY THE EMPIRE OF PAJAN, FREEING COMMONERS FROM ITS EXCESSES!
THE RANKS OF THE ARMY OF THE DEAD WILL NOT STOP GROWING!
I SAY UNTO YOU, BROTHER, NONE SHALL HALT THE BIRTH OF A NEW ERA OF PEACE...
...THE AGE OF KARASU!

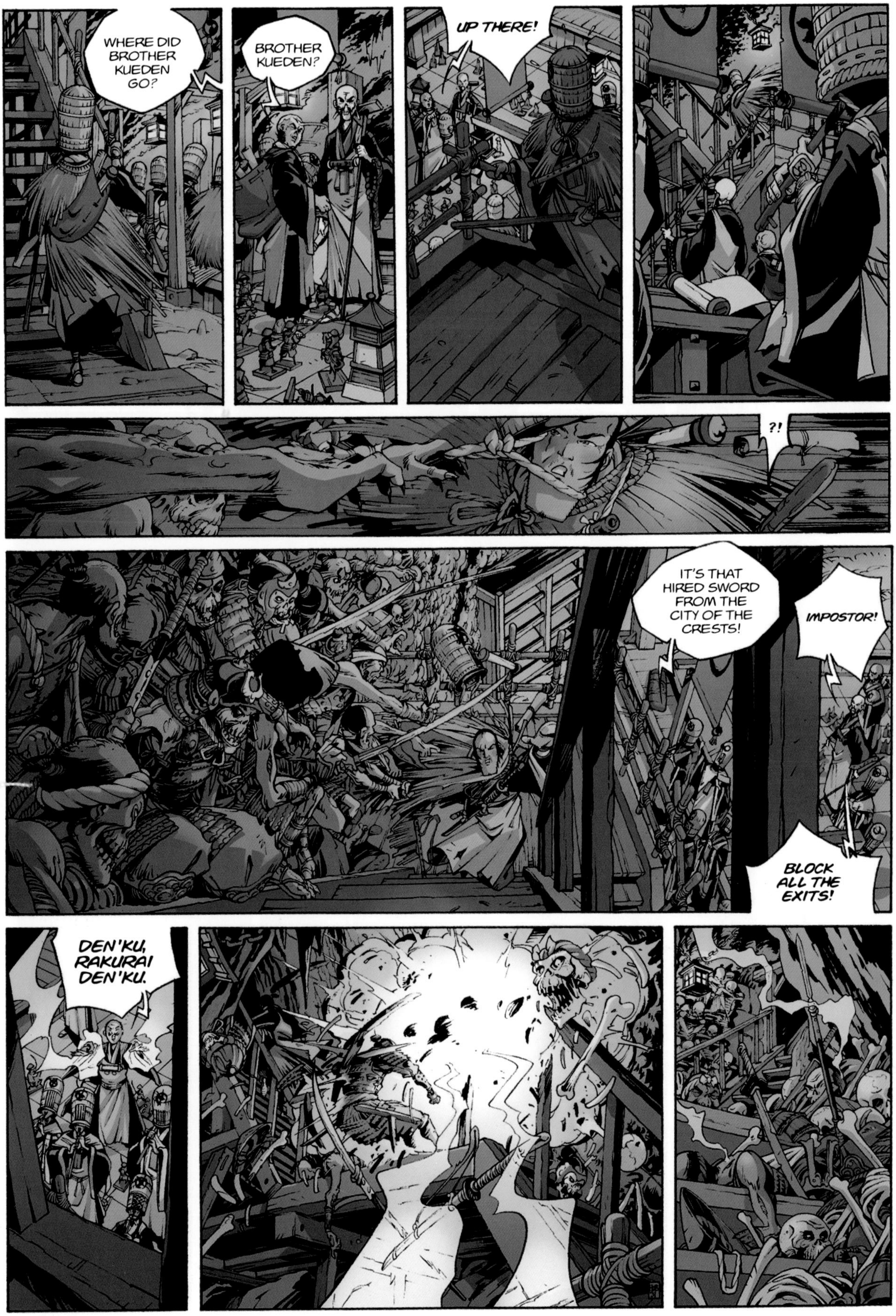
WHERE DID BROTHER KUEDEN GO?
BROTHER KUEDEN?
UP THERE!
?!
IT'S THAT HIRED SWORD FROM THE CITY OF THE CRESTS!
IMPOSTOR!
BLOCK ALL THE EXITS!
DEN'KU, RAKURAI DEN'KU.

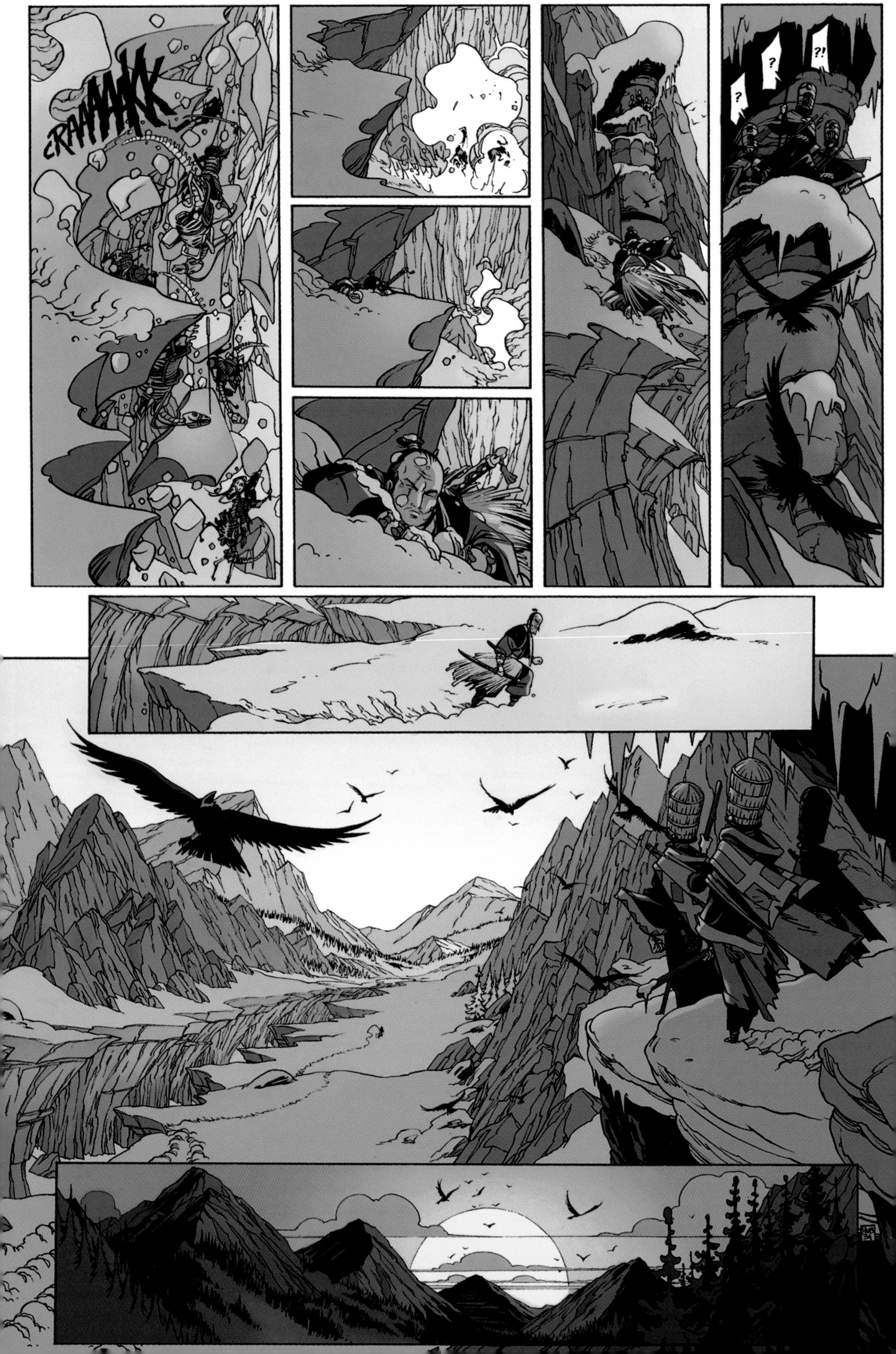
CRAAAAKK
?
?
?!

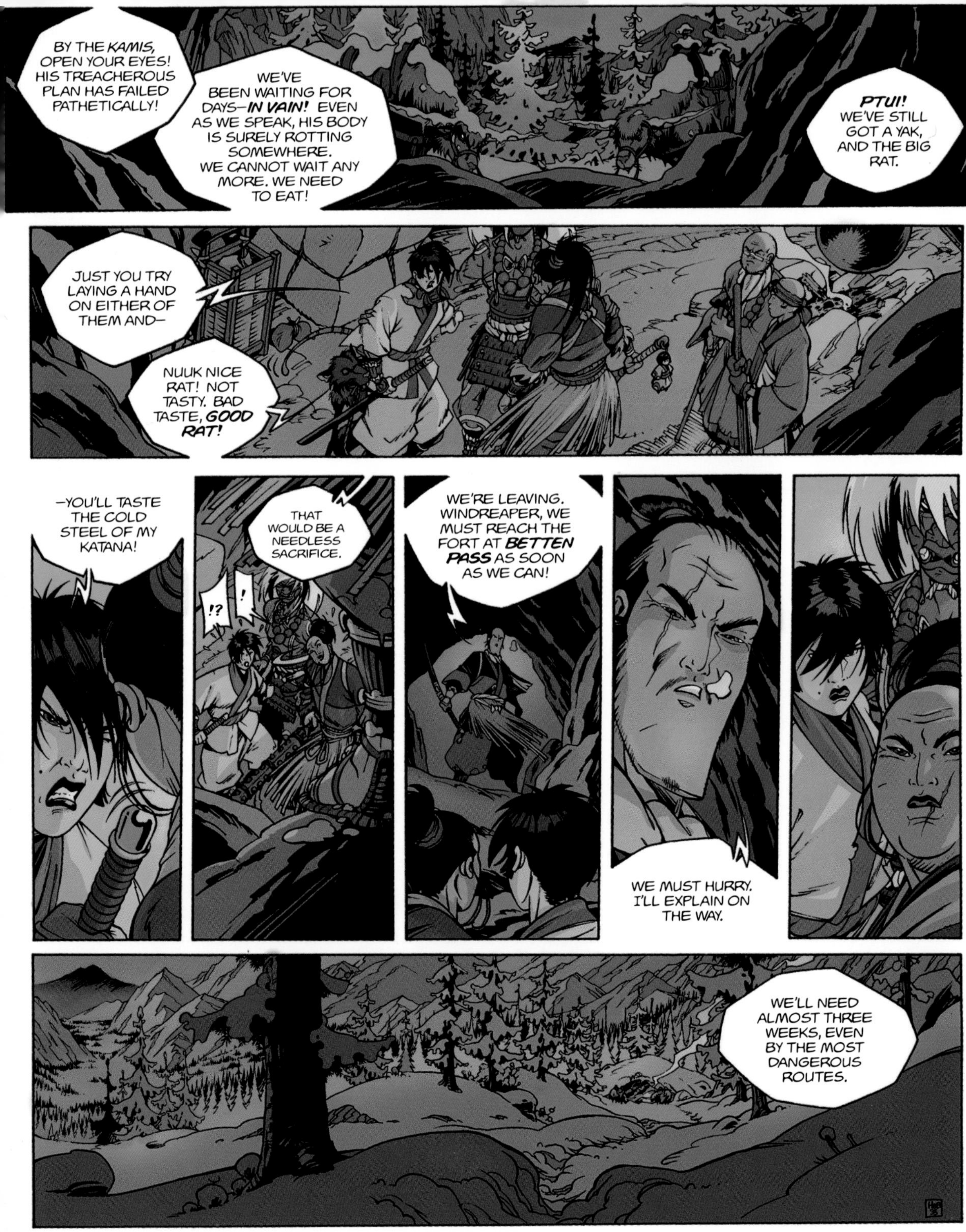
BY THE KAMIS, OPEN YOUR EYES! HIS TREACHEROUS PLAN HAS FAILED PATHETICALLY!
WE'VE BEEN WAITING FOR DAYS—IN VAIN! EVEN AS WE SPEAK, HIS BODY IS SURELY ROTTING SOMEWHERE. WE CANNOT WAIT ANY MORE. WE NEED TO EAT!
PTUI! WE'VE STILL GOT A YAK, AND THE BIG RAT.
JUST YOU TRY LAYING A HAND ON EITHER OF THEM AND—
NUUK NICE RAT! NOT TASTY. BAD TASTE, GOOD RAT!
—YOU'LL TASTE THE COLD STEEL OF MY KATANA!
THAT WOULD BE A NEEDLESS SACRIFICE.
!?
!
WE'RE LEAVING. WINDREAPER, WE MUST REACH THE FORT AT BETTEN PASS AS SOON AS WE CAN!
WE MUST HURRY. I'LL EXPLAIN ON THE WAY.
WE'LL NEED ALMOST THREE WEEKS, EVEN BY THE MOST DANGEROUS ROUTES.

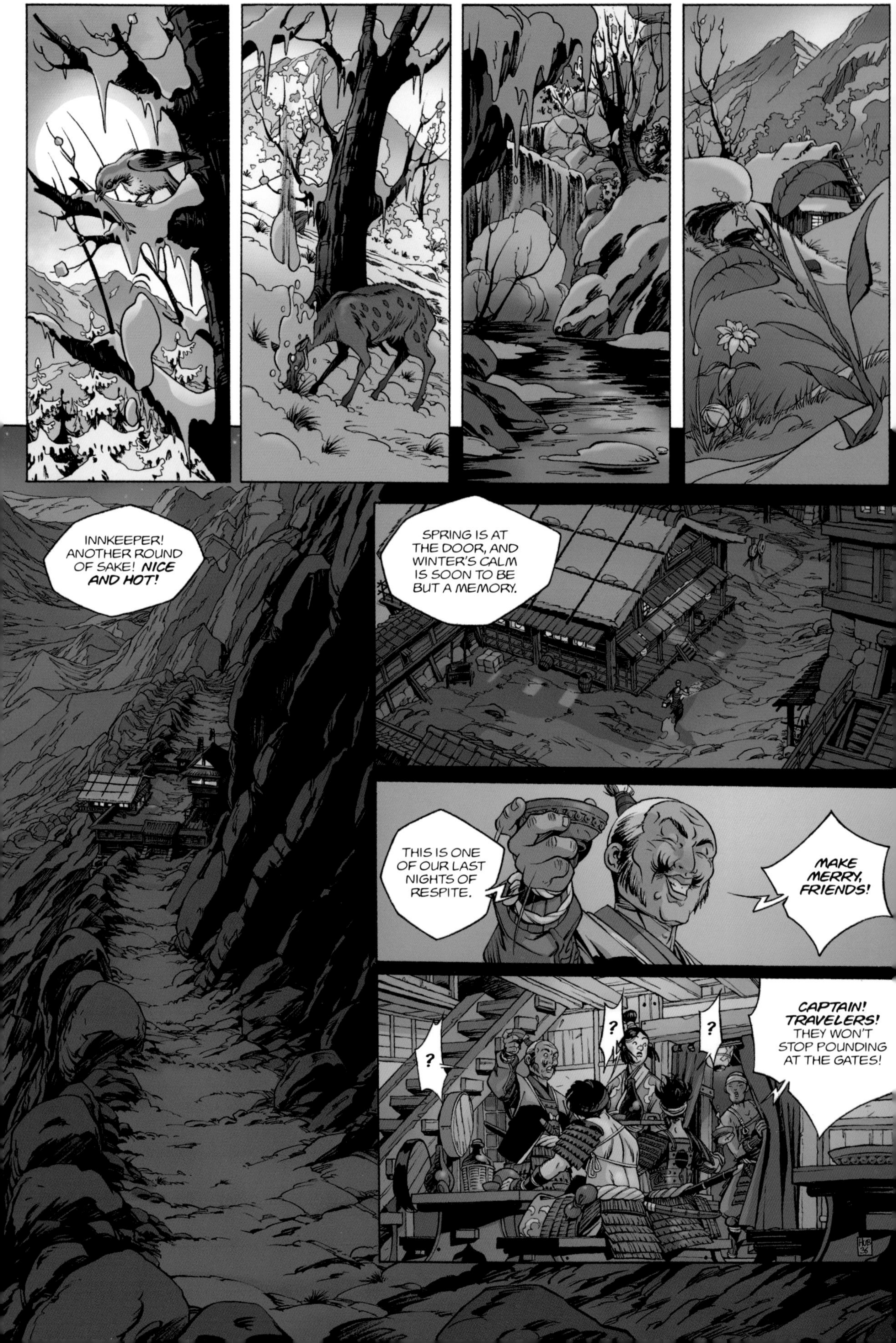
INNKEEPER! ANOTHER ROUND OF SAKE! NICE AND HOT!
SPRING IS AT THE DOOR, AND WINTER'S CALM IS SOON TO BE BUT A MEMORY.
THIS IS ONE OF OUR LAST NIGHTS OF RESPITE.
MAKE MERRY, FRIENDS!
?
?
?
CAPTAIN! TRAVELERS! THEY WON'T STOP POUNDING AT THE GATES!

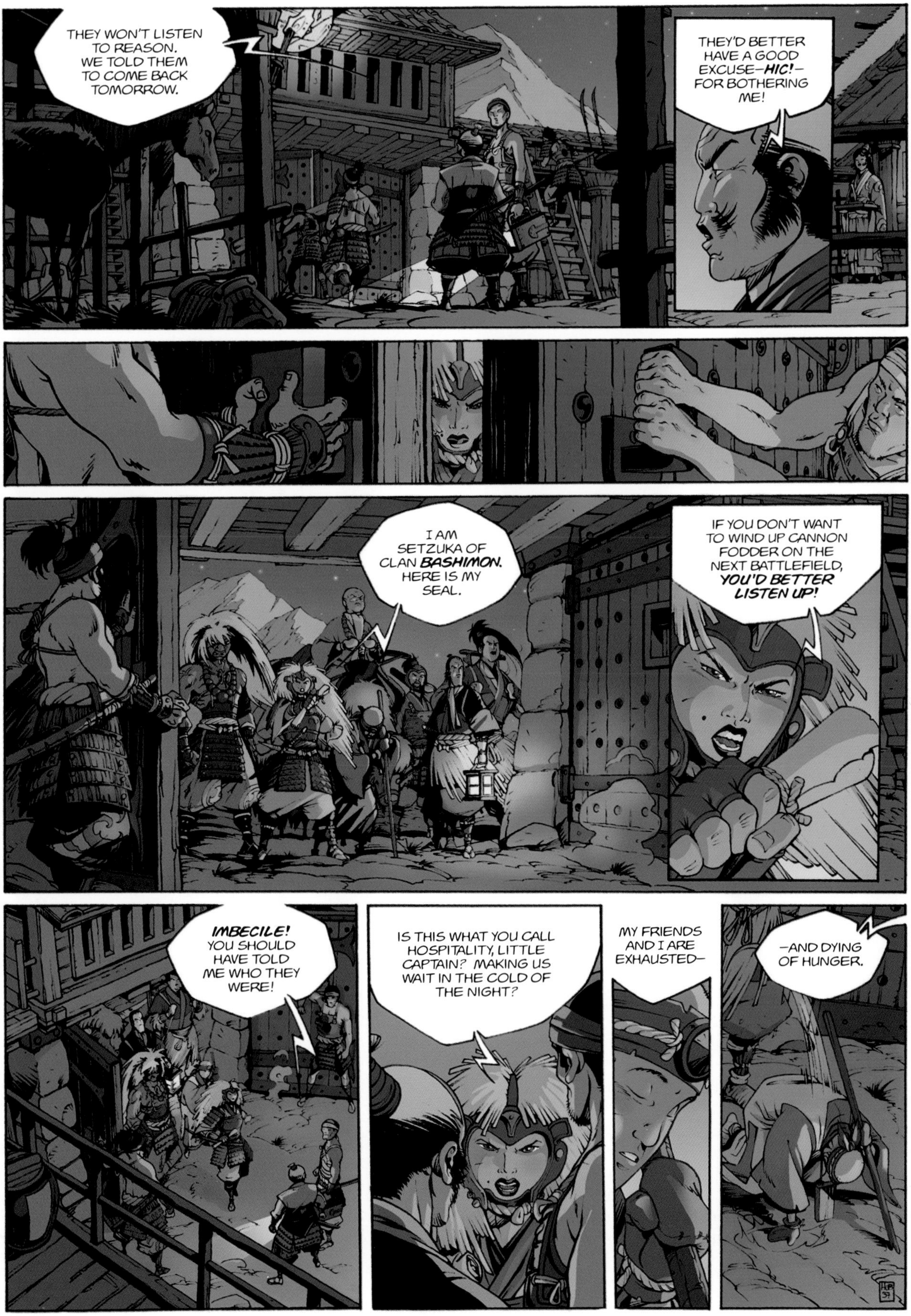
THEY WON'T LISTEN TO REASON. WE TOLD THEM TO COME BACK TOMORROW.
THEY'D BETTER HAVE A GOOD EXCUSE—HIC!—FOR BOTHERING ME!
I AM SETZUKA OF CLAN BASHIMON. HERE IS MY SEAL.
IF YOU DON'T WANT TO WIND UP CANNON FODDER ON THE NEXT BATTLEFIELD, YOU'D BETTER LISTEN UP!
IMBECILE! YOU SHOULD HAVE TOLD ME WHO THEY WERE!
IS THIS WHAT YOU CALL HOSPITALITY, LITTLE CAPTAIN? MAKING US WAIT IN THE COLD OF THE NIGHT?
MY FRIENDS AND I ARE EXHAUSTED—
—AND DYING OF HUNGER.

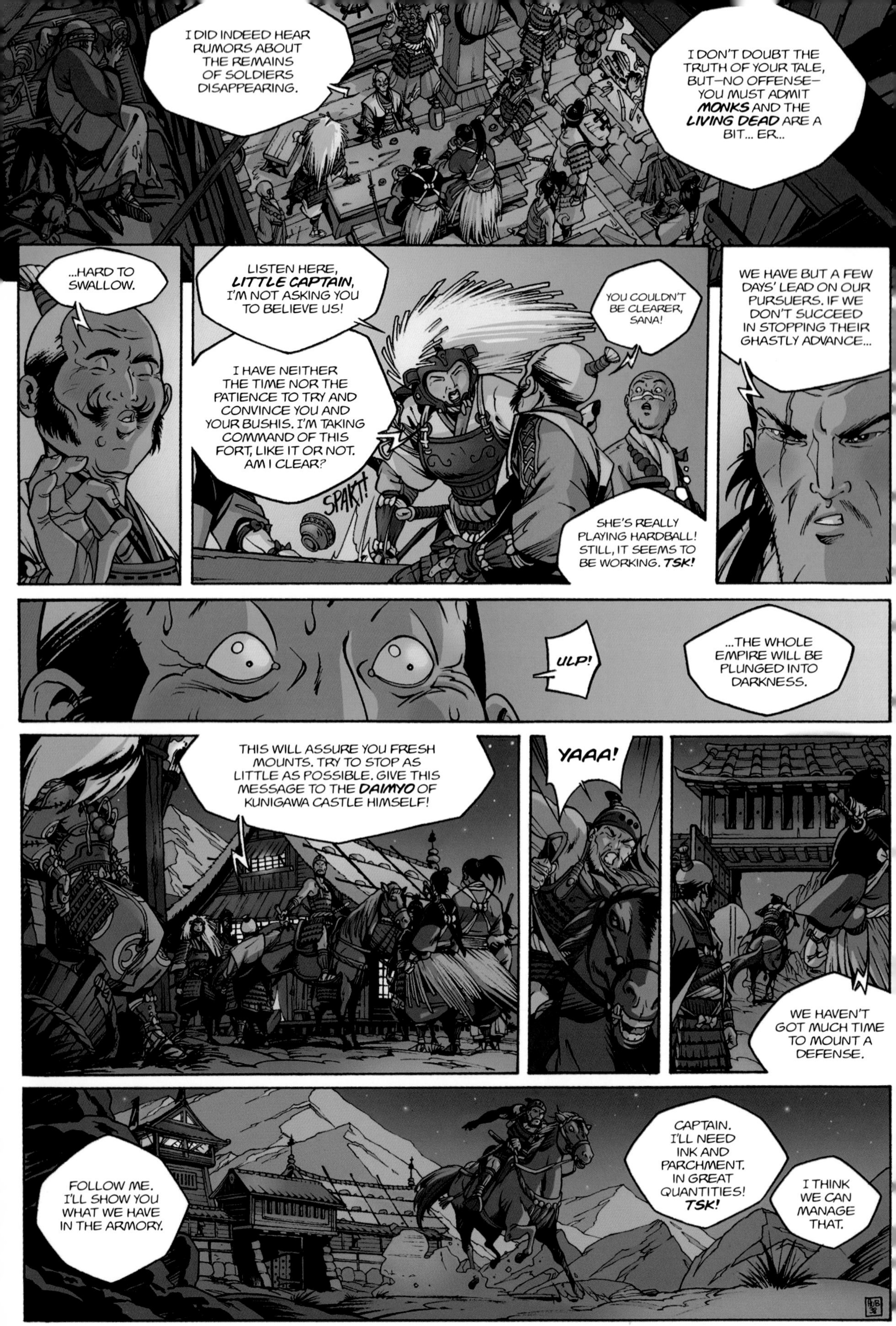
I DID INDEED HEAR RUMORS ABOUT THE REMAINS OF SOLDIERS DISAPPEARING.
I DON'T DOUBT THE TRUTH OF YOUR TALE, BUT—NO OFFENSE—YOU MUST ADMIT MONKS AND THE LIVING DEAD ARE A BIT... ER...
...HARD TO SWALLOW.
LISTEN HERE, LITTLE CAPTAIN, I'M NOT ASKING YOU TO BELIEVE US!
I HAVE NEITHER THE TIME NOR THE PATIENCE TO TRY AND CONVINCE YOU AND YOUR BUSHIS. I'M TAKING COMMAND OF THIS FORT, LIKE IT OR NOT. AM I CLEAR?
SPAKT!
YOU COULDN'T BE CLEARER, SANA!
SHE'S REALLY PLAYING HARDBALL! STILL, IT SEEMS TO BE WORKING. TSK!
WE HAVE BUT A FEW DAYS' LEAD ON OUR PURSUERS. IF WE DON'T SUCCEED IN STOPPING THEIR GHASTLY ADVANCE...
ULP!
...THE WHOLE EMPIRE WILL BE PLUNGED INTO DARKNESS.
THIS WILL ASSURE YOU FRESH MOUNTS. TRY TO STOP AS LITTLE AS POSSIBLE. GIVE THIS MESSAGE TO THE DAIMYO OF KUNIGAWA CASTLE HIMSELF!
YAAA!
WE HAVEN'T GOT MUCH TIME TO MOUNT A DEFENSE.
FOLLOW ME. I'LL SHOW YOU WHAT WE HAVE IN THE ARMORY.
CAPTAIN. I'LL NEED INK AND PARCHMENT. IN GREAT QUANTITIES! TSK!
I THINK WE CAN MANAGE THAT.

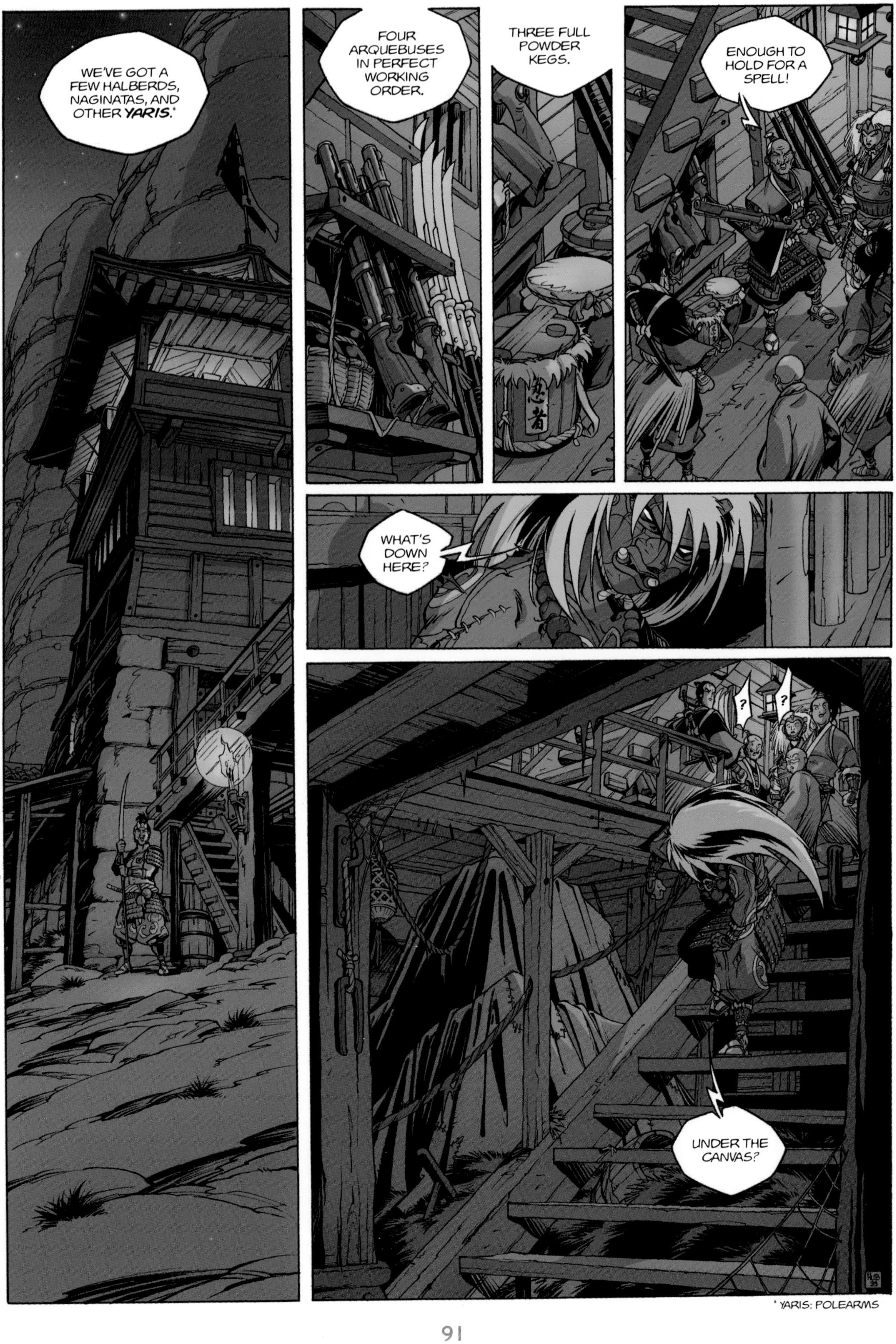
WE'VE GOT A FEW HALBERDS, NAGINATAS, AND OTHER YARIS.*
FOUR ARQUEBUSES IN PERFECT WORKING ORDER.
THREE FULL POWDER KEGS.
ENOUGH TO HOLD FOR A SPELL!
WHAT'S DOWN HERE?
?
?
UNDER THE CANVAS?
HUB

* YARIS: POLEARMS

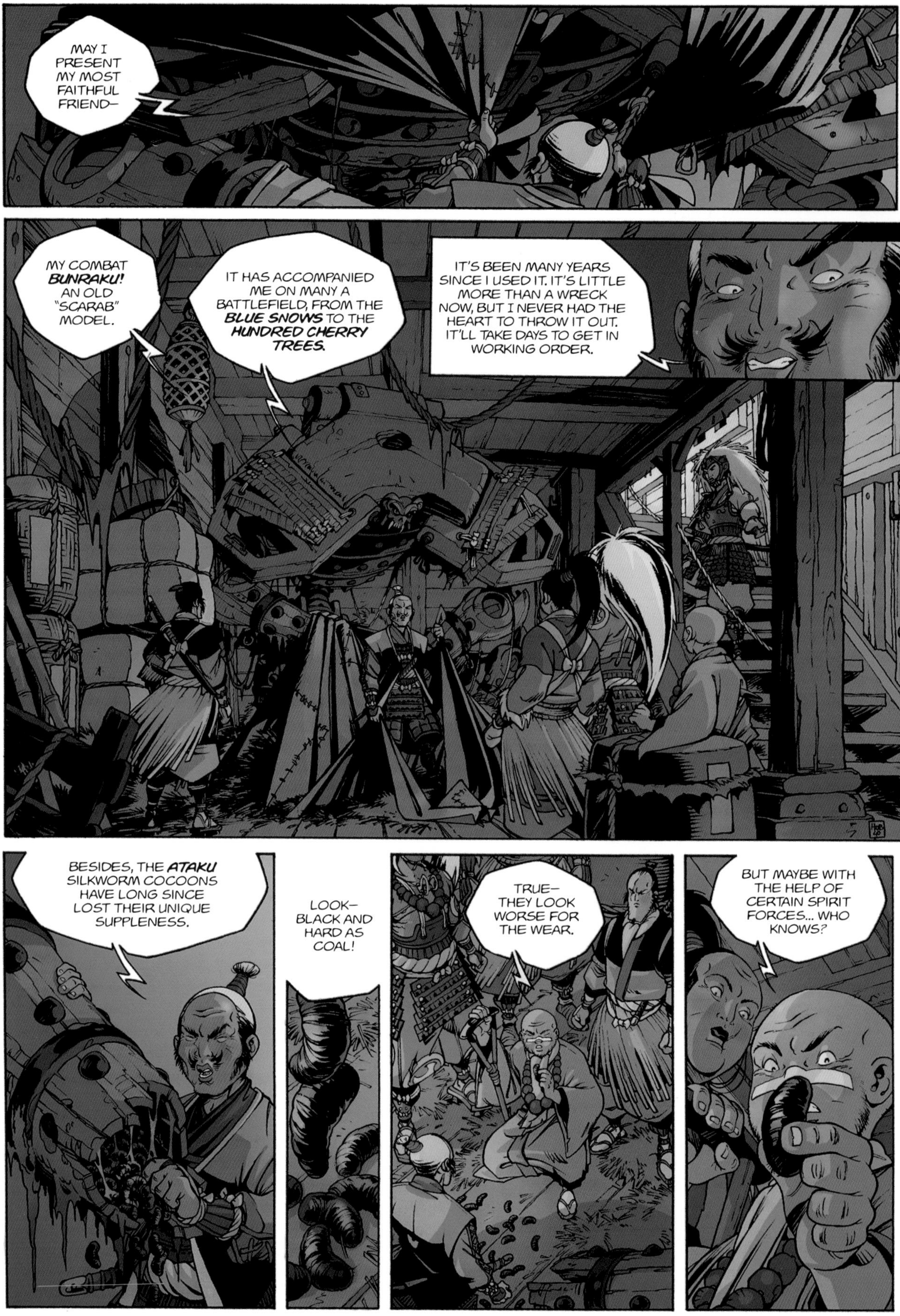
MAY I PRESENT MY MOST FAITHFUL FRIEND—
MY COMBAT **BUNRAKU!** AN OLD "SCARAB" MODEL.
IT HAS ACCOMPANIED ME ON MANY A BATTLEFIELD, FROM THE **BLUE SNOWS** TO THE **HUNDRED CHERRY TREES.**
IT'S BEEN MANY YEARS SINCE I USED IT. IT'S LITTLE MORE THAN A WRECK NOW, BUT I NEVER HAD THE HEART TO THROW IT OUT. IT'LL TAKE DAYS TO GET IN WORKING ORDER.
BESIDES, THE **ATAKU** SILKWORM COCOONS HAVE LONG SINCE LOST THEIR UNIQUE SUPPLENESS.
LOOK— BLACK AND HARD AS COAL!
TRUE— THEY LOOK WORSE FOR THE WEAR.
BUT MAYBE WITH THE HELP OF CERTAIN SPIRIT FORCES... WHO KNOWS?

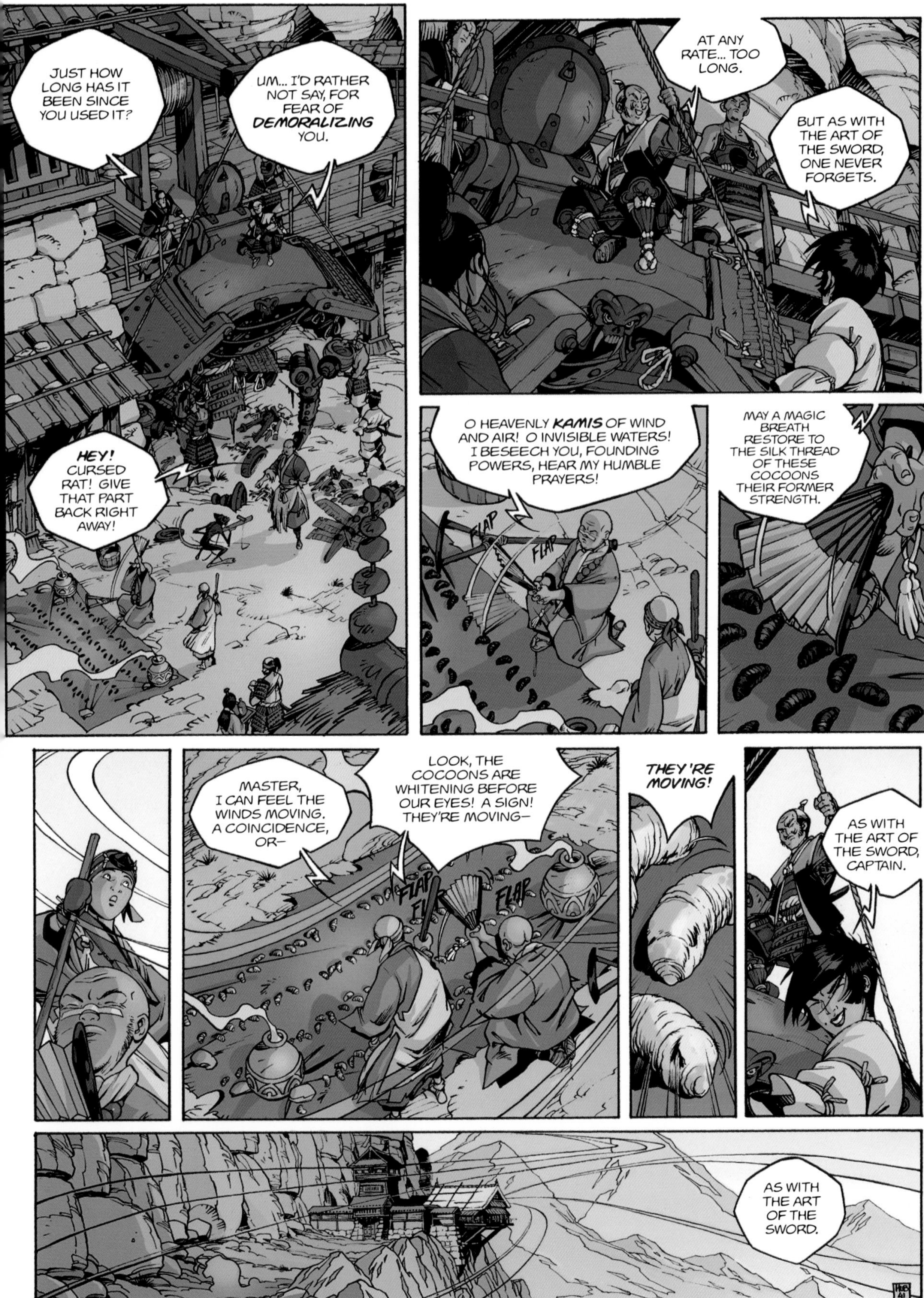
JUST HOW LONG HAS IT BEEN SINCE YOU USED IT?
UM... I'D RATHER NOT SAY, FOR FEAR OF DEMORALIZING YOU.
HEY! CURSED RAT! GIVE THAT PART BACK RIGHT AWAY!
AT ANY RATE... TOO LONG.
BUT AS WITH THE ART OF THE SWORD, ONE NEVER FORGETS.
O HEAVENLY KAMIS OF WIND AND AIR! O INVISIBLE WATERS! I BESEECH YOU, FOUNDING POWERS, HEAR MY HUMBLE PRAYERS!
FLAP
FLAP
MAY A MAGIC BREATH RESTORE TO THE SILK THREAD OF THESE COCOONS THEIR FORMER STRENGTH.
MASTER, I CAN FEEL THE WINDS MOVING. A COINCIDENCE, OR–
LOOK, THE COCOONS ARE WHITENING BEFORE OUR EYES! A SIGN! THEY'RE MOVING–
FLAP
FLAP
THEY'RE MOVING!
AS WITH THE ART OF THE SWORD, CAPTAIN.
AS WITH THE ART OF THE SWORD.

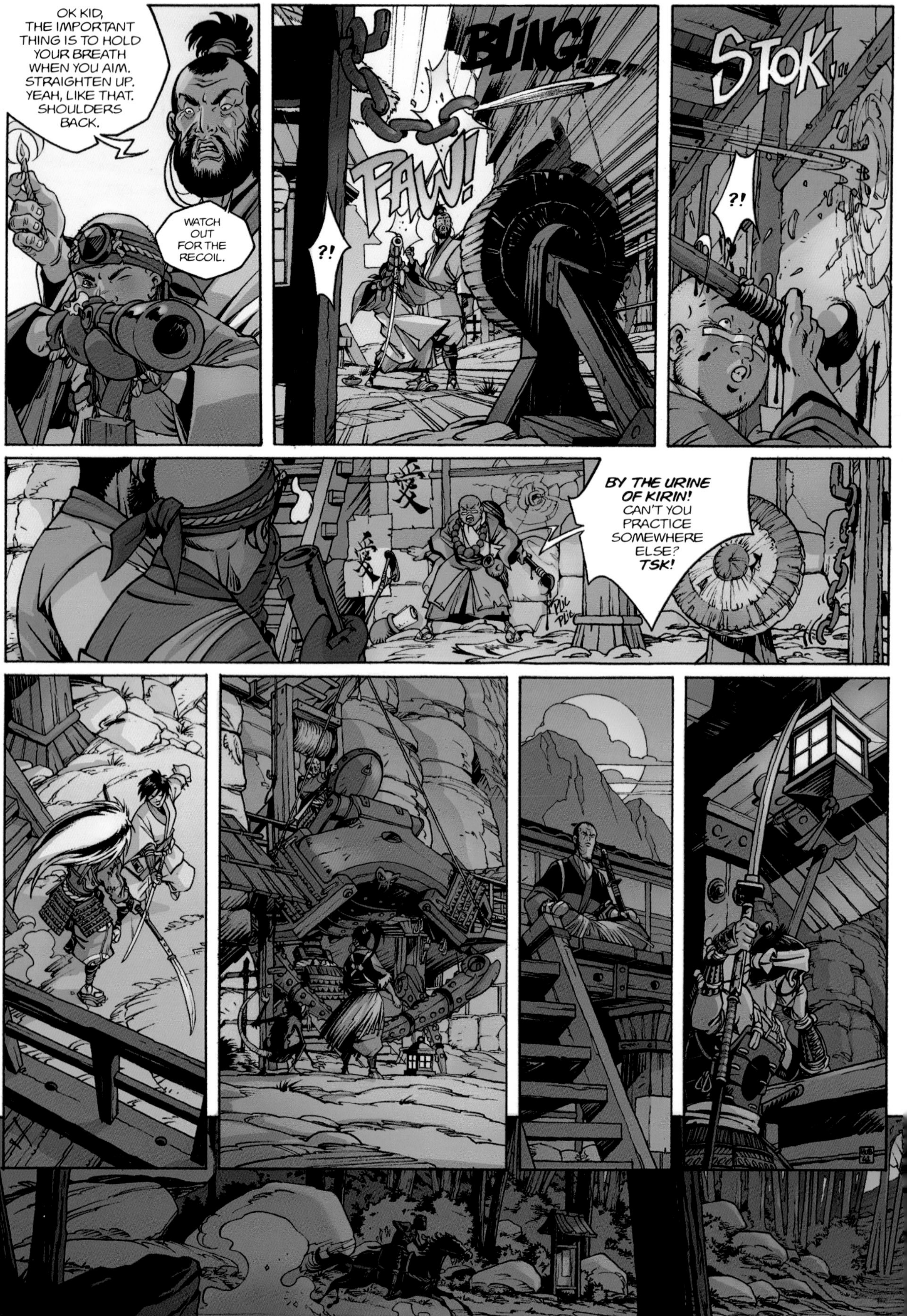

OK KID, THE IMPORTANT THING IS TO HOLD YOUR BREATH WHEN YOU AIM. STRAIGHTEN UP. YEAH, LIKE THAT. SHOULDERS BACK.
WATCH OUT FOR THE RECOIL.
BLING!
PAW!
?!
STOK...
?!
BY THE URINE OF KIRIN! CAN'T YOU PRACTICE SOMEWHERE ELSE? TSK!
PLIC PLIC

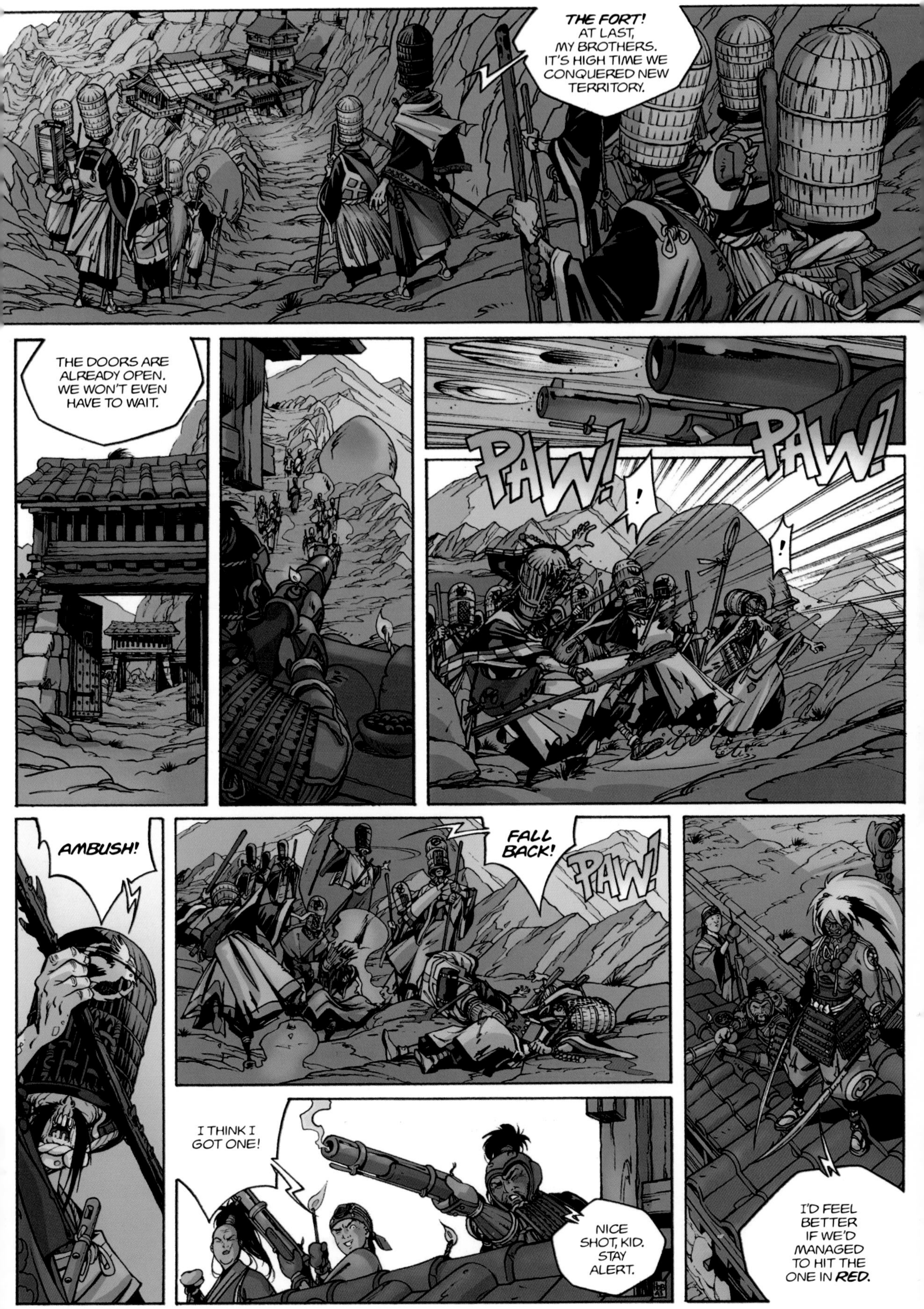
THE FORT! AT LAST, MY BROTHERS. IT'S HIGH TIME WE CONQUERED NEW TERRITORY.
THE DOORS ARE ALREADY OPEN. WE WON'T EVEN HAVE TO WAIT.
PAW!
PAW!
!
!
AMBUSH!
FALL BACK!
PAW!
I THINK I GOT ONE!
NICE SHOT, KID. STAY ALERT.
I'D FEEL BETTER IF WE'D MANAGED TO HIT THE ONE IN RED.

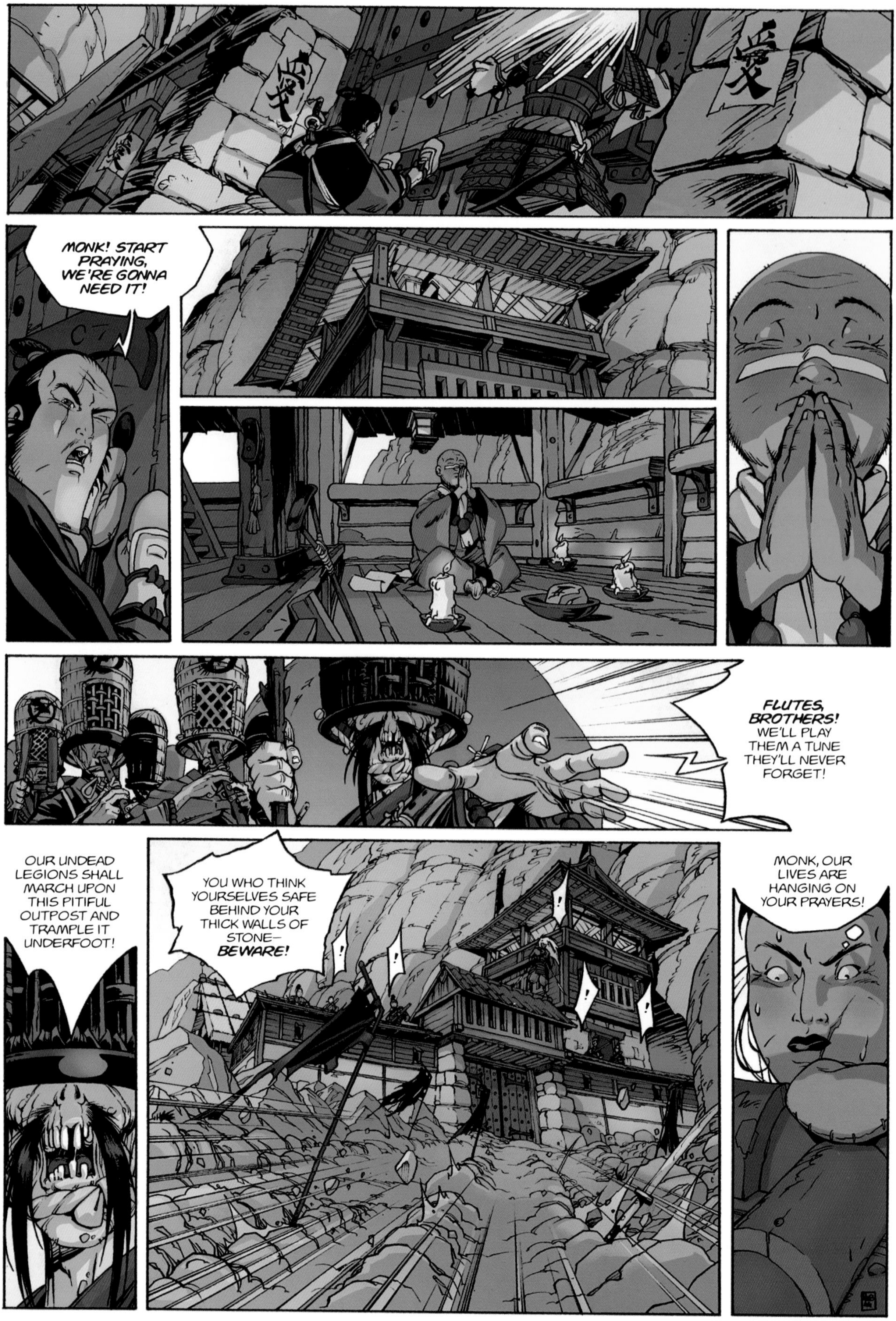

MONK! START PRAYING, WE'RE GONNA NEED IT!
FLUTES, BROTHERS! WE'LL PLAY THEM A TUNE THEY'LL NEVER FORGET!
OUR UNDEAD LEGIONS SHALL MARCH UPON THIS PITIFUL OUTPOST AND TRAMPLE IT UNDERFOOT!
YOU WHO THINK YOURSELVES SAFE BEHIND YOUR THICK WALLS OF STONE— BEWARE!
!
!
!
!
!
MONK, OUR LIVES ARE HANGING ON YOUR PRAYERS!

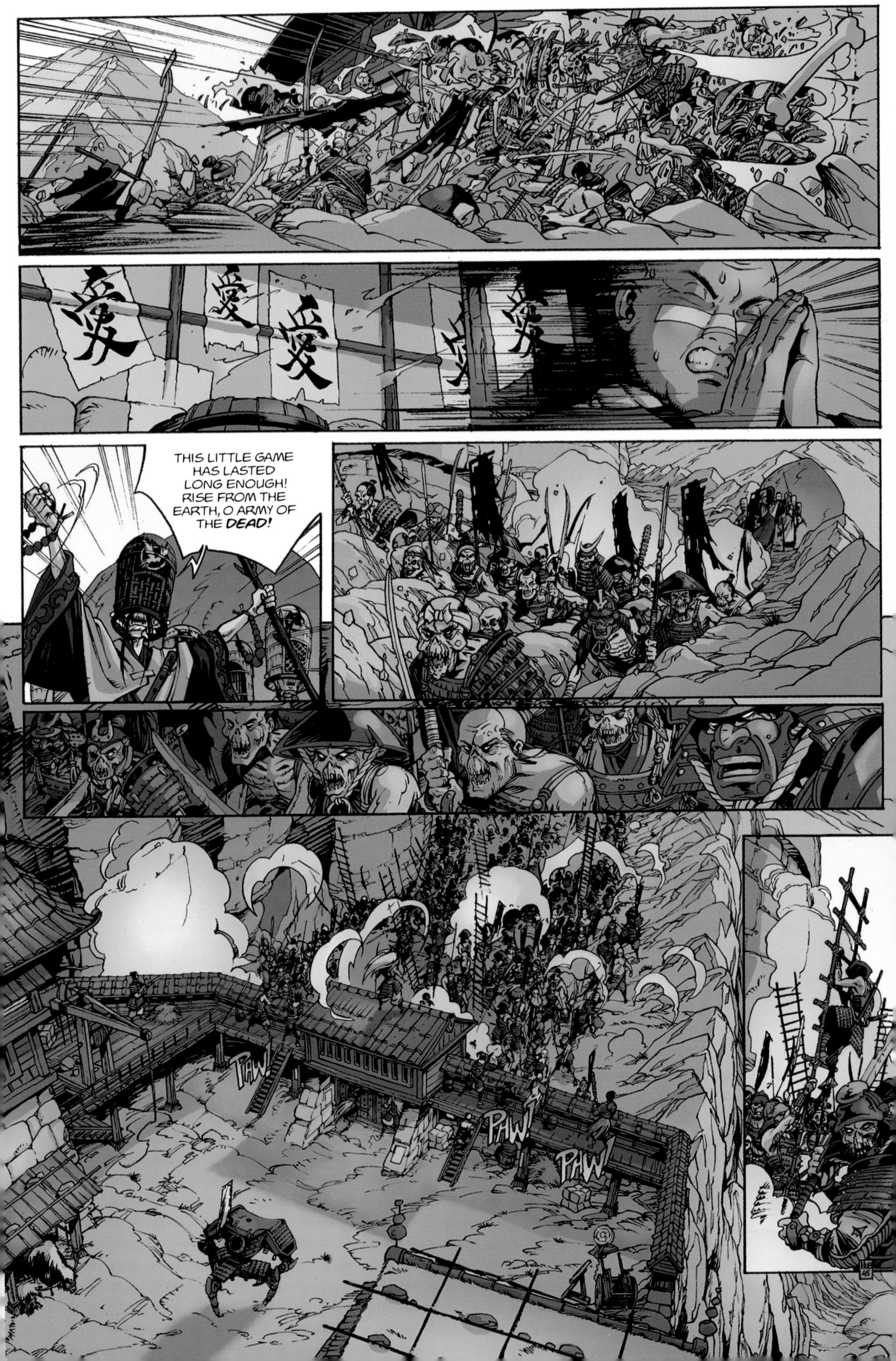
THIS LITTLE GAME HAS LASTED LONG ENOUGH! RISE FROM THE EARTH, O ARMY OF THE **DEAD!**
PAW
PAW
PAW

BLAM

BLAAM

THE DOOR WON'T HOLD FOR LONG!

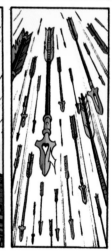

TCHAK TCHAK TCHAK TCHAK TCHAK TCHAK

AAH!

UNNNH!

PAW!

TUK TUK TUK TUK

THE POWDER!

DAMNED RAT!

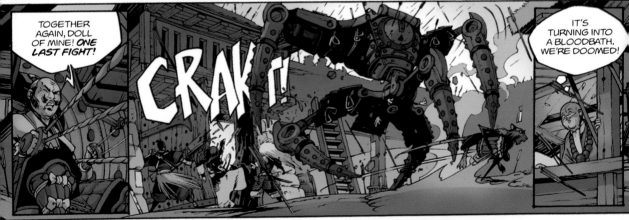

TOGETHER AGAIN, DOLL OF MINE! *ONE LAST FIGHT!*

CRAK!!

IT'S TURNING INTO A BLOODBATH. WE'RE DOOMED!

UNDEAD RIDERS!!

STAND ASIDE!

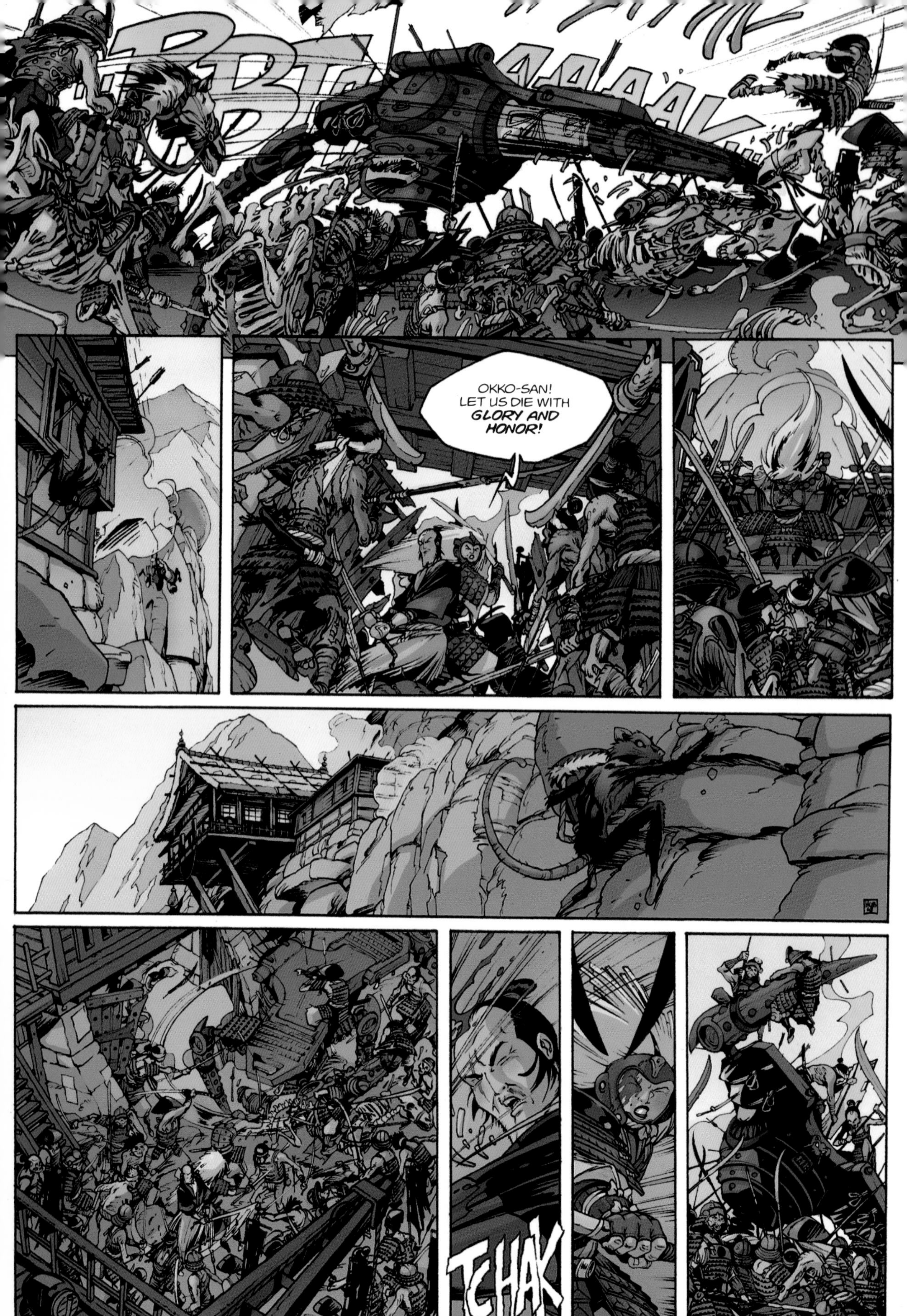
BRTCHAAAAAK
OKKO-SAN! LET US DIE WITH GLORY AND HONOR!
TCHAK

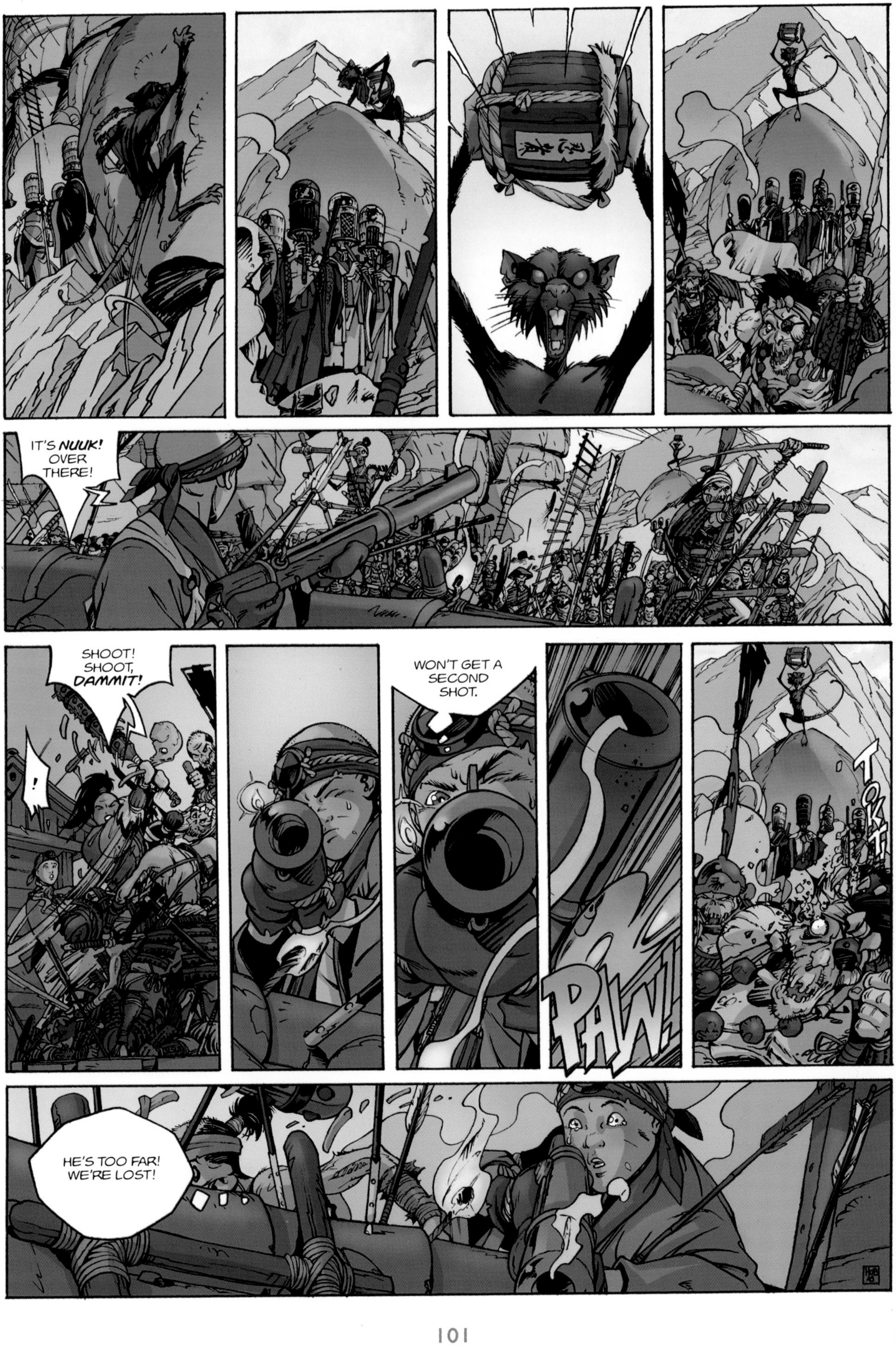
IT'S **NUUK!** OVER THERE!
SHOOT! SHOOT, **DAMMIT!**
!
WON'T GET A SECOND SHOT.
PAW!
TOK!
HE'S TOO FAR! WE'RE LOST!

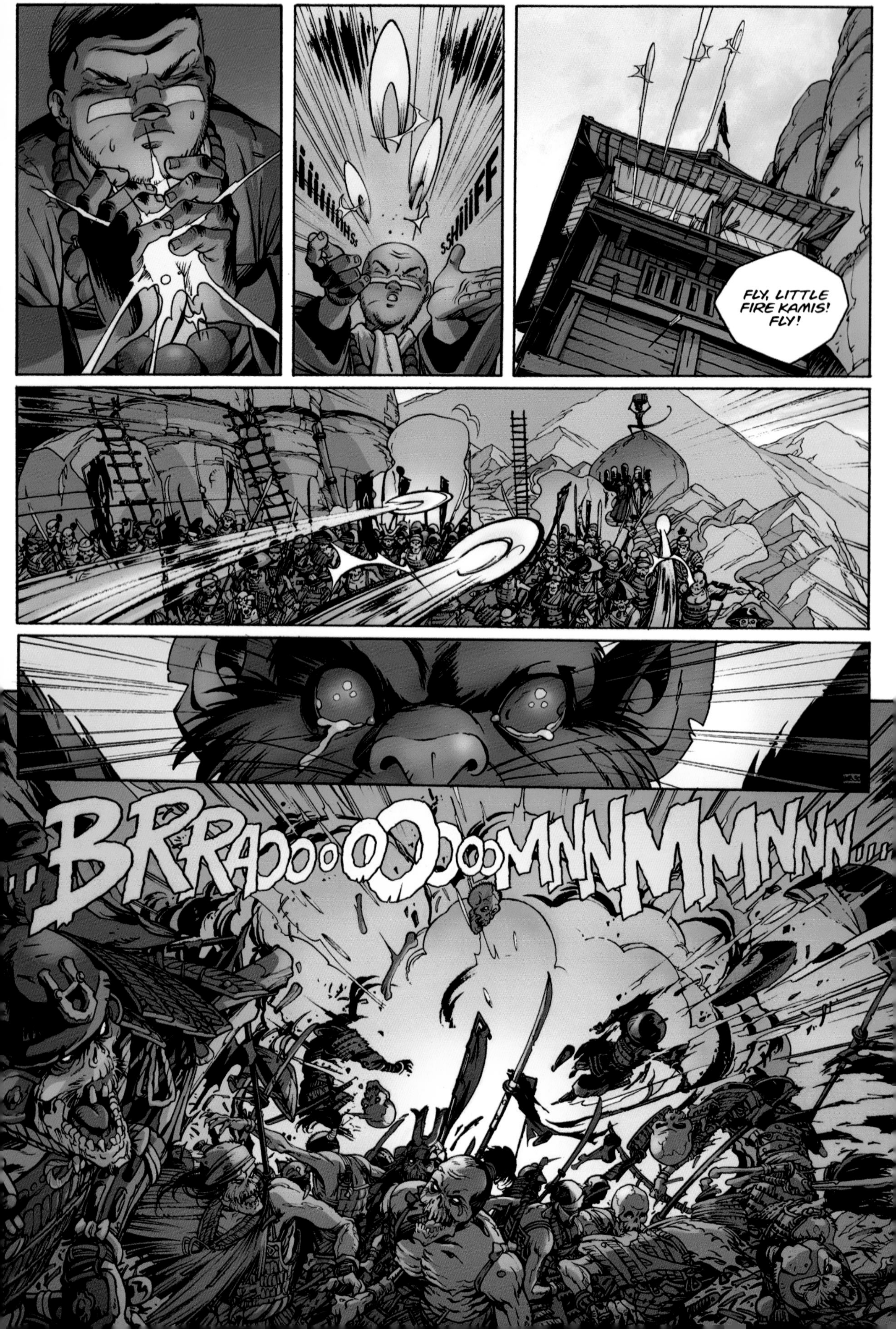

FLY, LITTLE FIRE KAMIS! FLY!
BRRAOOOOOOOOMNNMMMNNN...

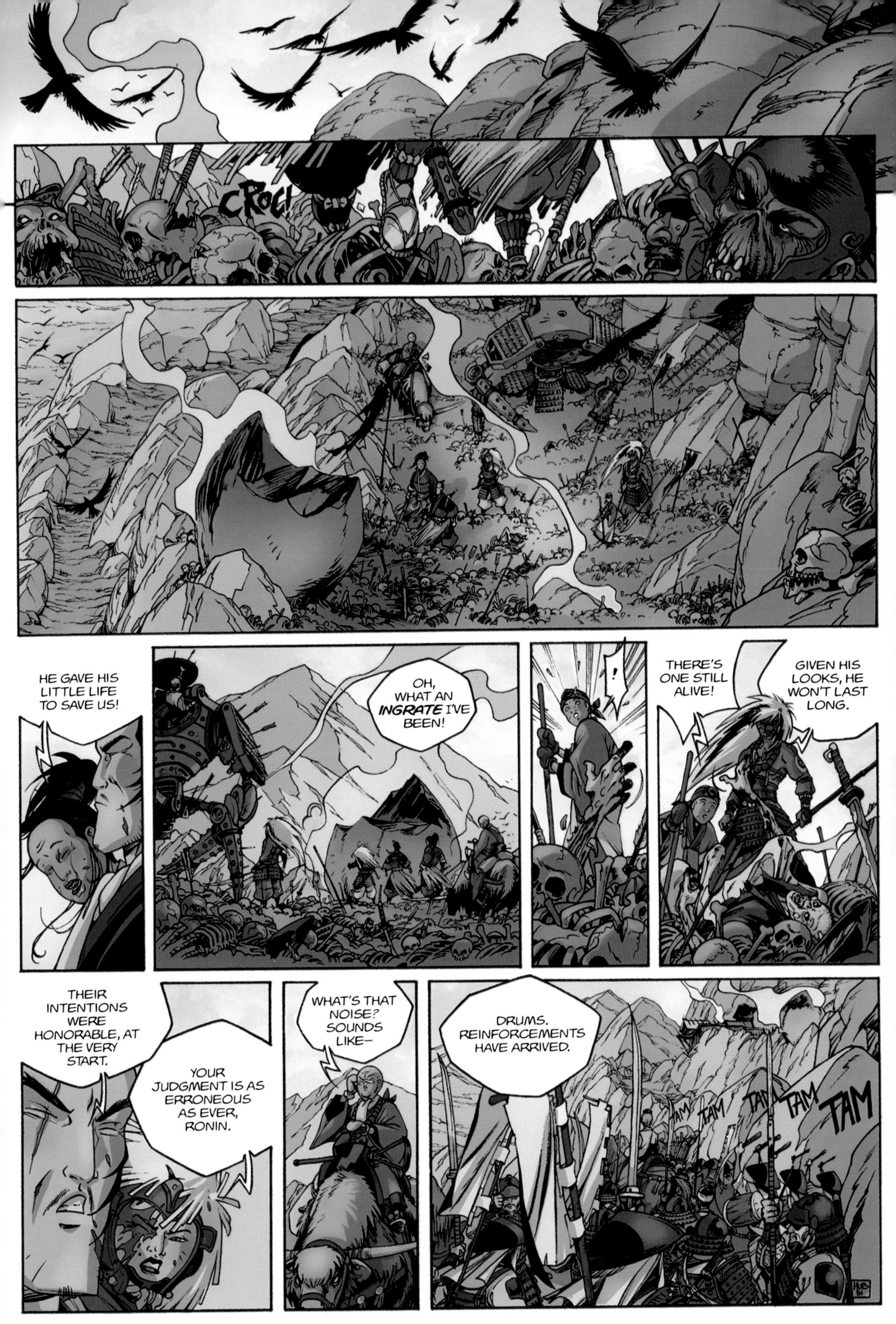
CROC!
HE GAVE HIS LITTLE LIFE TO SAVE US!
OH, WHAT AN INGRATE I'VE BEEN!
!
THERE'S ONE STILL ALIVE!
GIVEN HIS LOOKS, HE WON'T LAST LONG.
THEIR INTENTIONS WERE HONORABLE, AT THE VERY START.
YOUR JUDGMENT IS AS ERRONEOUS AS EVER, RONIN.
WHAT'S THAT NOISE? SOUNDS LIKE–
DRUMS. REINFORCEMENTS HAVE ARRIVED.
TAM TAM TAM TAM TAM

I DON'T WANT TO BE AROUND WHEN THE HORDES OF MAGISTRATES AND OFFICIAL INQUISITORS DESCENDS ON THIS PLACE.

IT'S TIME FOR US TO GO.

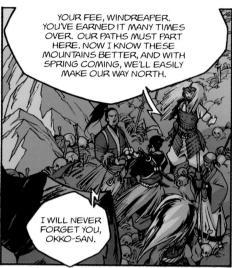

YOUR FEE, WINDREAPER. YOU'VE EARNED IT MANY TIMES OVER. OUR PATHS MUST PART HERE. NOW I KNOW THESE MOUNTAINS BETTER, AND WITH SPRING COMING, WE'LL EASILY MAKE OUR WAY NORTH.

I WILL NEVER FORGET YOU, OKKO-SAN.

NEVER!

THE LEGEND ABOUT YOU AND YOUR MOTHER— YOU NEVER GAVE ME AN ANSWER!

LISTEN TO YOUR HEART. IT WILL TELL YOU.

LISTEN TO YOUR HEART. IT WILL TELL YOU.

LISTEN TO YOUR HEART.

IT WILL TELL YOU.

LISTEN.

TAM TAM TAM

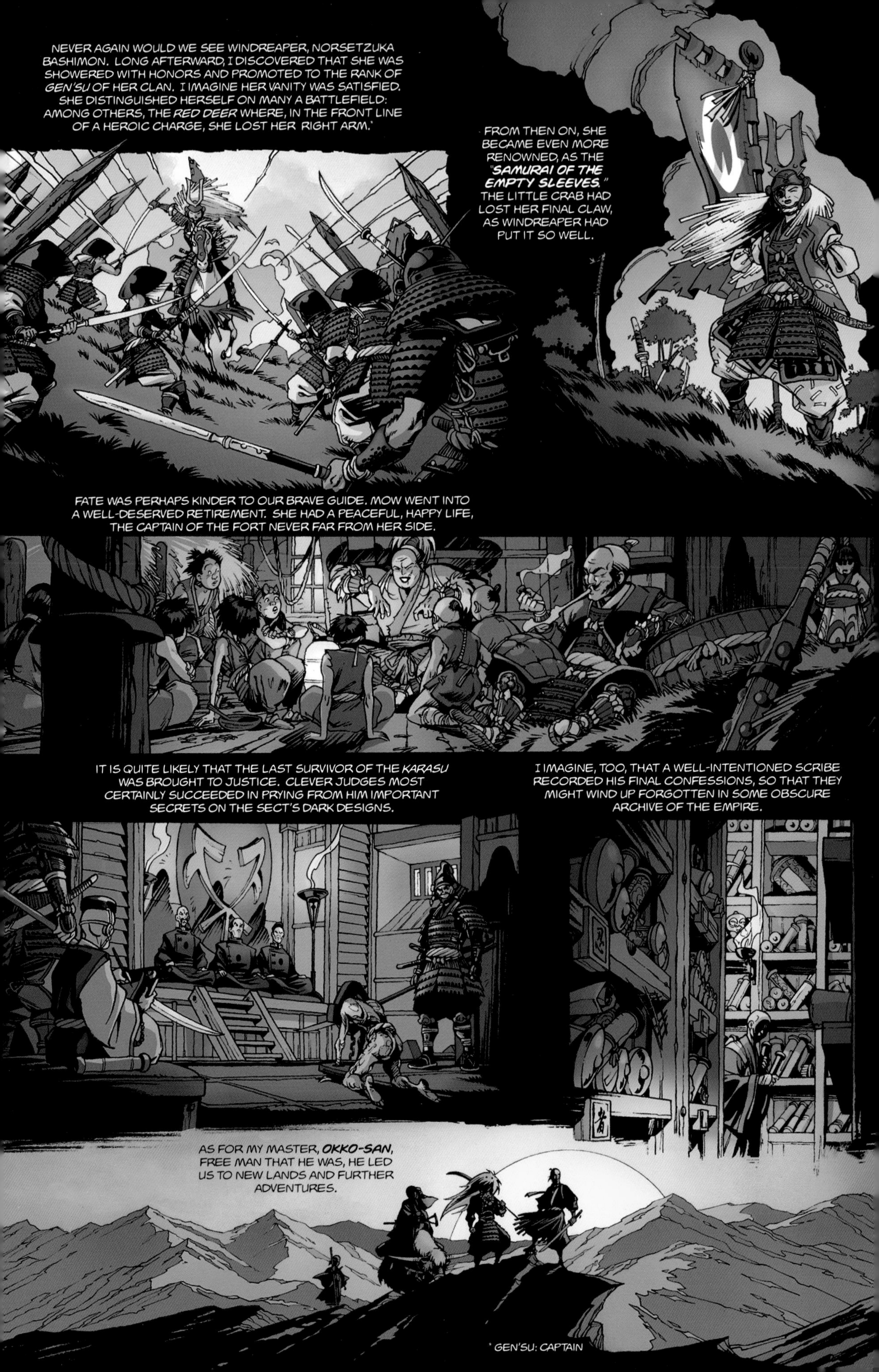
NEVER AGAIN WOULD WE SEE WINDREAPER, NORSETZUKA BASHIMON. LONG AFTERWARD, I DISCOVERED THAT SHE WAS SHOWERED WITH HONORS AND PROMOTED TO THE RANK OF GEN'SU OF HER CLAN. I IMAGINE HER VANITY WAS SATISFIED. SHE DISTINGUISHED HERSELF ON MANY A BATTLEFIELD: AMONG OTHERS, THE RED DEER WHERE, IN THE FRONT LINE OF A HEROIC CHARGE, SHE LOST HER RIGHT ARM.*
FROM THEN ON, SHE BECAME EVEN MORE RENOWNED, AS THE "SAMURAI OF THE EMPTY SLEEVES." THE LITTLE CRAB HAD LOST HER FINAL CLAW, AS WINDREAPER HAD PUT IT SO WELL.
FATE WAS PERHAPS KINDER TO OUR BRAVE GUIDE. MOW WENT INTO A WELL-DESERVED RETIREMENT. SHE HAD A PEACEFUL, HAPPY LIFE, THE CAPTAIN OF THE FORT NEVER FAR FROM HER SIDE.
IT IS QUITE LIKELY THAT THE LAST SURVIVOR OF THE KARASU WAS BROUGHT TO JUSTICE. CLEVER JUDGES MOST CERTAINLY SUCCEEDED IN PRYING FROM HIM IMPORTANT SECRETS ON THE SECT'S DARK DESIGNS.
I IMAGINE, TOO, THAT A WELL-INTENTIONED SCRIBE RECORDED HIS FINAL CONFESSIONS, SO THAT THEY MIGHT WIND UP FORGOTTEN IN SOME OBSCURE ARCHIVE OF THE EMPIRE.
AS FOR MY MASTER, OKKO-SAN, FREE MAN THAT HE WAS, HE LED US TO NEW LANDS AND FURTHER ADVENTURES.
* GEN'SU: CAPTAIN

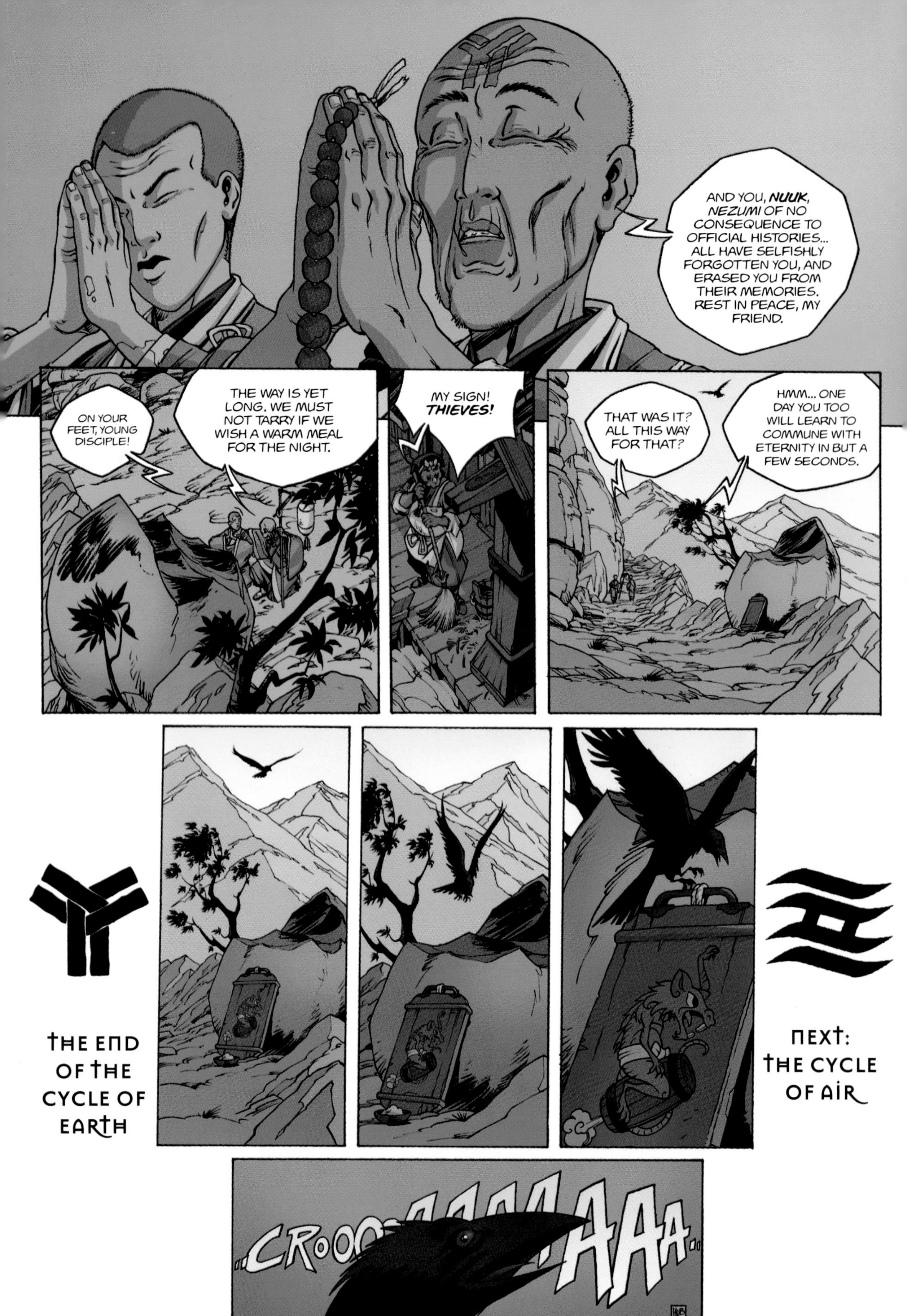
AND YOU, **NUUK**, *NEZUMI* OF NO CONSEQUENCE TO OFFICIAL HISTORIES... ALL HAVE SELFISHLY FORGOTTEN YOU, AND ERASED YOU FROM THEIR MEMORIES. REST IN PEACE, MY FRIEND.
ON YOUR FEET, YOUNG DISCIPLE!
THE WAY IS YET LONG. WE MUST NOT TARRY IF WE WISH A WARM MEAL FOR THE NIGHT.
MY SIGN! ***THIEVES!***
THAT WAS IT? ALL THIS WAY FOR THAT?
HMM... ONE DAY YOU TOO WILL LEARN TO COMMUNE WITH ETERNITY IN BUT A FEW SECONDS.
THE END OF THE CYCLE OF EARTH
NEXT: THE CYCLE OF AIR
..CROOO...AAA..

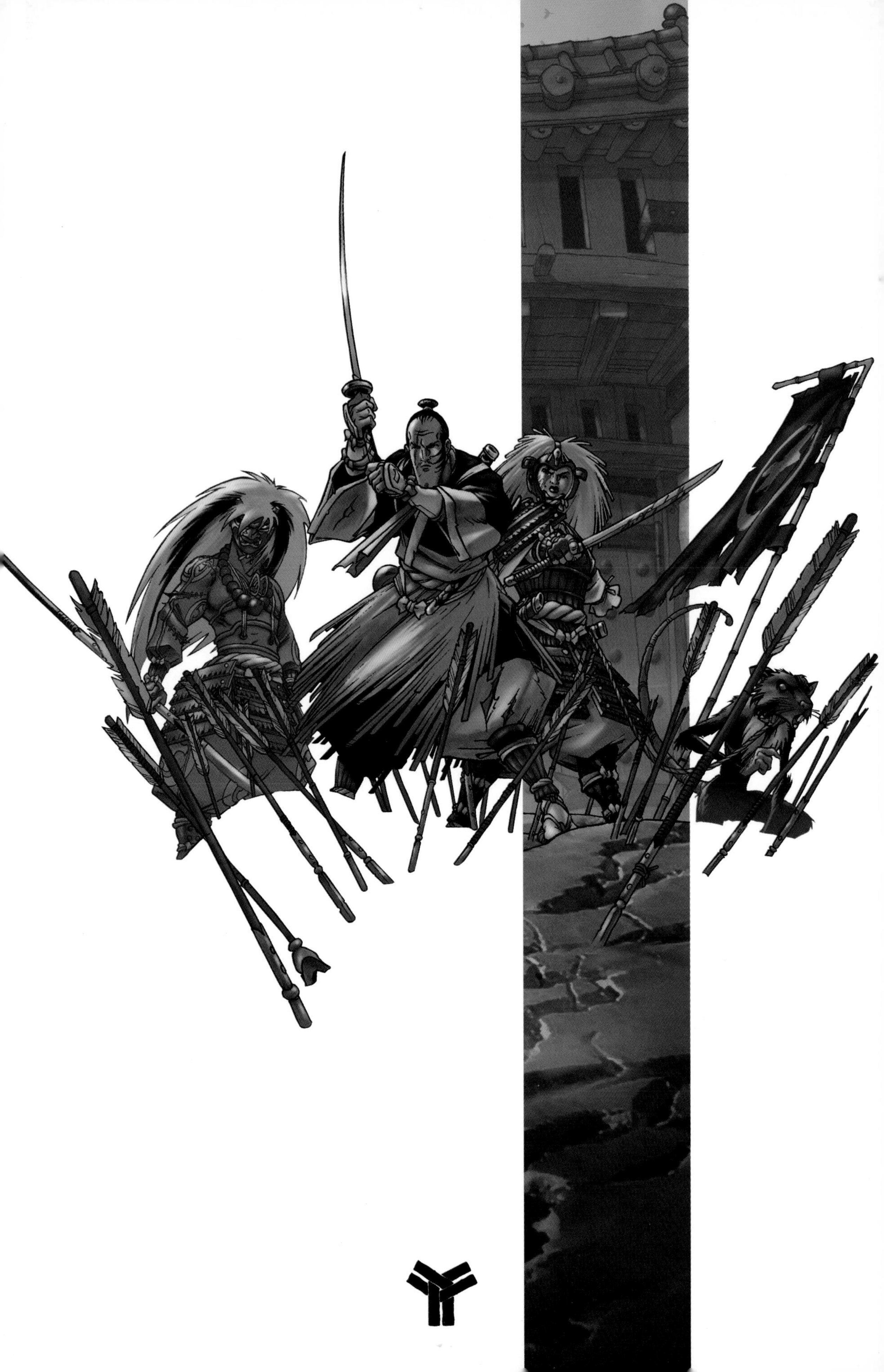